BETWEEN CARING & COUNTING:
TEACHERS TAKE ON EDUCATION REFORM

LINDSAY KERR

Between Caring & Counting

Teachers Take on Education Reform

UNIVERSITY OF TORONTO PRESS
Toronto Buffalo London

© University of Toronto Press Incorporated 2006
Toronto Buffalo London
Printed in Canada

ISBN-13: 978-0-8020-9123-9
ISBN-10: 0-8020-9123-7

Printed on acid-free paper

Library and Archives Canada Cataloguing in Publication

Kerr, Lindsay, 1951–
    Between caring & counting : teachers take on education reform / Lindsay
Kerr.

    Includes bibliographical references and index.
    ISBN-13: 978-0-8020-9123-9
    ISBN-10: 0-8020-9123-7

    1. Educational change – Ontario.   2. Education and state – Ontario.
    3. Teachers – Ontario.   I. Title.   II. Title: Between caring and counting.

    LA418.O6K47 2006   370.9713   C2006-900303-3

The University of Toronto Press acknowledges the financial assistance to
its publishing program of the Canada Council for the Arts and the Ontario
Arts Council.

University of Toronto Press acknowledges the financial support for its
publishing activities of the Government of Canada through the Book
Publishing Industry Development Program (BPIDP).

Contents

Tables and Figures

Acknowledgments

No work stands entirely alone, but builds on preceding works and is shaped by the everyday relations that are an integral part of the writer's world. From its inception to publication, the coming into being of this book has been a five-year process that involved numerous people who may see reflections of our conversations and exchanges in these pages. In particular, I am grateful for the input and support of those who contributed to this work. First, to the teacher-participants – Alice, Helena, Jessica, and Rachel – who made time in their busy schedules to partake in the focus group. I dedicate this book to committed teachers like them in Ontario, and elsewhere. Second, to Linda Muzzin (supervisor) and Nina Bascia (second reader) of my thesis conducted at OISE/UT, from which this book evolved. Their complementary expertise in the sociology of the professions and in teacher unions, respectively, provided insight and constructive criticism that informed the research phase. Special thanks to Linda for her unwavering support and for urging me to pursue publication. Third, to Stephen Kotowych, my editor at the University of Toronto Press for shepherding the manuscript through to publication, and to the anonymous readers assigned by him whose comments have been incorporated into the final manuscript. Last but not least, to my family, friends, and colleagues who engaged with me in dialogue throughout the writing process. The love and encouragement – as well as the challenges – of my life-partner Dereck, and my sons Blake and Eliot, make it all worthwhile. I am profoundly grateful to all whose input is interwoven into the fabric of the pages that follow; however, I accept full and ultimate responsibility for the final content that is now in the hands of the reader. Let the dialogue continue.

Acronyms

BNA	British North America Act
CUPE	Canadian Union of Public Employees
EQAO	Education Quality and Accountability Office
ETFO	Elementary Teachers' Federation of Ontario
FEUT	Faculty of Education/University of Toronto
ISO 9001	International Organization for Standardization
NDP	New Democratic Party
OAC	Ontario Academic Credit
OCT	Ontario College of Teachers
OECD	Organization for Economic Co-operation and Development
OECTA	Ontario English Catholic Teachers' Association
OISE/UT	Ontario Institute for Studies in Education/University of Toronto
OKNL	Ontario Knowledge Network for Learning
OPC	Ontario Principals' Council
OPSOA	Ontario Public Supervisory Officials' Association
OSSLT	Ontario Secondary School Literacy Test
OTF	Ontario Teachers' Federation
OSSTF	Ontario Secondary School Teachers' Federation
OTQT	Ontario Teacher Qualifying Test
P3s	Public-private partnerships
PC	Progressive Conservative Party
POR	Position of Responsibility
PLP	Professional Learning Program
RSP	Remedial Support Program
TAP	Teacher Advisory Program
TDSB	Toronto District School Board
TLP	Toronto Learning Partnership
TPA	Teacher Performance Appraisal

BETWEEN CARING & COUNTING:
TEACHERS TAKE ON EDUCATION REFORM

1 Introduction

It is clear that working in a school – while technically a ten-month job with some evenings and weekends off – is, as you and I know, a full-time occupation, one that can never be completely abandoned, escaped or shaken. It follows us like a silent shadow in the berry patch, on the bay, or into the middle of the night.

Roland S. Barth, 1990

Arriving at school the morning after the resounding defeat of the Ontario Progressive Conservative (PC) Party in October 2003, it was as if a dark cloud had lifted. The mood was one, not of jubilation, but of cautious optimism; eight years of blatant teacher-bashing had ended at the ballot box. As the bell rang and students scurried to their class-rooms as usual, I recalled the words of one of the teacher-participants in this study, expressed during the focus group more than a year and a half earlier, at a time when the PCs seemed unassailable. Helena's prophesy was: 'Politicians come and go. The education system always survived, no matter who was at the top of the government. Always, the education system survived. With all the laws, with all the vacilla-tions, we survived – they didn't!' Indeed we survived, but the struc-tural and policy changes implemented under education reform remain firmly entrenched across the system of public education.

The brunt of education reform hit when the Harris/Eves govern-ment reigned over Ontario, from 1995 to 2003. Events unfolding in Ontario are not isolated, but reflect the emergent international political economy of globalization[1] as governments the world over move to privatize public services. The legacy left by the PC government will not be transformed overnight. The 'new normal' has an ideological force that has become entrenched through the strategic restructuring of the institution of public education. This study provides a critical analysis of education reform, based on teachers' experiences as expressed during a focus group conducted in the winter of 2002, and textual analysis of documents internal to the institution. It shows how ruling relations have been orchestrated to discredit teachers and to destabilize public education. Utilizing the qualitative research methodology of institutional ethnography (Smith, 1987, 1999), the objectives of this study are threefold: to identify the 'ruling structures' that control the everyday work and lives of teachers in the public education system; to analyse and map the 'ruling relations' that operate within the public education system; and to identify the ideological code constitutive of the education system under reform. Understanding how power relations operate in and through the everyday policies and practices of societal institutions and identifying the ideological code are the core of institutional ethnography.

The ideology that underpins neoliberal policies extends across political parties and has a scope far beyond Ontario; it has a long history and a global geographical reach.[2] Cognizance of interconnections between the macro- and micro-levels are thus necessary to uncover the extensive 'ruling apparatus' upholding regimes such as the Harris/Eves PCs in Ontario – regimes that privilege corporate-business profits over the everyday lives of people. At the micro-level, the centrepiece of this inquiry is the lived experience of a focus group of secondary school teachers working in the public education system in Toronto. The impact of educational reform on their work and lives provides a window into the ruling relations of the new world economy as it affects one location on the globe. It is upon the efforts of teachers that the public education system depends; yet the perspectives of classroom teachers have been missing from the neoliberal rhetoric of education restructuring and policy reform. This inquiry redresses the imbalance by centring on teachers' experience.

At the macro-level, linking the experiences of local teachers with those of teachers in other parts of Canada and elsewhere, and with other public service workers, facilitates recognizing patterns in the power relations, policies, and practices by which the imperatives of globalization are perpetuated so as to control local communities and worksites. Interconnecting local and global perspectives enables a clearer view of how the system actually works; making genealogical links thus informs the inquiry, although the focus is teachers in Ontario. The purpose of unpacking education reform in Ontario is to find ways for advocates of a democratic and accessible system of education to resist the systematic decimation of public education, following the lead of the United States and United Kingdom. Education reform is not just a rearrangement of how educational services are delivered; as evidenced in the United States in particular, and as has become apparent in Ontario, the intention is the move toward privatization that threatens to infringe upon the basic human right to education enshrined in the United Nations Charter of Rights of the Child. Democracy itself is jeopardized to the extent that it depends on a solid public education system that is equitable and accessible to all (Dewey, 1997). Inherent in my critique of the neoliberal vision of education is a call for the democratization of government and its institutions, including education, to reflect and serve the heterogeneity of contemporary Canadian society and to encourage inclusive active participation in decision-making at all levels of governance, from diverse perspectives.

Excluded and remote from decision-making in the forward mapping model of policy formulation deployed by the PC regime are the so-called implementers of education reform – that is, the teachers. Elmore (1977) describes and questions forward mapping as a top-down strategy of policy formulation that begins with a clear statement of the policy makers' intent (outcomes), proceeding through a series of steps, to define what is expected of implementers. It relies on coercion, compliance, and centralized control of the bottom level of 'street-level bureaucrats' (in this case, teachers). The relations of ruling imposed through education policy reform in Ontario has subjected teachers such as myself to increased workloads, deteriorating working conditions, diminishing resources, declining relative wages, and loss of professional autonomy and discretion. Under these conditions, it is not surprising that low morale has been cited as a problem system-wide by teacher unions and education researchers (Naylor, 2001). This could be the reason why many are leaving the profession of teaching, and why an impending teacher shortage in Ontario was predicted in statistical studies conducted by the Ontario College of Teachers (OCT) in the late 1990s. Their prediction has precedents nationally and internationally, where similar education reform policies began being implemented earlier. According to McIntyre's (1998) projections, 41,000 teachers across the province would retire within five years, and 78,000 within ten years; meanwhile, the number of applicants to teacher training had dropped from almost 20,000 to less than 8,000 in each of the two years prior to his study. Factors cited as discouraging the selection of teaching as a career choice include the lack of opportunities for new teachers, low remuneration and prestige, the difficulty of the job, and the negative portrayal of teachers in the media – conditions actually exacerbated by OCT policies, as will become clear in subsequent chapters.

A second trend identified by the OCT is a widening gender gap among teachers (Giguère, 1999). Data analysis of the demographics of registered teachers indicates a steady decrease of male teachers across all age categories, from the over-fifty-five group to the under-thirty group. Whereas elementary school teaching has traditionally been a feminized profession, secondary school teaching is shifting in the same direction. The steady drop-off in numbers of male teachers and the increasing feminization of teaching over time (across age groups) and panels (elementary and secondary) has occurred within a political climate of relentless teacher-bashing and a decline in public valuing of the professional standing of teachers. The OCT has not conducted similar research into diversity along other axes of difference, such as race or ethnicity; however, what is inadvertently highlighted by the gender gap is the importance of taking gender relations into account in an examination of teachers and their work. Viewing the feminized profession of teaching in light of feminist analyses of women's work suggests questioning patriarchal constructions of teaching as work that is invisible, undervalued, and underpaid. Such gendered reproductive work is erased or marginalized in standard economic analyses limited to productive work (Marilyn Waring in Nash, 1995). A feminist perspective shifts the focus, first by recognizing and legitimizing the inherent value of teachers' work as maintaining and sustaining societies in ways that elude current quantification measures of accountability; and second, by acknowledging teachers as experts who possess first-hand knowledge, it counters exploitative relations commonly experienced by women workers.

The category of 'difficulty of the job' cited as discouraging teaching as a career choice is not explicated by the OCT in their 'objective,' 'neutral' demographic analyses, sidestepping broader socio-political issues that impact on teaching practice. During the 1990s in Ontario, increased teacher enrolment in additional qualifying courses at universities (such as special education, guidance, library, co-op education, and administration), suggests rising levels of stress associated with classroom teaching in an increasingly complex urban society. What these courses have in common is relief from classroom teaching. Ageist attributions of the tendency toward career moves out of the classroom to career progression or to an aging workforce devalue experience acquired through practice; teachers are configured as disposable human resources replaceable by new recruits. The question of how to sustain teachers throughout their careers and how to make the most use of their accumulated expertise is thus overlooked by the OCT.

It is reports from the perspective of teachers conducted for teacher federations across Canada that the 'difficulty of the job' is explicated (King and Peart, 1992; Gallen, Karlenzig, and Tamney, 1995; Naylor, 2001). Summarizing findings from these reports, the demands on the teacher's role has expanded beyond traditional education to include additional responsibilities reflecting broader societal changes. Many of these changes, such as the breakdown of 'traditional' family and kinship patterns (in the absence of alternate support structures), increasing international migrations, rising unemployment and poverty, increasing credentialization, and the proliferation of mass media, all impact on schools and contribute to extra work for teachers. A broader range of needs, whether psychological, social, emotional or physical, that were formerly mediated by other institutions (such as community centres, religious organizations, or social service agencies) has been downloaded onto teachers. The diverse needs of groups such as visible minorities and newcomers to Canada, special needs of students staying in school longer due to youth unemployment, and changes in the job market, all contribute to a more complex role for educators. Cutbacks to social services, coupled with high unemployment, directly affect some students and their families, becoming manifest in schools through socio-emotional and behavioural problems, hunger and poverty, drugs, gangs, and violence.

Situated within the milieu of the 'new' political economy in Ontario, at the end of a particularly trying year, the school at which I teach, which normally has a stable staff, was faced with an almost 40 per cent turnover in its teachers in June 2001. During that academic year (2000–1), teachers faced significant intensification of work under education reform: the imposition of an extra half-course to teach; the implementation of new curricula and new computerized report cards for Grades 9 and 10; and the addition of extra duties such as the Teacher Advisory Program (TAP) and on-call assignments. Adversarial labour relations precipitated the CUPE strike of educational support workers and teachers' withdrawal of voluntary extra-curricular activities. Protracted collective bargaining negotiations ended in what many teachers viewed as a less-than-satisfactory contract.[3] Apart from more typical year-end requests, staff changes included early retirements, requests for unpaid leaves of absence, downshifting to part-time status, transfers to other schools, resignations for alternative employment (such as to private schools or the college system), and a disability leave. Such high teacher turnover, whether through resigning, transferring, or downshifting,[4] is not school-specific but is occurring province-wide, denoting widespread dissatisfaction among teachers in the public education system. The consequence of significant staffing disruption is likely to be instability and uncertainty for years to come. Not only is there a drain of expertise from the system, but new recruits may not be available to cover attrition.

A compounding factor is 'poaching,' in the form of a growing international demand for and recruitment across borders of teachers (as well as nurses), especially on the part of the United States and the United Kingdom. These countries, which began implementing neoliberal policies in the 1980s, are suffering the longer-term consequences. To rectify the fallout of staffing shortages there, high salaries and signing bonuses are offered as incentives to lure teachers from abroad, as evidenced by advertisements in the employment opportunities pages of Toronto newspapers. A report published by the UK Institute for Public Policy Research,[5] analysing statistics on teacher recruitment, resignation, and retirement, predicts that with rising enrolment in secondary schools, staffing difficulties will continue to be acute. According to this report, the problem cannot be resolved in the short term by expansion of training; instead, the report advocates a shift in emphasis to reduction of wastage from the profession and maximization of the return of those out of service (that is, attracting back teachers who have left teaching). This shift in emphasis from recruitment to retention suggests that improvements to the job itself are necessary to redress the problem of teacher exodus.

Quantitative demographic and statistics studies do have a place, but studies of the aggregate miss the texture, nuance, and detail afforded by qualitative research. This study turns to a group of practising teachers as the starting point to unpack ruling relations in education, based on their experience as well as my own. At the outset, it is necessary to explain my location: I have been a secondary school teacher for twenty-five years, having taught in an inner London comprehensive school in England, in public schools in Vancouver and Toronto, and in a private school in Rome, Italy. My teaching subjects include mathematics, science, physics, chemistry, communication technology (privileged subjects in education reform), as well as special education and guidance (low priorities in education reform). I have also been engaged in curriculum design and pilot projects for the former Toronto Board of Education.[6] I have chosen not to rise up the hierarchy of administration, preferring the challenges, trials, and tribulations of daily interaction with students in the classroom. Horizontal expansion of expertise and exploration through in-school research has defined my career path and guided my professional development. As an insider, I have personally experienced the deleterious effects of education reform due to reduced availability of time, resources, and support for teacher-led projects. For me, these changes have taken some of the joy and intrinsic rewards out of teaching. This inquiry is therefore also in part an autoethnography, reflecting on my own experiences in teaching and figuring out where to go from here.

In my teaching practice, adherence to critical/feminist pedagogy has at times meant transgressing the taboo of bringing politics into the classroom. To advocate critical thinking in a standardized skills-based curriculum that is assumed to be politically neutral is to tread a delicate line. As a woman in the traditionally male-dominated fields of mathematics and science, I encourage students to participate actively and question the prevailing ethos, to include different perspectives, and to consider the social and environmental consequences of technoscientific progress. In my personal experience, it has become commonplace to hear clichés such as, 'This is how we do business' and 'It's business as usual,' uttered by educational 'leaders'[7] in the face of hardships imposed by the systematic dismantling of the public sector. The language of the boardroom (accountability, quality control, standardization, effectiveness, efficiency, excellence) is assumed to be 'common sense' as if it were an uncontestable 'fact' that education is business. Under these conditions, I find myself compromised in my work and conflicted about my place in it. Personal experience thus instigated and informs this inquiry, so I make no claim to neutral objectivity. For me, teaching is not just a job but my chosen occupation. Teaching is not just skills training for the job market but a relation and a transformative praxis. Students are not funding units nor products on an assembly line; they are living human beings, each possessing unique potentialities. It is their education in the broad holistic sense that is at stake when teachers are standardized into deliverers of curriculum content or incapacitated by the constraints of education reform.

This inquiry is not, however, just a series of personal narratives; it also draws on critical/feminist discourses on social relations, globalization, and democracy. These interconnected discourses are complementary in challenging hegemonic assumptions and in striving for socio-economic equity and justice. The shared premise is an ontology that considers reality to be socially constructed, and an epistemology that values subjective experience as legitimate knowledge. As such, critical/feminist theory and praxis constitute an alternative to the dominant scientific-deductive paradigm. The methodology of institutional ethnography is particularly conducive to critical/feminist research since it starts with subjective experience to unpack power relations. Unlike most purely academic research, institutional ethnography provides a framework for activist research in analysing how power works in complex societies, so as to bring about socio-political consciousness of people as active agents in their lives and work.

Placing education reform within the larger socio-political context of globalization, by making international comparisons and linking emergent events across national borders, reveals that it is an integral part of economic restructuring. Economic restructuring exhibits common characteristics globally; government downsizing, trade liberalization, deregulation, austerity measures, and the privatization of public services and resources are common tendencies of national governments that have been colonized into the globalization agenda. The scientific management of 'human resources' governs power relations so as to control and regulate people to serve the economy, and undermines democracy. Derived from the manufacturing industry, scientific management determines government policy, permeates public discourse, and shapes societal institutions. Discerning local manifestations in actual policies and practices facilitates unpacking the social relations orchestrated by education reform.

Under the guise of accountability, this inquiry exposes the economic rationalism of 'accounting logic' as the governing principle for education policy-makers. As described by Broadbent and Laughlin (in Broadbent, Dietrich, and Roberts, 1997), accounting logic that governs contemporary notions of accountability is based on two assumptions: '1. That any activity needs to be evaluated in terms of some measurable outputs achieved and the value added in the course of the activity; 2. That it is possible to undertake this evaluation in and through the financial resources actually used or received' (p. 37). The applicability of such a reductive criterion derived from the private for-profit corporate sector to the domain of public education must be contested, given the different raison d'être of these sectors. What emerges through centring teachers' perspectives is a paradigm clash between the dominant economic paradigm of accounting logic deployed by policy-makers and an ethic of care at the centre of education practice.

The restructuring of education (like that of healthcare) poses a fundamental dilemma for teachers (like nurses): on the one hand, they are torn between a deeply imbued ethic of care for their charges (students or patients) and fiscal restraint policies that impose conditions of declining facilities, resources and support; on the other hand, they are torn between serving others and self-care in terms of financial, physical, and mental well-being for themselves as 'caregivers.' For frontline workers in the caring professions, it is conceivable that the consequence of coping with the downloading of responsibility and the intensification of work[8] is a net care deficit. This can be internalized in destructive ways that induce demoralization, exhaustion or burnout, resignation or downshifting, and sometimes rage. A more constructive alternative to these individualized responses is some form of collective action to oppose the juggernaut of neoliberal reform.

Economic restructuring and the dismantling of public services impacts directly on woman workers in the feminized professions of teaching, nursing, and social work. A gender analysis reveals how manufacturing consent and galvanizing public support for government policies has relied on essentialist attributions of the 'feminine' qualities of caring, nurturing, and self-sacrifice (for children or the sick), while simultaneously denigrating and devaluing the contribution of (primarily) women workers in these fields. Historically, similar constructions of women have been deployed in nationalist discourses enlisting women as caregivers responsible for reproduction, not only in the biological sense but also in terms of sustaining societies (Anthias and Yuval-Davis, 1993). Valorizing women by elevating them on pedestals as paragons of self-sacrificial virtue, while simultaneously devaluing their backstage work, typifies the contradiction inherent in patriarchal relations. For the feminized professions, gender relations play out in declining relative remuneration and systematic attacks on the labour rights of teachers (and nurses) voicing opposition. Moreover, centring public debate in this way obscures and denies the negative impact on the recipients of care – that is on students (and patients)

– while proceeding with undermining the social democratic value of equal access to education and healthcare, regardless of ability to pay. It is thus necessary to integrate an ethic of care with socio-economic justice, so as to differentiate between the personal meaning of care/caring in the domestic domain and institutionalized forms of an ethic of care that can serve to exacerbate exploitation and political injustice.

Based on teachers' experience in the public education system, this inquiry exposes paradoxes inherent in education reform. First, as public funds invested in education decline, government control over the public education system increases via 'accountability' measures. The ascendancy of standardization, as the ruling principle for curricula and the measuring stick for evaluation, not only reproduces hegemonic mainstream thinking but also increases surveillance over teachers (and students) and enhances Foucaultian 'governability.' Second, increased regulation of public education is coupled with deregulation of private education. The trend toward privatization not only creates divisions between public and private education, but also arguably perpetuates socio-economic inequity by reinforcing existing hierarchies of privilege and power. To this end, government legislation has been wielded to control and regulate teachers in public schools. Interpretations of legislation not in line with the intent of squeezing more out of public school teachers for less cost were castigated as 'creative non-compliance' by PC minister of education, Janet Ecker. Attempts on the part of some school boards and principals to minimize the negative impact of legislation met with hostility, threats, and further restrictive legislation. Education policy formulated on high is entrenched in law so as to enforce compliance, quash dissent, and curtail union activism.

Regardless of the left-right orientation of political parties in power, similar patterns and trends are occurring nationally and transnationally. Recognizing similarities across borders facilitates naming the power relations by means of which the 'ruling apparatus' (Smith, 1987) controls and manipulates the everyday lives of teachers within their local contexts. The absence of government accountability to the public that it purports to serve and the erosion of public services are evident across first and third world countries.[9] Placing reforms within the larger socio-economic context of globalization enables detection of exploitative policies and practices that operate to control people's lives from a distance, and facilitates identifiying the ideology that drives education reform. Like their colleagues in other parts of the world, Ontario teachers through their unions have participated actively in opposing globalization (Martell, 1995) and continue to challenge the values inherent in advanced capitalism that privilege corporate profits, infringe on human rights, and impact on social services including education. Awareness of the negative consequences for women and other marginalized groups opens the field to alternate futures based on social and ecological values, rather than techno-scientific constructions of the future that promote economic values above all else.

Consistent with critical feminist inquiry, this study began by identifying a problem and posing questions to guide the research process: Why are teachers quitting/downshifting? What are the concerns and issues raised by teachers? How are ruling structures coordinated to control teachers' activities? How are power relations orchestrated across the institution of public education? Whose interests are served by education reform? How do gender/class/race relations operate within the education system? How are teachers' work and lives governed through texts, policies, procedures and practices? How are teachers drawn into complicity in their own coercion? Although teachers are the focus, analysis of power relations at work will undoubtedly have relevance for and resonate with the experiences of practitioners within the other feminized caring professions of nursing and social work.

Having laid the ground from which this inquiry arose, chapter 2 situates educational restructuring within the local context of Ontario as integrally connected with events unfolding nationally across Canada and internationally in the global arena. Educational restructuring, as orchestrated by the PC governments under the leadership of Mike Harris and Ernie Eves, is traced genealogically to the report of the 1994 Royal Commission on Learning, *For the Love of Learning*, produced under the previous labour-oriented New Democratic Party (NDP) government of Bob Rae. The pervasiveness of the ideology of educational reform becomes apparent as co-extensive across political parties and nation-states.

Chapter 3 explicates the primary methodology of institutional ethnography developed by Dorothy E. Smith that is conducive to critical/feminist research and activism. The secondary methodology of auto-ethnography and related methodological constructs deployed in the textual analysis are also described. The research process is recounted, from focus group testimony through to supplementary documentary analysis. Brief bibliographic sketches are provided of the teacher-participants at the centre of the study as insider informants of the internal operations of the public education system.

Chapter 4 describes the ruling structures of the institution of public education in Ontario that pertain to teacher-participants. Education restructuring legislation implemented by the PC government is linked to specific recommendations of the Royal Commission on Learning. The various ruling structures governing teachers' lives and work are analysed in terms of genealogy, mandates, and mission statements, as well as the constitution of their executive boards at the time of writing. The ruling structures with jurisdiction over the teacher-participants in the focus group include: Ontario Ministry of Education, Toronto District School Board (TDSB), the Ontario College of Teachers (OCT), Ontario Secondary School Teachers' Federation (OSSTF), Ontario Principals' Council (OPC), Ontario Parent Council, Education Quality and Accountability Office (EQAO), Ontario Institute for Studies in Education at the University of Toronto (OISE/UT), and the business lobby. A complex net of interlocking ruling relations emerges through mapping money flows, text flows, and mobility of personnel across ruling structures at the upper echelons.

Chapter 5 cuts through the façade of public relations rhetoric by undertaking textual analysis of documents internal to the institution of public education. It begins with three specific texts identified by teacher-participants in the focus group as particularly troublesome: the OCT letter of 15 October 2001; the TDSB letter of 22 June 2001, and the Remedial Support Program–Teacher Log. These three documents constitute the starting point for a textual analysis and segue into related texts internal to the institution. Each document provides a gateway to the operation of ruling relations, and reveals how power relations are coordinated intertextually (through discourse) across the various ruling structures. The OCT letter exposes how teachers' professional identity is constructed as 'deficient' and how a partly privatized teacher training industry was set up by this government-controlled body. The TDSB letter discloses adversarial labour relations between teachers and their employers that frames teachers as 'law-breakers' and reveals the imperative to crack down on unions. The RSP–Teacher Log demonstrates how accountability operates in teachers' daily work. The imposition of clockwork and paperwork on extra help offered to students not only contradicts how extra help works in actual practice, but the logs constitute false records and could serve to justify phasing out special education by downloading responsibility onto classroom teachers. What is uncovered through textual analysis of these three documents is how teachers are inscribed in texts and how they are constructed in ways that augment surveillance and control over their lives and work. These documents and others that ensue from them enter the realm of permanent records held by the institution. From this textual analysis, the ideological code constitutive of the institution of public education becomes apparent, as carried in actual policies and practices of the institution.

Chapter 6 challenges official discourses emanating from the university that disseminate the ideology of education reform, in particular school renewal and professional development. Imbued with the authority of 'expert' knowledge, education reform pundits acquire acclaim, inform (or reinforce) government policy, and influence public opinion. This chapter will contest the occupational strategy of 'professionalism,' viewing it as integral to the ruling apparatus and as perpetuating hierarchies of power and privilege. Unionism is revisited as a counterweight to advanced capitalism. As a counterpoint to 'accounting logic,' the notion of an ethic of care is reclaimed from its distortion in neoliberal discourse. Without being prescriptive, alternative egalitarian social relations are proposed that empower teachers as self-reflexive practitioners and as proactive agents of social transformation, through withdrawing complicity with the ruling apparatus and democratizing the institution of public education from within.

The Afterword updates events since the focus group was conducted and shows how the changes implemented during the main onslaught of education restructuring remain largely intact and enshrined in legislation. While decision-makers persist with the ideology of education reform, teacher resistance has achieved some gains. The struggle continues.

2 The Socio-political Context of Ontario

Few would doubt that education is instrumental in shaping society, from which it follows that education is politically charged. Who has access, what is taught and by whom, says a great deal about the values and structure of society. Education policy tends to reflect national priorities, although distinctions between national systems seem to be converging in the age of globalization. Central to inculcating the dominant values and mindset in the populace is controlling teachers; in Ancient Greece, Socrates was sentenced to death by poison for corrupting youth by encouraging them to question the prevailing ethos and to develop independent thought. Historically, formal education was a privilege bestowed upon the few, invariably the sons of the aristocracy. The notion of public education as a basic human right that should be accessible to all has a relatively short and incomplete history globally. Article 26 of the United Nations Universal Declaration of Human Rights (1948) declares that 'Everyone has the right to education. Education shall be free, at least in the elementary and fundamental stages. Elementary education shall be compulsory. Technical and professional education shall be made generally available and higher education shall be equally accessible.'[1]

Whereas the history of public education in Ontario is beyond the scope of this inquiry, a brief overview locates education reform within the socio-political context. In Ontario, Egerton Ryerson is generally credited as the founder of the public school system in the 1840s. For the times, Ryerson's vision of public education was broad and inclusive:

> On the importance of education generally we may remark, it is necessary as the light – it should be common as water and free as air ... Education

among the people is the best security of a good government and constitutional liberty. It yields a steady, unbending support to the former and effectively protects the latter. (Cited in the conclusion of the OSSTF presentation to the Standing Committee on Social Development on Bill 104, entitled *Bill 104: Education Quality at Stake*)

But in the late 1800s, education was politically contested (Gidney and Millar, 1990), as it is today. Gidney and Millar conclude:

Out of the transformation of Upper Canadian grammar schools between 1840 and 1880, in sum, came the Ontario high school, a school that was broadly accessible, highly selective, engaged in offering both boys and girls a revised version of liberal education, preparing students for the universities, professions, and white collar work, and promoting both social mobility and social reproduction. It was an institution that would endure largely unchanged for nearly a hundred years until the early 1960s when Ontarians embraced the notion of an extended secondary education for all young people. (p. 319)

Although the particular issues today may be somewhat different, the essential tension lies between proponents of a system that sorts and selects the 'best' from the rest, and proponents of a broadly inclusive system through both secondary and tertiary levels of education.

The structure of the public education system also has its origins in the political tensions of 1800s. Whereas Ryerson advocated non-denominational though Christian-based public education, the British North America Act of 1867 in placing education under provincial jurisdiction also guaranteed special education rights for Roman Catholics. At the time, education was religious-based and offered through denominational schools that were mainly Protestant in Upper Canada. In Ontario, public funding to Roman Catholic schools accrued gradually up through the grades, until Bill 30 (1985) extended funding to include the senior grades (11, 12, and OAC). The effect of increasing funding to Catholic schools was to reduce funding to secular public schools. Despite constitutional challenges to the anachronistic BNA Act that granted preferential treatment to Catholics over other religious groups, the separation of secular public and Catholic schools remains.[2] In addition, Bill 75 (1986) accorded some measure of autonomy to Franco-Ontarians, through separately elected trustees. When combined, the effect is four types of publicly funded schools in Ontario that reflect the colonial past: English public, French public, English Catholic, and French Catholic.[3] Since teacher-participants are part of the English public system, this study focuses on one of the four, although all are subject to education reform legislation.

Since the advent of public schools, a multitude of commissions and task forces have produced a plethora of studies, reviews, and reports, as successive governments moved to leave a mark on public education. Some recommendations proceeded through to implementation, while many did not. In the post–Second World War period, official documents pertaining to secondary education include the Hope Commission (1950); Robarts Plan (1961); Hall-Dennis Report (1968); Circular H.S.1 (1969–70) and its successor H.S.1 (1974–5); Secondary Education Review Project (SERP, 1980); the Renewal of Secondary Education (ROSE, 1982); Ontario Schools: Intermediate and Senior Divisions (OS:IS,1982); Radwanski Report (1987); Transition Years (1989); Common Curriculum (1993); Royal Commission on Learning (1994). From this listing, it is evident that education was not at a standstill. Some equity gains were being achieved in accessibility and relevancy of education for a more diverse student population during the progressive expansionism of the 1960s and 1970s. In the mid-1970s, from my distant vantage point in London, England, as a recent graduate teaching in an inner-city comprehensive school, the Ontario system seemed appealing in terms of student progression by subject not by grade, with the option of pursuing different subjects at different levels of difficulty, and with the provision of publicly funded alternative schools. The pace of change in educational governance, credit systems, curriculum review, and programs picked up in the 1980s. Bill 82 (1980) mandated that school boards provide special education programs and services for 'exceptional' students. The pace reached fever pitch with the pendulum-swing back to a standards-based, back-to-basics model of education during the full onslaught of education reform (1995–2003).

The provincial election of 1995 brought the Progressive Conservative party to power based on a political platform outlined in the document entitled the *Common Sense Revolution*. The policies implemented under this reform agenda amount to the systematic dismantling of public services, with severe cutbacks to public education, healthcare, and social services. Neither 'common sense' in terms of representing popular wisdom nor 'revolutionary' in the sense of advocating radical social change in the direction of equity, the policies in this document constitute an oppressive backlash against socio-economic democracy by a small but powerful elite. Premier Mike Harris resigned in April 2002 amid growing public criticism of the negative impact of PC policies: in particular, the public inquiry into contaminated water at Walkerton that killed eleven people following privatization of water testing; calls for a public inquiry into the shooting death by Ontario Provincial Police of an unarmed Aboriginal activist, Dudley George, at Ipperwash; and the coroner's inquest into the suicide-death of a pregnant woman, Kimberley Rogers, while under house arrest for welfare fraud. Kimberley Rogers's crime was collecting welfare while on a student loan in her attempt to rise out of poverty through gaining an education – a situation that was legal prior to the Harris welfare reforms. Backed by a well-financed campaign machine and marketed as a different new leader, Ernie Eves (former minister of finance in the Harris cabinet) continued to perpetuate the political economic policies that dominated the 1990s.

Resistance and defiance toward the restructuring of public services is evidenced by unprecedented labour unrest in Ontario throughout the PC government's term in office. Teachers' and nurses' unions have constituted significant voices of dissent.[4] Physicians too, through the Ontario Medical Association, protested cutbacks to healthcare. The fact that physicians were successful in gaining concessions is undoubtedly attributable to the different gender composition and power of the medical profession as compared with teaching and nursing. In contrast, throughout the PC reign, the legislative power of the province was wielded via a litany of legislation designed to restrict, regulate, and control the everyday work and professional lives of teachers. Rotating teacher strikes and withdrawal of voluntary services register objections to education legislation. In particular, opposition to Bill 160 (Education Quality Improvement Act) prompted full strike action by 126,000 teachers across Ontario between 27 October and 7 November 1997. Nevertheless, the bill passed into law in December 1997. This controversial bill of 219 pages (Robertson, 1998) proposed sweeping changes to education. In a key manoeuvre, the provincial government seized control over education spending that was previously under the jurisdiction of local school boards. Under a new funding formula, richer boards – such as Toronto and Ottawa – were severely cut back while smaller rural boards benefited. Contested education reform legislation has induced a power struggle among the provincial government (with its agencies), local school boards, and teachers' federations that has waged since the mid-1990s when neoliberal education reforms commenced with full force.

The threat to the public education system became explicit in Bill 45 (2001) that allowed a tax break of up to $3,500 to parents who chose to send their children to private schools. Couched in the neoliberal rhetoric of 'choice,' Bill 45 exposed the agenda of privatization of public education that was implicit in Bill 160. Synonymous with the American voucher system, white upper/middle class families are the beneficiaries of private education. Excluded are politically disenfranchised and underprivileged groups in society – visible minorities, recent immigrants, the working poor or unemployed, and single parent families – for whom private education is not a 'choice.' The bill passed into law, despite opposition to the implications that it would reduce funds for public education further and promote unequal access to quality education. A tiered education system, as in England and the United States, widens the gap between the rich and the poor. The monoculture of mind of the beneficiaries of private education are further advantaged by the prestige and improved post-secondary opportunities that potentially translate into highly paid influential job prospects.

In parallel with legislation enabling the privatization of education, the public education system was subjected to relentless attacks by government and the media. Discrediting public education served as a ploy to manufacture consent for education reform; indeed, the first PC minister of education, John Snobelen, declared the intention at the outset: to 'create a crisis' in education to stimulate change. From a critical perspective, in *The Education-Jobs Gap*, Livingstone (1999) exposes fallacies and contradictions in the rhetoric of corporate executives who blame public education for the unsatisfactory quality of job entrants. Livingstone inverts the problem to that of underemployment due to increasing credentialization; an oversupply on the job market of educationally qualified candidates suggests struggles over paid work are being waged to preserve the 'competitive advantage' of dominant groups over those in subordinate social positions. This possible ulterior motive for education reform seems plausible, given the glaring contrast between closures of public schools in lower socio-economic areas and the burgeoning of new private academies in Toronto.

Prior to Harris, however, the shift towards corporate-capitalist values in the public sector had already begun under Bob Rae's NDP government in Ontario in the early 1990s. It was the Rae government that undemocratically delivered the social contract. Under the social contract, mandatory unpaid holidays, referred to as 'Rae Days,' were imposed across the public sector to justify salary cuts, significantly affecting schools. Martell (1995) traces relations between Rae's government and the OSSTF, which, as part of the Public Services Coalition, actively participated in bringing the NDP to power and later in ousting them. The NDP's betrayal of its electoral base by distancing itself from the labour movement once in power, and shifting allegiance towards the pro-business 'new right,' marks a significant turning point for that party and for the province of Ontario. The counterweight of official political opposition to the dominance of corporate-capitalist values over social democratic values that was offered by the leftist NDP evaporated. Government policy, beginning with Rae and continuing with Harris/Eves, would henceforth be informed by transnational business leaders, through venues such as the annual World Economic Forum in Davos, Switzerland (Martell, 1995; Ralph, Régimbald, and St-Amand, 1997). Economic growth through global competitiveness and 'comparative advantage' became normalized as 'common sense,' regardless of the human cost.

Aside from the social contract, the legacy left to education by the Rae government was the report of the Royal Commission on Learning: *For the Love of Learning*, which proposed major changes to education. The significance of this document for future educational reform in Ontario was predicted by Martell (1995) in advance of the 1995 election that brought the PC government to power: 'Whatever government took office after June 8 would now follow the pattern laid down by the Rae administration in educational restructuring ... A new education politics in Ontario had been born' (p. vi). Indeed, as subsequent chapters reveal, almost all of the changes orchestrated under education restructuring by the PC government can be traced to specific recommendations made by the Royal Commission on Learning.

Bestowed with re-envisioning public education and appointed by then NDP minister of education and training,[5] Dave Cooke, the royal commissioners exhibit a singular lack of teaching experience in public schools. As indicated by their biographic sketches, preference was given to politicians, bureaucrats, and casualized academics.[6] A breakdown by gender shows that of the five commissioners, three were women and two men. The composition of the commissioners suggests a semblance of equitable representation by gender and race, although it is questionable whether all were full and equal participants. One of the women was unlikely to have participated equally in power relations: as the sole token student representative, Manisha Bharti was singled out for patronizing accolades in the preface:

> It is normally invidious to single out individuals for special mention ... we make special mention of our colleague, Manisha Bharti. During the course of our work, friends invariably asked whether Manisha was as good as her reputation suggested. Our answer, invariably, was "Better." We witnessed her steady growth from 17 to 19. We would like to think she learned something from us; certainly we learned enormously from her ... The title of the report is due entirely to her ... When Manisha becomes Prime Minister, one of us will recommend you [Raf DiCecco, Executive Director] as Chief of Staff. (Royal Commission on Learning, 1994, Short Version, pp. xii–xiii)

The condescending tone and false modesty suggest the watchful gaze of the commissioners over the student representative's 'growth'; real power resides with 'one of us' to ordain her future. The student representative's only actual cited contribution to the document is the title, *For the Love of Learning*, which has been denounced by educator-critics as a misnomer for the type of education system envisaged by the commission. This report superseded the earlier Hall-Dennis Report (1968), replacing what was a progressive, child-centred educational model with a reactionary, technocratic model driven by a one-size-fits-all approach.

The 'four engines' driving the royal commission's vision of education are early childhood education, teacher professionalization/education, technology, and community alliances. The model of education espoused resembles the resurgence of a narrow back-to-basics education that advocates a return to the three Rs, with the addition of technological literacy. The bias toward a consumer-driven corporate vision of education is evidenced by the prevalence of corporate boardroom language throughout the report: outcomes, standards, testing and assessment, stakeholders, private partnerships, quality control, performance indicators, accountability, and so on. Acquiescence to corporate values and the promotion of community (read business) alliances opens the door to corporate intrusion into public education, and paves the way to privatization.

The limited attention accorded by the royal commission to equity pertains mainly to the Roman Catholic and francophone communities (reflecting the dominant founding nations and the identities of the commissioners themselves), with only cursory mention of aboriginal groups and visible minorities. It overlooks the range and diversity of contemporary Canadian society and implicitly promotes assimilation, rather than questioning eurocentric, androcentric middle-class assumptions about education; it is assumed that what is good for white middle-class students is good for everyone. Which recommendations have not been implemented by the PC government is telling. An example is Recommendation No. 137, on the provision of in-service training on equity and anti-racism education, which suggests 'that trustees, educators, and support staff be provided with professional development in anti-racism education.' Even this token gesture toward equity has been ignored in the subsequent reforms. On the contrary, sweeping changes that rolled back equity legislation, affirmative action, and labour rights without public debate, has characterized the PC regime.

Recommendations of the royal commission that have been taken up under education restructuring include: the implementation of a new curriculum (of academic and applied courses and an emphasis on technology); the elimination of the fifth year of high school (OACs); the instatement of the teacher-advisory program (TAP); standardized testing; the literacy test and mandatory community service for students; career education; and the establishment of new bodies to monitor accountability, such as the Ontario College of Teachers (OCT), the Education Quality and Accountability Office (EQAO), and parent councils.

While purporting to operate independently of government, the proposed new bodies to monitor accountability operate closely with the ministry to control and regulate teachers and their work (as will be explicated in chapter 4). The centralization of education under the Ontario Ministry of Education marks a decisive shift in school governance from relatively autonomous local school boards to control by the province. This resembles the loss of autonomy of local education authorities in the United Kingdom under Thatcher with the imposition of national testing of a national curriculum under central control by the Qualifications and Curriculum Authority (Woods, Jeffrey, Troman, and Boyle, 1997). In the United States, where education falls under state jurisdiction, devolution of power to state authorities similarly diminishes the autonomy of local communities, although the specifics vary from state to state, just as they do from province to province in Canada. In New Brunswick, school boards were eliminated altogether (Robertson, 1998, p. 39). In Ontario, centralized power to the province is augmented by decentralized local school management with respect to day-to-day operations that are overseen by school administrators under advisement of parent councils. The alignment of principals with parent councils thus constitutes a means to side-step the intermediary level of school boards, and to exclude teachers from participation in decision-making in the schools where they work.

Contrary to the royal commission's stated intention to combine stability provincially and flexibility locally (vol. 4, p. 25), the emphases in the report and the consequences of implementation suggest the restructuring of school governance is predicated on authoritarian control and standardization, at the expense of teacher empowerment and responsiveness to specific needs and local diversity. The veneration of teachers as 'heroes,' whose collaboration is essential in bringing about educational reform, masks an underlying representation of teachers as technopeasants or technocrats, whose work requires regulation and control by the proposed new bodies. As stated by Commissioner Gerald Caplan, 'There is nothing in the report that is not being done somewhere in Ontario' (OISE/UT Forum on the Royal Commission on Learning, January 1995). Whereas this statement creates the illusion of a bottom-up democratic process of consultation, it may be construed as an admission of appropriation; many of the ideas in the report are selectively plagiarized from individual handpicked teachers, or developed in flagship schools which have the advantage of special sponsorships, supports, and resources. Those initiatives that inform the report fit into the technocratic utilitarian vision of education favoured by the commissioners, with a short-sighted emphasis on technology, skills ('outcomes') and community 'partnerships.' The extent to which *For the Love of Learning* constitutes the game-plan for educational reform becomes apparent when comparing specific recommendations in the report with legislation. As will become clear in subsequent chapters, this textual document commissioned by the former labour-oriented NDP government comprises the blueprint for PC education reform in Ontario.

The vision of education promoted by the Royal Commission on Learning is neither specific nor responsive to the local context of Ontario, but reiterates education reforms begun earlier in the United States and the United Kingdom. An international policy analysis of education reform conducted by Levin (1997) identifies three prevalent strategies deployed in English-speaking countries that are members of the Organization for Economic Co-operation and Development

(OECD): '1. decentralization of authority to schools and the creation of school or parent councils to share that authority; 2. various forms of choice or other market-like mechanisms; 3. increased achievement testing with publication of results and its corollary, more centralized curriculum' (p. 6). From a policy perspective, these strategies are construed as promising useful 'outcomes' for improving student learning – an oft-quoted but ill-defined goal of education reform. Although Levin warns against copying policy reforms from other countries without taking into account differences in 'organizational, political, social and educational traditions,' the basic tenets of educational reform go unchallenged. Whereas there is ample evidence of the pitfalls of education reforms in Britain and the United States, Ontario (and other provinces in Canada) follow the dominant international trend. To cite one indictment of education reform, the *Myth of the Texas Miracle in Education* exposes the public relations conceit of improved standardized test results as concealing high drop-out rates and system failure to meet the needs of marginalized youth, in particular for males of African and Hispanic descent in that state (Haney, 2000). From an equity perspective, a heterogeneous society such as Ontario cannot ignore evidence of systemic bias inherent in standards-based education reform. Tracing the genealogy by which policies and practices become systemically embedded in societal institutions thus requires cognizance of the socio-political context – globally, nationally, and locally.

Within the contemporary context, the retrenchment of the public sector and the move toward privatization of public services in Ontario is situated within and integrally connected to the larger national context of Canada, and the international arena of globalization. Whereas at the beginning of the century the imperatives of colonialism and industrialization were governing 'progress' and affecting people's lives and work, at the end of the century globalization and computerization are espoused as driving change. Meanwhile, the civil rights movement struggled for universal access to education, not exclusively for the privileged few but to be inclusive toward gender/class/race/ethnicity, and educator groups globally continue to challenge external interference in education by the state, religious institutions, and/or multinational corporations. The struggle to oppose corporate intervention is not new. Writing in 1918, Veblen denounced the intrusion of the 'captains of industry' into the university. The importance of education to the globalization agenda of today is substantiated by the extent to which big business has manoeuvred to encroach into and co-opt universities (Slaughter and Leslie, 1997; Newson and Buchbinder, 1988; Turk, 2000; Tudiver, 1999). In their comparative study of post-secondary education in the United Kingdom, the United States, Australia, and Canada, Slaughter and Leslie (1997) identified the trend toward 'academic capitalism,' defined as 'market and market like behaviours' on the part of faculty and institutions. Since Conservative governments were in power during the time period of the study in Britain, the United States, and Canada, but a Labour government in Australia, they attribute the trend toward academic capitalism to the supranational phenomenon of globalization. From this critical perspective, with the emergence of the knowledge economy, the 'products' of education – whether knowledge (as a commodity) or labour (as an educated workforce) – are increasingly determined by and put into the service of the for-profit private sector.

At the provincial level, the Premier's Council (with representatives from business, labour, education, and community organizations) produced two reports that hinge education on the global economy: *Competing in the New Global Economy* (1988) and *People and Skills in the New Global Economy* (1990) (cited in the Royal Commission of Learning, vol. 1, p. 23). At the federal level, the report entitled *Knowledge Matters: Skills and learning for Canadians* (2002) outlines the strategy to position Canada as a leader in the global economy. Based on a human capital theory, three imperatives are highlighted: a well-educated and well-skilled workforce in all parts of the economy and all parts of the country; a looming demographic crunch that will exacerbate skills shortages; and a learning system to meet the skills and labour-force demands of the next decades. Data for predictions are drawn from Statistics Canada, the Conference Board of Canada, and the Canadian Federation of Independent Business. Within this business logic lies the contradiction between extolling the importance of the knowledge economy and reduced government funding through reductions in transfer payments to the provinces for education. Behind the figures lurks a disconcerting social engineering approach to education that is driven by speculative economic forecasts at both levels of government. A myopic deterministic view of the future has risen to dominance that prescribes the 'mission' of education as to enhance competitiveness in the global marketplace. In this narrow utilitarian view, all levels of education are reduced to training a flexible, compliant, and technologically skilled workforce to serve economic growth. Institutional claims of neutrality and objectivity conceal the politically motivated and ideologically driven nature of education reforms geared to serve the interests of the political economy.

From a critical/feminist perspective, there is a significant downside to globalization. The negative consequences of neoliberal public policies on marginalized groups (whether based on gender, race, ethnicity, class, sexual orientation, or other axes of difference) have been an exacerbation of socio-economic inequities. Canada, one of the richest countries in the world and a member of the G8, is not immune: witness the rising incidence of homelessness on the streets of Toronto and lengthening lineups at food banks. Recent census data from Statistics Canada confirm the widening disparity between rich and poor. Mass protests around the globe indicate that as the number of people affected grows, the anti-globalization movement (more proactively referred to as the global justice movement) is expanding to a magnitude that can no longer be dismissed as an anomalous 'interest group.' The turnout at mass protests in Seattle, Prague, Genoa, and elsewhere testify to a growing popular resistance to the imperatives of globalization. Closer to home in Quebec City, protesters converged in opposition to the Summit of the Americas in April 2001, where they were confronted with a heavy police presence and a concrete barricade wall marking the socio-ideological divide. Represented among the protesters were teacher-activists.

In order to make sense of women/teachers' everyday lives and work it is necessary to pay attention to the international political economy (Pettman, 1996). Third world feminists such as Chandra Mohanty and Vandana Shiva argue convincingly that it is women workers in the third world who are most negatively affected by globalization. Women are exploited as a primary source of cheap malleable labour in export-processing zones, where mostly young women workers are managed through the curtailment of labour organizing and the casualization of work (Mohanty, 1997b; Klein, 2000). Control is exercised through disrupting job security in order to keep wages down, thus maximizing profits for private transnational corporations with headquarters in the first world. As in export-processing zones in the third world, the gendered division of labour confers low remuneration, poor working conditions, and disregard for labour rights on women workers in the 'pink ghettos' of what Swasti Mitter (1986) refers to as the 'Third World in the midst of the First.' Comparing women workers in the global marketplace with women in the feminized professions of teaching, nursing, and social work exposes similarities. The economic imperative of minimizing taxes to stimulate the economy and attract investment comes at the price of the erosion of the public sector. The high percentage of women employed in public service work are among those who have suffered the consequences. The impact on teachers transnationally comes into sharp relief in Charlton and Charlton (2001) by the extent of teacher protest action globally. In Africa, teachers have taken strike action over wages and working conditions in Côte d'Ivoire, and non-payment of wages in Guinea-Bissau (p. 206). In India, teachers participated in united strike action with mill workers, bank workers and street hawkers, since 'teachers are not getting their salaries. Besides they suffer from the uncertainties of the contract system ... We don't count.' (p. 240). In China, where over 10,000 primary school teachers gathered to march on the capital to protest reforms threatening their jobs, 'police beat up and severely injured many of the teachers to prevent them getting to Beijing' (p. 230).

Not to diminish the severity of such police brutality, 'teacher bashing' in Canada has taken the form of continual attacks on teachers' professional integrity waged through the media. Adversarial relations prevail in singling out teachers as particular targets for restrictive legislation, threatening to deny their right to strike by declaring teachers as 'essential workers,' and imposing fines or other sanctions for non-compliance. Nevertheless, teacher strikes and protest action have erupted across the Canadian provinces. For example, early in 2002, in British Columbia, 35,000 teachers participated in marches and rallies throughout the province to protest Liberal government policies there; in Alberta, teachers in twenty-two school jurisdictions drew public attention to the decade-long deterioration of public education under Klein's PC government by going out on strike, but were forced to comply with a back-to-work order. The measures may be different, but the effect is similar: to quash dissent and enforce compliance.

Comparing teachers in different regions highlights similarities across nation-states and political party lines, and substantiates the contention that public policy formation is coordinated supranationally according to a particular ideological worldview. Whether imposed on debt-ridden third world countries through Structural Adjustment Programs (SAPs) of the International Monetary Fund (IMF) and the World Bank, or 'voluntarily' adopted by wealthy first world countries (including Canada), the influence of transnational banking institutions has been identified as paramount in orchestrating the global political economy (Chossudovsky, 1997). The global justice movement (led in

Canada by Maude Barlow and the Council of Canadians) challenges the orchestration of power relations by international financial institutions, transnational companies, and supranational organizations such as the World Trade Organization. The economic dictates of these supranational forces are held responsible for the erosion of democracy and basic rights of citizens, curtailing labour unions, dismantling the social infrastructure, relaxing health and safely standards, and rising levels of poverty – tendencies that are evident to varying degrees across nation-states worldwide (Engler, 1995; Greven and Purdy, 2000; Klein, 2000). Corporate-capitalist relations constitutive of globalization increasingly pull the strings at the supranational level and determine public policy.

The Canada–US Free Trade Agreement (FTA, 1989) marks Canada's entry into the competitive arena of globalization under U.S. dominance (Laxer, 1993). This document, initially signed by the federal PC government of Brian Mulroney, was expanded by the Liberals under Jean Chretién to include Mexico in the North American Free Trade Agreement (NAFTA, 1994), and negotiations are under way to incorporate Latin American countries in the Free Trade Agreement of the Americas (FTAA). In joining trade blocs and embracing globalization, the social democratic values embodied in the systems of social welfare, healthcare, and education that distinguished Canada from the United States began to be eroded. Government regulation of economic development in the public interest became subordinate to transnational corporate interests. Both the federal and provincial levels of government, whether Liberal or PC, are therefore implicated in the move away from social democratic values toward corporate-capitalist values in pursuit of 'competitive advantage' in the global arena. The debt and deficit 'crisis' was manufactured (McQuaig, 1995; Laxer and Harrison, 1995) to galvanize public acceptance of extreme austerity measures: government downsizing, the privatization of public services, and severe cutbacks to healthcare, education, and social programs. In the case of the Ontario government, the role of international financial institutions as enforcers of compliance with policies similar to SAPs is identified by Clarke (in Ralph, Régimbald, and St-Amand, 1997):

> Indeed the Harris government's budget strategy is primarily designed to respond to the demands of Wall Street. The world's two leading bond rating agencies, Moody's and Standard and Poor on Wall Street in New York, had already issued a stiff warning to the Rae government by lower-

ing Ontario's cherished credit rating. In the new global economy, these agencies operate as private sector police forces over government finances. (p. 34)

Within the political context of Canada and the division of powers between federal and provincial levels of government, education falls under provincial jurisdiction. By reducing transfer payments to the provinces, the federal government set the conditions for the rise to power of provincial governments favouring big-business interests (Ralph, Régimbald, and St-Amand, 1997) and advocating 'mean and lean' policies toward social services (Harrison and Kachur, 1999). Regardless of the left/right orientation of political parties, neoliberal policies have been implemented provincially, whether PCs under Ralph Klein and Harris/Eves (Harrison and Kachur, 1999), or New Democrats under Bob Rae (Martel, 1995), or Liberals under Gordon Campbell. Through downloading responsibility onto the provinces for making ends meet in education and healthcare, the federal government has managed to distance itself from public criticism, while arguably carrying out the main plank of dismantling the welfare state and divesting from public services. A precedent is the United States federal government's abdication of fiscal responsibility while instating ideological control over education that has been traced to the report entitled *A Nation at Risk: The Imperative for Education Reform* of 1983. Commissioned under the presidency of Ronald Reagan, this report contains substantial input from and reflects the interests of corporate America (Altbach, Kelly, and Weis, 1985; Robertson, 1998).

In Alberta, the provincial government of Ralph Klein holds the dubious distinction of spearheading into Canada neoliberal policies that originated in the 1980s in Britain and the United States. In *Contested Classrooms*, Harrison and Kachur (1999) trace the entry of education reform into Canada via New Zealand and they identify the strategy adopted in Alberta and copied in Ontario: 'Long before Mike Harris, Ralph Klein's government was the first in North America to adopt the political strategy of Roger Douglas in New Zealand: create a crisis, then strike fast and hard before opposition can be mobilized against the new policies' (p. xiii).

Protest and strike action across Ontario and elsewhere suggests that political strategists and public policy-makers underestimate teachers' opposition to autocratic rule and to an ideology of education reform that undermines public education. Locating the education system as a whole within the larger context contributes to disrupting taken-for-granted assumptions and to understanding how the ruling apparatus actually operates. Beginning with the experiences of teachers, subsequent chapters set out to unpack the power relations and to expose the ideological code of education reform in Ontario.

3 Research Methodology

As pointed out by Audre Lorde (1984) in her oft-quoted essay entitled 'The Master's Tools Will Never Dismantle the Master's House,' critical/feminist analysis requires alternative tools to break through dominant paradigms. The research methodology of institutional ethnography offers an alternative that is particularly suitable for qualitative research from a critical/feminist perspective. Moreover, institutional ethnography is conducive to direct action since it provides a coherent framework of analysis to inform socio-political activism. Thus the purpose of explaining the research methodology here is not only to recount how this study was conducted, but also to elucidate how it can be taken up by practitioners working in complex organizational structures, to analyse how the system works and to inform action. This inquiry centres the subjective experiences of a group of women secondary school teachers practising in public schools in Toronto, Ontario. Sources of data include a focus group of teachers and documentary texts internal to the institution. Writing an analysis can be a process of discovery; as a teacher myself, the method of autoethnography is also actually part and parcel of this analysis, integrating my self-reflexive personal knowledge and experiences as an 'insider' within the institution of public education. Incorporating autoethnography into institutional ethnography is consistent with the methodological approach of Smith (1987).

Institutional ethnography, pioneered by Dorothy E. Smith (1987, 1999), constitutes an alternative to mainstream social science research performed on people construed as objects by objective observers who claim to represent a neutral 'truth.' Androcentric assumptions underlying the construction of knowledge and of academic disciplines, including sociology, fail to take into account alternative perspectives. From the alternative 'standpoint of women' (Smith, 1987), institutional ethnography interrogates the 'taken-for-grantedness' of theories, constructs, concepts, and categories embedded in discourses and texts. Although gender constitutes the lens through which inquiry is conducted, it is acknowledged that gender is not a monolithic, unified category but intersects with other axes of difference in various ways. Since the majority of teachers are women, while those in positions of responsibility are primarily men, the perspective of women is particularly relevant in understanding the practice of teaching within a male-dominated power structure.

The primacy of theorizing in research is rejected by Smith (1999) as a universalizing, reified abstraction that displaces and constrains inquiry according to predetermined theoretical paradigms. Theory removed from the everyday world obfuscates understanding the social world as lived by people. Rather, Smith argues that theory and practice are integrally connected. Drawing selectively on feminism, Marxism, and Foucault, Smith's alternative research methodology is an inquiry that begins from the subjective experience of people as they go about their actual daily activities, within the contexts of particular local sites. It is a sociology that shifts the focus from structures to people, centring people's subjective experience as active knowers. Starting from lived experience, the extended ruling relations by which individual activities are coordinated across multiple sites are mapped. The concept of ruling relations affords a useful tool for analysing how power works in complex societies. It is defined as follows:

By the 'ruling relations,' I mean that internally coordinated complex of administrative, managerial, professional, and discursive organization that regulates, organizes, governs, and otherwise controls our societies. It is not yet monolithic, but it is pervasive and pervasively interconnected. It is a mode of organizing society that is truly new for it is organized in abstraction from local settings, extralocally, and its textually mediated character is essential (it couldn't operate without texts, whether written, printed, televised, or computerized) and characteristic (its distinctive forms of organizing and its capacity to create relations both independent and regulative of local setting depend on texts). (p. 49)

Texts thus constitute the bridge between everyday local actualities and ruling relations as 'text-mediated relations' embedded in policies that regulate everyday practices. It is at the 'fault-lines' (Smith, 1987, 1999) between subjective experience and official policy that the underlying structures and mechanisms of control can be accessed. This begins with identifying as markers the disjunctures, discrepancies, and contradictions between people's (in this case teachers') accounts of their everyday worlds, and the discourses perpetuated in and through the official texts of the institution (such as policies, reports, records, computer technologies). The operation of ruling relations is rendered explicit by mapping social relations through the materiality of texts so as to make visible how social relations are organized locally by remote control of the extralocal ruling apparatus.

It is through texts and discourses that the organization of consciousness and coordination of activities across local sites is achieved, sustaining the ruling apparatus by regulating the work of people. According to Smith (and consistent with Foucault), ruling operations occupy no particular place, but organize local sites articulated to it through the authority of legitimized texts and discourses, thus 'regenerating a discursive politics to which we are opposed' (1999, p. 171) by assuming an unquestioned taken-for-grantedness in the workplace. Embedded in texts are ideological codes, or political assumptions, that are carried into local sites where the ideology itself, if made explicit, might not otherwise be assimilable (1999, p. 175). The ideological codes embedded in texts are also inherent in those daily practices in which people are 'active in the ongoing concerting of activities with others' (1999, p. 109), within and across various sites. People (in this case teachers), operating with dual consciousness and 'lacking access to the original site or the original events, are committed, as a course of listening, to the palimpset of the layered reported speech and its one-way dialogic' (1999, p. 181). Thus people are drawn into participating in sustaining ruling operations, sometimes unbeknownst to themselves and/or against their own interests.

With the advent of new technologies, the proliferation and replicablility of text-mediated relations are facilitated, objectifying teachers and instrumentalizing their work. A critical exposé of policies and practices that go against the grain, that contradict the experience of practising teachers, or that constrict their work, contributes to an understanding of how power relations operate in the public education system. This inquiry therefore includes as its centre-piece a dialogue among teachers, picking up cues as markers directly from their experience as voiced in the focus group setting, to guide the analysis. What is troubling to, and/or arouses feelings of unease among teachers, are taken up as constituting markers for further analysis of ruling relations. Teacher-participants therefore constitute 'informants,' revealing problematic fault-lines between the everyday world of teaching and policy mandates, thus providing key access points for making visible the ruling relations.

Central to exploring relations of ruling is starting within the particular accessible world of participants (rather than, for example, surveying them). In this study, access to the lived experience of teachers was gained through a semi-structured focus group as described by Morgan (1988). The advantage of the focus group is not only conducting multiple interviews simultaneously but, more importantly, generating data from the interaction among participants. In this respect, the focus group is different from the individual interview: it has the advantage of access to the substantive content of dialogue between participants, as well as the opportunity to observe how teachers talk about their everyday lives and engage in constructing reality in relation to each other. Through close attention to what participants consider interesting, relevant or important, and through the emergence of similarities and discrepancies or agreement and disagreement between participants in the moment-to-moment face-to-face interaction, the structures and social relations that operate to regulate their work may be identified.

The responsibility of the moderator of the focus group is to create an informal atmosphere conducive to participant dialogue, open exchange, and disclosure. The moderator ensures even participation and encourages different opinions. Attending not only to what is being said but also to what is not being said is important (for example, through being attuned to incongruencies between body language and verbal responses or pauses). Discussion in the group was focused by posing open-ended questions and probes designed to encourage group interaction about the lived experience of teachers. These questions served as a framework for maintaining discussion around the topic, but without limiting responses to a simple question-answer format or inhibiting exchange between participants.

The focus group involved one session with four experienced practising secondary school teachers working in public schools in Toronto. The session was conducted at my home at a time and date convenient to participants' schedules – a Saturday in February 2002. Refreshments were served, creating an informal and relaxed atmosphere. The focus group discussion was audio-taped and subsequently transcribed by me. Recruitment of participants was enabled by using contact information from staff lists acquired during my prior teaching engagements. Six potential participants were contacted initially. The invitation to participate was followed by telephone contact, in which questions and/or clarifications were addressed and a date set for the focus group session. All were willing to participate, but two were unable to attend on the scheduled date.[1] The focus group finally consisted of Alice, Helena, Jessica, and Rachel (pseudonyms). Telephone contact was followed up by a letter explaining details of the research study and including an informed consent form.

Ethical considerations are paramount in institutional ethnography to avoid objectifying participants as disembodied data to be interpreted by a 'neutral' observer. Respect for the subjective experiences and privacy of participants is coupled with the obligation of the researcher to accurate reporting. Participants in this study were fully informed about the purpose of the study in advance and could withdraw at any time. Written informed consent was obtained prior to commencement, including permission to audio-tape the focus group session. Confidentiality on the part of participants was also stated as a requirement. Participants were invited to review the transcript of the focus group for accuracy if they wished to do so. At no time were participants judged or evaluated on their effectiveness as teachers. Benefits included the opportunity to share experiences and engage in dialogue with peers, in a relaxed atmosphere that is not usually afforded in the workplace. Details that might reveal the identities of individual participants or their schools have been omitted, or have been altered in such a way as not to change the substantive content.

Careful selection of participants is crucial to the success of a focus group. The selection criteria established in advance were women, with at least ten years teaching experience, and with qualifications in more than one subject (including various combinations of mathematics, computer science, social services, physical education, special education, English, and French). Based on these criteria, there was not one woman of colour on the staff lists from which selection was made. Although one of the participants is Jewish, and another is an immigrant to Canada, visible minorities appear to be underrepresented in teaching. This may be indicative of the demographics of the teaching profession in general. In the absence of official race-based statistics, this observation corroborates minority parents' call for more diverse role models in education. Because of a longstanding familiarity with the system, all four teacher-participants possess an 'institutional memory' that enables them to reflect on recent changes in the school system in relation to past policies and practices. All have taught at other schools in Toronto during their careers and two of the four have also taught abroad, thus contributing a comparative perspective. The teacher-participants were known to each other as current or former colleagues, but not as personal friends. The teacher-participants are also known to me by acquaintance as former colleagues; however, I do not hold a position of responsibility, nor am I in a position of power or privilege in relation to any of the participants.

A shared reference point is that all participants (as well as myself) taught at the same school during the bulk of the Harris/Eves educational reforms. The school, for which the pseudonym Beaconsfield Collegiate is used, is located in a middle-class neighbourhood in Toronto. Beaconsfield Collegiate is considered a 'good school' by teachers. What does this mean? The facilities are in relatively good repair, the staff is stable, a high proportion of students continue on to post-secondary education, and the school takes pride in its academic standards and protects its reputation. Discipline problems are generally not a major issue. There is an English as a Second Language (ESL) program at the school, since the student body is somewhat diverse. As compared with downtown Toronto schools, however, the student population is less reflective of the full range of socio-economic and cultural backgrounds, and program offerings have traditionally emphasized academic subjects.

Of the four participants, one chose to take early retirement, two have downshifted to part-time, and only one is teaching full-time. All are also parents, with children of varying ages at elementary or secondary school, university, or have graduated. In order to provide a sense of who the participants are in this inquiry, the following brief biographic sketches have been assembled from the focus group discussion.

Alice teaches modern languages and held a position of responsibility as head of department. As a member of a curriculum writing team, she participated in the development of the new curriculum. Alice communicates a love of languages for the access they provide to other cultures and perspectives. Her desire to 'get kids hooked' on the contemporary usefulness of languages informs not only her teaching practice but was brought to curriculum writing, despite the limitations she describes as having been imposed by the ministry. Based on experience in different schools and having taught in Europe, Alice brings a comparative perspective and critical reflection on educational restructuring in Ontario. Although she was ahead in her 'game plan,' she took early retirement in June 2001, due to deteriorating conditions in education, combined with pressures in her personal life, including assisting ill and aging parents. To supplement her decreased pension income (because of early retirement), she now does supply teaching. Rather than LTOs (Long Term Occasional supply teaching), Alice elects assignments of a day or two so that she has time for herself to read and go to the theatre, instead of marking and preparation at night and on weekends that consumed her life as a full-time permanent teacher. Much to Alice's dismay, her daughter has followed her footsteps and is currently enrolled in teacher training.

Helena teaches mathematics and computer science full-time. As an adult immigrant to Canada, she recognizes that the politically oppressive tendencies she 'ran away from' when she emigrated are emerging in Ontario. Her school-age children are in elementary and secondary public schools. At the end of the day, she has limited energy left to help her own children with homework. The only full-time teacher in this group, Helena is also the only one to use the language of survival in managing changes that necessitate her working 'until 2 o'clock in the night' to prepare lessons and materials for her classes. Jessica describes Helena's classes as quiet and attentive, indicating her level of dedication and preparedness. Helena believes it is important to keep up with innovations in computer technology and the utilization of interesting applications derived from the real world. Having worked in industry before entering teaching, Helena sees a return to industry ('at double the pay') as her way out if the oppressive political climate in schools continues.

Jessica has taught social sciences, 'gifted' education, and physical education. In order to make time for her family and volunteer work in the community, she downshifted to part-time. Her children are in secondary school and are also involved in competitive extra-curricular sports. An optimistic and energetic person, she has a lively sense of humour and takes an active part in co-curricular activities in the school. During her days as a student, she was somewhat of a rebel, lending a non-conformist spark to her teaching practice. Her belief that education should be fun is reflected in the animated interaction in her classes. Active engagement in her own learning is evident in the fact that she holds a masters degree and she 'loves taking courses.'

Throughout her career Jessica has expanded her repertoire of teaching areas. If her teaching schedule becomes too restrictive or if her subject preferences are not honoured, Jessica will simply quit.

Rachel teaches mathematics, science, and computer science, part-time. She recently became a grandmother. A friendly and spontaneous maternal demeanour characterizes her relations with students; she will give students a 'pat on the back' for effort, although she finds herself more reserved and cautious in the current climate of surveillance. Fairness and a concern for disadvantaged students denote her caring approach. Previous experience teaching in vocational schools carries over into a concern for what happens to those students under the recent changes. Confident in her position, Rachel is not a 'pushover.' Diversions from the standard curriculum bring her classes alive through student projects connecting mathematics with the magic of numbers and with art, to which end she engages in personal research on her own time. Helena comments on the 'amazing projects' Rachel's students have produced. Due to time pressures in the new curriculum, she laments the loss of this creative aspect of her teaching practice and the connection it affords with students.

Based on the focus group testimony of these teacher-participants, the subjective experiences and issues raised in the group constituted a starting point for selecting documentary texts for follow-up analysis. These documents in turn led to other documents/texts referred to, through the intertextuality of text-mediated relations. Sources of textual data from the public domain were derived from three major categories: form letters, newsletters and memos published and/or circulated internally to teachers by the school, TDSB, OSSTF, or the OCT; public documents from the Ministry of Education and the media; and electronic texts available at the websites of the various structures and constituencies that govern teachers. Access to textual data was obtained through utilizing printed material previously collected by me as a teacher with the TDSB, and current textual material searched out as needed. Public archival resources and internet websites of various institutions affecting teachers were also accessed. Documents did not include private or confidential records on participants or their schools.

Data analysis comprised four interconnected processes: coding the transcript of the focus group session and identifying markers of ruling relations; identifying ruling structures pertaining to the public education system; mapping ruling relations between structures of ruling through textual analysis of documents; and finally, identifying the ideological codes in the data.

The first part of the data analysis involved transcribing and coding the audio-tapes immediately following the session, providing a word-by-word immersion in the text. The transcript was compared and integrated with field notes taken at the time, annotating discursive details of the interaction as it unfolded. Details included verbal expressions in the dialogue (for example, emphases, intonation, overlapping speech, hesitation, and type of language used), as well as emotional tone (for example, laughter, pacing, volume, body language), and group dynamics between the participants (for example, support/confrontation, agreement/disagreement, who is dominant/quiet, arrival/departure). This time-consuming process provided an in-depth and nuanced transcript of the focus group while the experience was still fresh in memory. The focus group analysis guided the direction of the document analysis, with participants acting as informants of problematic educational policies and practices that impact on the day-to-day work and lives of teachers. The transcript was coded by comparing and interconnecting actual experiences, activities, and observations and clustering similar patterns into themes. By tracing repetition, recurring issues, related threads in the dialogue and the emergence of meanings as clarified over the course of the exchange, themes and sub-themes were extracted (for example, surveillance; caring and counting; clockwork). Sub-themes were grouped and distilled into major themes, or alternatively themes were broken down into sub-themes.

Markers were also detected where tensions were experienced by teachers (for example, between declared intentions or policy requirements and actual behaviours). These gaps between appearances and actuality indicate fault-lines that conceal/reveal the operation of underlying ruling relations. Expressions of uneasiness or heightened emotional content (either verbal or non-verbal as detected in speech patterns and body language), confusion, uncertainty, contradictions and discrepancies within and between teacher statements were cued as markers that determined the direction for further documentary textual analysis.

The second process identified the ruling structures governing the public education system (the institution). The composition of executive boards, mandates, and sources of authority of the various ruling structures were analysed. Tracing the genealogy of ruling structures within the larger politico-economic context is described by Foucault as an 'analysis of descent' (in Rabinow, 1977, p. 83); rather than pursuing elusive, essentialist 'origins' back through linear-historical time, genealogy seeks connections and broadens the field in order to identify the discursive practices or discourses that dominate institutionalized structures. Although structural analysis is not normally part of an institutional ethnography, it facilitates recognizing how power is constructed and foregrounds patterns and/or omissions across the institution as a whole.

Through mapping connections between structures, the ruling apparatus is made visible as dispersed over various sites far removed from the day-to-day reality of the classroom. The extent to which interlocking structures that govern the education system are linked by flows of paper, technology, money, and the mobility of personnel (especially at the upper echelons) became apparent. Increasingly linked through technology transfer, the organizational policies and procedures of the ruling apparatus are coordinated in complex ways that objectify teachers and control their everyday work from a distance.

The third analytic process mapped the ruling relations (Smith, 1999). Comparing the experiences of teachers with related documentary texts (policies, procedures, legislation, statistics, reports, classifications, and so on) draws attention to contradictions and disjunctures that are indicators of the operation of ruling relations. Analysis of discrepancies between subjective knowledge (experience) of focus group participants and objectified knowledge (official texts) thus makes visible the mechanisms by which control is exercised over teachers' work and lives; for example, institutional claims to be student-centred are contradicted by teaching practice according to standardized curricula and computerized report cards. The fault-lines or gaps between teachers' experience, including the activities performed in actual practice and related official documentation, provide access to knowledge about what is really going on. Official documents – as textual 'facts' – govern, coordinate, and control teachers' work. By tracing the social relations that connect the work of participant teachers with the work of others, the 'invisible' processes of the education system were located, revealing how routinized organizational procedures regulate the everyday work and control the lives of teachers beyond the classroom.

The fourth process integrated and extended the analysis to highlight recurring motifs across text-mediated relations so as to discern the ideological code constitutive of public education restructuring in Ontario. The social reorganization of knowledge within public education, orchestrated through generalized organizational policies and procedures, is coordinated across multiple sites through the texts of the institution. These texts carry ideological beliefs, norms, and values that are introduced into local sites where they are reproduced through the activities of participants within the institution. Making visible the ideological code is the core of an institutional ethnography, since it is the key to raising socio-political consciousness and empowering teachers.

These four processes were neither discrete nor sequential, but dialogical and cyclical throughout the process of data analysis, informing and extending one another. Whether coding the focus group transcript, identifying ruling structures, mapping ruling relations, or deciphering the ideological codes, discourse analysis was applied.

According to Smith (1999), discourse is 'intertextuality.' The organization of discourse, as 'a field of relations' of 'objectified worlds known-in-common,' is coordinated in and through institutional scripts and official texts. 'Discourse is understood as determined intertextually and beyond the intention of individual speakers or writers' (p. 103), thus occupying no particular place but rather is widely dispersed:

> Texts generated in different settings –for example government systems of collecting statistics, social scientific research at universities and think tanks, policy making in government, and mass media – are coordinated conceptually, producing an internally consistent picture of the world and providing the terms of policy talk and decisions. (Smith, 1999, p. 157)

For discourse analysis, Smith draws on the discourse theory of Mikhail Bakhtin. Analogous to Bakhtin's 'secondary speech patterns,' Smith recognizes discourse, not as sets of abstract ideas, but as actual practices organized in and through texts – that is, as coordinated intertextually. It is through analysis of the specific 'utterance' in relation to language usage, and of actions in relation to normative conventions, that the dichotomies between individuals and society can be connected. According to Bakhtin (in Holquist, 1981), through dialogue (whether spoken or textual) within diverse historical and socio-cultural language contexts, meaning is constructed such that 'actual social life and historical becoming create a multitude of concrete worlds, a multitude of bounded verbal-ideological and social belief systems' (p. 288). Dissociating from dominant language usage and identifying appropriation involves a process of 'naming' and reclaiming language:

'expropriating it, forcing it to submit to one's own intentions and accents is a difficult and complicated process' (p. 294).

In textual analysis of the focus group, staying close to the everyday experience and language of participants is therefore essential to avoid overlaying, interpreting, and framing through the language of academic discourse or theory. Focus group discourse analysis involved listening closely to the 'utterances' of participants in order to extract meaning and to understand meaning-making in-process from the vantage point of participants. Understanding shared meaning through the particular sense associated with words and utterances, vocabulary and metaphors, is important to attune to inter-subjective experience as accurately as is possible.

The shared socio-ideological specificity of language usage of teachers was evident by the extent to which mutual understanding flowed through the dialogue, leaving gaps to the outsider's ear. Language specificity was also evident when participants were 'breached' (Garfinkel, 1967) in certain dialogical segments involving collaborative efforts at making sense of their experiences, and in attempts at translating or interpreting the 'foreign' language/discourse of policy directives. This highlights the importance of context in interpreting dialogue and texts, and also explains how miscommunication occurs across socio-ideological divides. Uncertainty, hesitation, stuttering, and searching for words suggested disjunctures between experience and the official line of policy-talk. Alternatively, excited pitch or tone, increased volume, and acceleration of pace occurred when meanings were unequivocal. Identified as markers, instances of breaching offered clues or access points for further exploration, either through probing questions or through follow-up textual analysis.

The concept of breaching is particularly useful to explicate disjunctures between experience and official texts. Garfinkel's breaching experiments, that began with the game of tick-tack-toe, progressed into closer to real-life situations involving casual conversations and student counselling. Among these latter series, experimenters were instructed to insist on the clarification of commonplace remarks made while engaged in casual conversation with acquaintances. In conversation, fundamental presuppositions are implicit, due to a 'reciprocity of perspectives.' When breaches of 'interpretive trust' in mutual understanding of commonplaces occurred in these experiments, three types of reaction ensued. First, participants' emerging doubts about discrepancies between 'appearance' and 'reality' were attenuated for as long as possible, as they continued to (co-)operate according to the assumed 'rule' or trust, granting the benefit of the doubt to the experimenter/ transgressor. When this was no longer possible, not only did interaction break down rapidly, but agitation, strong sanction, and moral outrage were aroused at the rupture of 'perceived normality.' As stated by Heritage (1984), 'If a socially organized and intersubjective world stands or falls with the maintenance of this interpretive trust, then it is not surprising to find that it is attended to as a deeply moral matter. We should, indeed be surprised if it were not' (p. 97). Alternatively, when a breach of trust of reciprocally understood implicit 'rules' occurred, dissonance and anxiety were dispelled by interpreting the manoeuvre as a joke, enabling participants to make sense of it. Similarly, Bakhtin (in Holquist, 1981) identifies the 'mockery mode' as one of the strategies in the unofficial sphere for coping with or subverting the dominant 'monologic' of the official discourse. During the focus group, for example, participants laughed and mocked the illogicality (according to them) of a new policy of the TDSB that in the case of snowstorms, teachers are now required to produce a doctor's note to avoid pay deduction!

All three reactions identified by Garfinkel in the breaching experiments – benefit of the doubt, the mockery mode, and moral outrage – were manifested during the focus group session, when official policy directives violated the reciprocity of perspective as understood by the teacher-participants. Garfinkel's notion of breaches of interpretive trust offers an explanatory construct for the disconnect between the mutually exclusive discourses of policy constructors of education reform and practising classroom teachers (the so-called policy implementers).

A reciprocity of perspectives among teacher-participants was evident in the focus group. Conversation was animated and involved candid disclosure, sharing of experiences, and collaborative sense-making. In sustained group exchange, utterances are not simply attributable to a single voice but emerge through interaction between participants in the process of meaning construction within the 'collective subjective' experience (Gramsci, in Buttigieg and Callari, 1975). At moments of intense exchange, the conversation was reminiscent of the discursive style attributed to women by Deborah Tannen (1990), as overlapping and interjecting speech patterns, supportive comments, confirmations, affirmations and redirections uttered simultaneously, unlike the taking turns at centre stage that Tannen claims characterizes men's conversation patterns. This made it difficult to transcribe some sections of the tape when emotional energy was high and several voices were speaking at once. When occasional differences of opinion or disagreement occurred, rather than a confrontational argumentative style, collaborative negotiation in the effort to figure out 'what's going on' was evident in the focus group transcript. Similar gender differences in conflictual interactions were also identified by Tannen (1990). Participation was even and active. Sense-making emerged through dialogue without an identifiable dominant member, nor was there evidence of 'group think' operating in the group.

On its own momentum, the focus group lasted more than an hour longer than originally scheduled. There was laughter and camaraderie that teacher-participants remarked is missing nowadays, given rushed daily schedules and the isolated physical layout of schools, with separate classrooms, subject-specific work areas, and a staff room in a remote part of the building. The staff room as a venue for interdisciplinary exchanges (whether regarding subject disciplines or students) apparently has diminished with new time constraints; exchanges now tend to be limited to momentary random crossing of paths in the photocopy room or the washroom. The informality of the exchange provides a privileged eavesdropping on teacher-talk. While similar to a staff-room conversation, the longer time frame than is normally available in the school setting allowed greater in-depth exploration of issues, enabling more sustained comparisons of experiences and reflections on changes, drawing on the past and other school contexts. Although questions were prepared in advance, the focus group took on a life of its own that addressed the questions spontaneously, with the added benefit of revealing additional material that may not have emerged had a rigid adherence to a question/answer format prevailed. My role became one of bringing the focus back periodically and seeking clarification on changes to which participants were privy that had emerged in the five months since I took study leave to conduct this research.

Not only did the focus group provide research data but it was found useful to the participants. This was expressed directly by them and is evident in the intensity of exchange, in the active sense-making process that materialized through comparing experiences, and also in subtle shifts that emerged through dialogue, as for instance in the dawning realization that collegiality between teachers and principals is compromised by the new managerial role of school administrators. The ease of exchange may be attributable at least in part to careful selection of participants in advance. Not only were they known to each other but also they are compatible by gender, experience, and dedication to classroom teaching, with no 'aspiring administrators.'[2] Advising participants in advance of who else might be participating facilitated group cohesiveness by providing the opportunity to withdraw or to make recommendations of others who might be interested. Some strong language was used – 'bull shit,' 'it's a pissing context,' 'bloody' (followed by a prompt apology) – indicating that participants were not presenting a public relations front, but engaged in a free-flowing exchange uninhibited by the presence of the tape recorder. I take this as a privilege of trust in me to represent the focus group in a respectful way.

Markers of the operation of ruling relations were identified in relation to three specific documents referred to as problematic by teacher-participants during the focus group: the letter from the OCT stipulating requirements for the Professional Learning Program; the letter from the TDSB deducting a day's pay; and the form of the Remedial Support Program – Teacher Log recording extra help offered to students. These three texts constituted the starting point for the textual analysis (see chapter 5). Since the OCT letter had been thrown in the garbage by both participants who received it, alternate avenues of data collection had to be explored to obtain a copy. Fortunately, participants knew of a colleague who had received the letter and who 'never throws anything out.' Thus, I was able to obtain a copy.

Each of the letters was identified according to letterhead, date, addressee, signator/s, to whom it was copied, and what enclosures or attachments were included. Textual analysis involved coding the type of language used and the sources of power and authority upon which claims were based (such as legislation, related documents, or other professions). The contents were contextualized to antecedent events, identifying the actions described or prescribed in the text, and the consequences threatened (for example, for non-compliance). The paper trail of the letter itself was mapped, as well as related documents that preceded or followed the letter, or that were referenced intertextually. A similar analysis was applied to the Teacher Log form. Mapping these three documents revealed extensive links between the ruling structures of the education system and the complex interplay of text-mediated relations governing teachers' work and constructing their identities. From this analysis, what emerged is how teachers become inscribed and objectified in documents in ways that assume an independent textual reality of permanent files and records of the institution. Detached and apart from teachers' experiences and remote from the sites within which they practise daily, these records come to construct teachers in ways that exert power over their daily work and careers, and over which teachers have limited control.

The process of comparative analysis of the text-mediated relations of the institution continued to the point of saturation, when variations and contradictions within and between the subjective experiences of teacher-participants and the official texts of the institution were sufficiently clear that the ideological code became apparent. Credibility is not based on traditional scientific criteria of 'reliability' and 'validity' but relies on triangulation, using a combination of research methodologies and techniques that operate as correctives to the limitations inherent in any one approach: institutional ethnography, autoethnography, focus group, informal interview, documentary analysis, and micro-macro-analysis. Teacher-participants' testimony expressed in the focus group transcript as the primary reference point was cross-referenced with print or electronic texts of the institution, and field notes from informal in-person or telephone interviews with representatives of the ruling structures or other professions. The analysis proceeded until clarity emerged that reconciled discrepancies between participants' testimony and official claims. This approach differs from 'objective' rules of evidence, such as reliance on official authority or statistical sampling. Its strength lies in breaking through surface 'common sense' to access a 'truth' beneath that which appears to be the case at face value. As such, it would not have mattered which texts were selected as the starting point for textual analysis, since any text that arouses unease for any insider informant could provide access to the interconnected text-mediated relations that carry the ideological code of the institution. The aim is not generalizability of findings, but to represent a particular context and location that is generalized to theory. The researcher is 'responsible in terms of "truth," accuracy and relevance' (Smith 1999, p. 25) toward insider informant accounts, and for following up with thorough analysis.

Through the process of writing this inquiry, *autoethnography* emerged as an integral part of the analysis. As a teacher myself, the day-to-day reality of teaching practice is within my realm of experience – physically, cognitively, emotionally, socially – so that the boundary between institutional ethnography and autoethnography seemed blurred at times, and at other times complementary (for example, enabling access to my personal documents and files held by the institution, without violating participants' privacy). My personal knowledge of the school, of recent and past events, of various people and places referred to in the discussion permitted a level of interpretive trust and reciprocity without getting bogged down in commonplace details. During the analysis, I became aware of the extent to which I share an understanding of implicit meaning, so that much goes unsaid and is assumed to be understood by 'insiders' of a particular social group (in this case teachers) that is inaccessible to or misunderstood by 'outsiders.' Insider understanding, however, is both an advantage and a disadvantage: the advantage is access to the experiential world of the social group; the disadvantage is taking for granted the assumptions of the social group. Being on study leave for the year permitted a degree of detachment and distance from the daily reality of teaching and provided the luxury of time for critical reflection.

Autoethnography as a genre of writing (Richardson, 1997; Ellis, 1997) and a critical methodology (Denzin and Lincoln, 2000) extends beyond the traditional personal narrative that tends to privilege the individual 'voice,' point of view, or experience; it expands the personal-subjective to include inter-subjective and self-reflexive analyses of the socio-political context and the power relations that shape one's experience. How we-teachers are 'othered' or objectified in official accounts and how we-teachers participate in maintaining existing power relations by 'othering' constitute dual aspects that mirror each other. To the extent that writing involved identifying the social, historical, political, and economic forces affecting teachers lives, it has been a process of 'conscientization' (Freire, 1972) for me. As an insider-outsider of the teaching profession, through the process of writing, I came to understand the complexity of influences that have shaped me through my work (and vice versa). Just as shape emerges to the writing in-process, so too is the writer shaped by it.

Thus, the process of writing itself is a 'method of inquiry' (Richardson, 1997) and also a transformative practice. It extends beyond reporting earlier findings, or proving/disproving foregone conclusions as in the scientifico-deductive method, but rather is integral to the exploration and discovery. Writing as inquiry is open-ended, entering into uncertainty with no known outcome. For me it can best be described as a kind of 'academic sleuthing,' following a trail, delving into dark corners, connecting a myriad threads (*which threads are selected?*) and weaving them into a meaningful document (*meaningful to whom?*).

New questions continually arose in the process: How do I honour participants' experience and analyse their words without privileging theory, or my own theory-in-use? Am I contributing to objectifying participant-teachers too, editing and selecting what suits me? How do I balance hope (empowerment) with despair (hegemony)? Who is the intended audience? If this text is to do more than sit on a library shelf with a myriad of other studies, accessible only to academics (or collecting dust), where do I take it? What do I do with this new understanding? How do I move further toward transformative praxis in my personal/professional life?

These are some of the personal real-life challenges raised by the writing process. Indeed, this book is another phase in the process; through readers it enters the intertextual world in ways that I trust will contribute to alternative critical discourses to the dominant discourse of education reform.

4 Ruling Structures and Relations

Analysis of ruling relations is facilitated by identifying the ruling structures, or power brokers, of the institution of public education as a whole. The 'analysis of descent' begins with discerning contradictions between what the ruling structures say they do and how teacher-participants perceive them. Public relations pronouncements by the various structures in print or in electronic form at their websites provide access to the ruling relations that pertain within and between the ruling structures. Websites proved to be a prolific source for collecting data about ruling structures in claims they make about their operations and histories, intentions declared in mission statements, the composition of executive boards including biographic sketches of directors and board members, and disclosed funding sources. What electronic links are made available (or excluded) at the various websites offer clues to the relations among ruling structures, indicating which are closely connected and which are excluded or marginalized. Print materials including magazines, memos, and newsletters that circulate internally are also drawn on and cross-referenced. Names begin to pop up (like usual suspects) and are tracked across ruling structures and through the text-mediated relations of the institution. The extent to which educational restructuring can be traced to specific recommendations of the Royal Commission on Learning becomes evident through comparing legislation enacted by the PC government with recommendations in the report produced by the commission appointed by the earlier NDP government.

In order to execute the reforms envisaged by the royal commission, fundamental restructuring was proposed to the power relations between the major power brokers in education, identified as the ministry, school boards, and teachers' unions:

> The relationship between the Ministry and the federations is important but difficult. It seems obvious to us that, if the education system is to improve in the many ways we have prescribed, it is essential that both sectors must focus on building collaboration within the system. The Ministry, boards, and the federations must work together in the service of better learning for students. (vol. 4, p. 119)

The solution proposed to this 'difficult' relationship is centralization of power to the ministry to take 'a leadership and management role' (p. 119) and to ensure that 'collaboration is non-negotiable' (p. 123). What does this oxymoron actually mean? Non-negotiable with whom? Who determines the meaning and terms of 'collaboration?' What is the difference between non-negotiable collaboration and coercion? The positive spin on collaborative relations orchestrated through the restructuring of pre-existing educational structures and the formation of new structures masks the unequal power relations and decidedly anti-union, anti-democratic sentiments that are associated with authoritarian regimes.

Pre-existing Ruling Structures

When the Progressive Conservative government came to power it did not hesitate to strike fast and hard: the swift passage of complex legislation such as Bill 26 (Savings and Restructuring Act, known as the Omnibus Bill, 1995), Bill 104 (Fewer School Boards Act, 1997), and Bill 160 (Education Quality Improvement Act, 1997) among others, bestowed unprecedented power on the Ministry of Education, diminished the role of school boards, and marginalized teachers' unions. Restructuring, first by creating the new superministry renamed the Ministry of Education and Training (initiated under the Rae government) and then reshuffling into the Ministry of Education/Ministry of Training Colleges and Universities, undoubtedly created significant upheaval within the bureaucracy of the ministry, at the same time as sweeping education reforms were being mandated according to arbitrarily imposed deadlines from 'command central.' It is the ministry that is responsible for overseeing the implementation of education legislation through coordinating the various educational structures. At the ministry website, the new bodies of the Education Quality and Accountability Office (EQAO), the Ontario College of Teachers (OCT), and the Ontario Parent Council all have links, suggesting that they operate in concert to enforce compliance with legislation.

Ministerial control over education was secured through the centralization of funding and the enforcement of fiscal restraint, thereby controlling the purse strings. The economic rationalism of the arbitrarily devised 'new' *funding formula* allocates money to schools based on to a standard allotment according to square footage per student enrolled. According to Hugh Mackenzie's (2002) critique of school funding, when the effects of increased enrolment and inflation are taken into account, the seventy-two school boards across Ontario had lost $1.28 billion in funding since 1997, with 69 per cent of the total loss concentrated in the Greater Toronto Area. Presented as public service announcements, the PC advertising campaign during the 1999 election misrepresented to the public the impact of the funding formula as reducing class sizes to an 'average' of twenty-two in secondary schools. Conflating 'average' class size with 'maximum' class size misrepresents what teacher-participants experience in their classrooms:

HELENA: It depends on the subject. In mathematics I had 35, 28, 30 [students].
JESSICA: Well, they let 35 [students] start and then you'll end up with 30. Every time I've taught Human Geography, I've always had over 30 ...
RACHEL: Well, and teachers who have Special Ed ... I know somebody who [teaches Special Education]. She has only six kids and she said to me, well she said, 'Yes, but it's hard because they're disabled.' Well, I had 30 *and* I had 8 that were disabled *in* the classroom! So, there's your average! You've got your person with six or eight [in Special Education classes] and you've got your other person with 30 or 35 and the average is 20, right!
HELENA: And with 28 to 32 students in the classroom, it's almost impossible! With 30 students you cannot practically take care of those 6 or 7 who obviously are not interested.

With large class sizes, caring for students is compromised and 'at-risk' students are the ones who are most negatively affected. Even the government's own Education Equality Task Force commissioned to review the funding formula confirmed in its report (referred to as the Rozanski Report, released in December 2002) the inadequacy of funding to public schools and the impact on the classroom that teachers' unions, parent groups, and some school boards have protested all along. Nevertheless, the Harris/Eves regime continued to deny the impact on classrooms (that is, students and teachers) and sidestepped Rozanski's recommendations to amend the funding formula to take into account the real costs of education.

Aside from funding and overseeing the implementation of government legislation, a primary function of the ministry is developing curriculum policy. To this end, the self-proclaimed accomplishments of the minister include the implementation of a teacher-proof new *curriculum* and the institution of a standardized new *report card* for students across the province. These documents that govern the everyday work of teaching and evaluating students reduce teacher autonomy and discretion, standardizing education at the expense of the individual needs of students. Teacher-participants contest curriculum change as amounting to no real pedagogical change, suggesting a lost opportunity to radically rethink education. The process of curriculum writing is described as a hit-and-miss process, coordinated according to the business practice of bidding for contracts, with private companies in some cases entrusted to design the new curriculum. The only criterion laid down by the ministry was a distinction between academic and applied courses that marks a return to streaming. Alice describes her experience on a curriculum-writing team and the struggle to integrate theory and practice into both types of courses, while maintaining this arbitrary distinction imposed by the ministry:

ALICE: I have no problem embracing new things and when the new curriculum came out I was fully prepared to say Yeh! This could be really great! Now, I got in on an interesting thing, because, what happened was that the ministry I guess concocted this, the Conservative government. The ministry came down with a few rough ideas to change the curriculum, and then somebody had to define what it was going to be. They must have had some educational specialists working on things and then they simply farmed out the development of the [curriculum] documents to various companies; sometimes it was school boards who were allowed to bid on these things and some school boards did win. But for example in Moderns, it was a private company that won the bid. Now I happen to know one of the women who was heading up this company and she did assemble a terrific team of educators from all across the province. We created the document [Moderns curriculum]. And all we knew when we went in on this was there are two things required: we must have an academic program and we must have an applied program. Great, this sounds terrific, you know. Something new, different. Great! Applied. Wow! What is that? [In the end] I think it did come out the way we wanted it to. It does have gaps here and there. However, we had to spend hours and hours agonizing to find out what it was that we wanted. And we submitted a number of things, sent it back to them [the ministry] and they sent it straight back to us and said, 'No, no, no! This is not what we want.' But at the same time they couldn't give us any definition [of academic and applied]. Well, take *that* to the classroom!

The new curriculum in mathematics is described as the same old stuff recycled and compressed down into earlier grades. Especially in cumulative subjects, the effect on students of the level of difficulty of the new curriculum and an unrealistic timeframe to cover the course leaves teachers with the dilemma of meeting their responsibility of delivering the curriculum on time or addressing student needs and filling the knowledge gaps:

RACHEL: And I also thought that it would change. I was hoping for it and it didn't. The topics that have been pushed down onto the [grade] 11 are hard, they're *very* hard. The new 11 is more difficult than the old 12 in terms of the content. Certainly in our subject, it occurs maybe more than in anything. It's like (enacting a teacher-student exchange) 'We're onto a new topic'; 'Yuh, but I don't understand the one [before]' (Laughter); 'That's *too bad*! – you know – Let's just go onto the next section.' I can also tell you that [the head of the mathematics department] said he was going to go to a meeting to complain bitterly about the amount of material that the ministry said we had to teach in that grade 11 course (Laughs). There's *no way*! There was virtually a new topic every single day. And I mean the kids were just sort of like (sympathetic groan).

HELENA: Well, what do you do in inverse functions [in mathematics], when they don't know what a function is (Laughter) – never mind inverse?

Not only is the pace and sequencing of the new curriculum a problem, but Rachel describes the lack of distinction between mathematics courses offered at different levels or streams, given similar content and the same textbook. Referring to the two new Grade 11 courses of 'Functions,' and 'Functions and Relations':

RACHEL: It's the identical book, the identical questions. The absolutely only thing that was different was the conics section; the [Functions course] was to have no conics.

Despite the nebulous distinction between courses, as early as Grade 9, students are streamed by course codes that are tied to destination 'pathways': university, college, or the workplace. In particular, the new curriculum discriminates against students with interest, skill, and ability sets that are non-conforming, or different from the similar set necessary for success in academic and applied courses in Grades 9 and 10 (or university and college courses in Grades 11 and 12). In the absence of alternatives, teachers are left with responsibility for students who are struggling in a 'curriculum that is not suited to them':

ALICE: I said earlier that I embrace change. Fine! If there's something better for the system let's do it. Um – I think what we're creating here, is a system where there is absolutely no net to catch the kids who aren't right up at the top of things. Look back 10, 15, 20 years in teaching. We had general level schools, the vocational schools – like Brockton [Rachel: Which I worked at.] Yeah, and I think served a fantastic purpose. [Rachel: Fantastic!] ... [Now] they come to Beaconsfield and we tear our hair out, because the responsibility is downloaded to us as individual teachers to get them through on a curriculum that is not suited to them.

Teacher-participants' frame of reference is student-centred in advocating for curricular diversity to suit student needs, rather than forcing students to fit into the 'monoculture' of the new curriculum and to kowtow to the expectations of arbitrarily imposed standards. Their concern is for students falling by the wayside under education reform.

The issue of overrepresentation of students from minority groups in the old general and vocational level programs is framed differently, as overvaluing traditional academic programs and professions while stigmatizing non-academic programs and trades:

ALICE: There is absolutely no stigma about going to a technical school [in Switzerland]. So you are going to be a plumber. But you know what? A plumber earns more than I do! [Rachel: Absolutely!] And you'd better not try to get a plumber on the weekend, because he has a certain status over there. He's a professional in his job. Nobody else can do it. The kid who goes to the commercial school might be the guy who punches your ticket on a train. But I can't go and take his job because he's been trained in that. And he's gone through a very rigorous curriculum, including a lot of language teaching because he's up front representing the country on trains, and he has to speak some English, some Italian, some French, some German, whatever. But his curriculum is not a dumbed-down, watered-down program. It's your chosen course. [Helena: It's specialized] That kind of change I think would have been wonderful! [Helena: Yes!] [Rachel: I absolutely agree!] Those kinds of trades you've got nobody working here – you can't get a plumber, an electrician, a marvel granite worker.

The kind of radical change envisioned by teacher-participants includes new curricula for technical and commercial programs that are 'specialized' and 'rigorous' to subvert societal prejudices and legitimize a diverse array of ways to contribute to society. Such courses are neglected by education reform with its emphasis on curricula designed for students bound for post-secondary education, revealing who is considered worthy of the investment.

Rather than the latitude of previous course guidelines, curriculum policy is specified in terms of 'benchmarks' and learning 'outcomes' that are inscribed in textbooks. With the new curriculum, the ministry declared as invalid Circular 14 listing ministry-approved books and support materials. New textbooks were produced for the new courses, as politically identifiable documents that prescribe the curriculum to be delivered to students, at a substantial public cost of up to $150 per book depending on the subject area. Economic priorities of the publishing industry governed textbook production. To meet rushed deadlines and compete for purchase orders, surface appeal and glossy pictures took priority over substantive content in textbooks released just-in-time. Preview copies were sent to schools from multiple publishers in the busy days at the end of the academic year. Departments had to make hasty decisions about which version to order, or risk having no textbooks for the new curriculum in September. The combined effect of drastic time compression for publication and teacher scrutiny shows in a shoddy product:

JESSICA: Even the textbooks we did get were so slap-dash that there were so many mistakes. I don't know if you found this. Oh my, the geography was embarrassing! I thought, oh for sure they're going to recall them all, and give you, you know pages of errata, just pages of it.

HELENA: The examples in computer science are so boring in the new so-called books, which means, as a teacher you end up writing [your own] textbooks.

At the level of the classroom, inadequate support materials, errors in textbooks, and the dearth of questions to assign to students mean that it falls on teachers to create their own supplementary materials.

Alongside standardized curricula, the other self-proclaimed achievement of the minister is the standardized new report card. Computerized comments on report cards limit teachers' feedback to parents and students to prescribed notations. With the proliferation of comments for the new report card, teachers find they have to wade through pages and pages of unedited, disorganized comments, looking for one that fits. It would be less time-consuming and more personalized to do hand-written comments, but that would give teachers too much autonomy:

JESSICA: Comments, and then you can't find the one that you want!

RACHEL: And they managed to miss the comments that you really want to make; nowhere to be found on there!

ALICE: You had to rifle through that [list of comments]. And then again, from the department heads' point of view, you have to translate that into something that your department, your staff members, are going to use because they're all, like [name of teacher], totally cynical about the whole thing, saying, 'This is a pile of shit and I'm not using

any of it!' (Laughter) But as department head, you know, you're saying, 'Let me help you here.' And so I couldn't tell you how many
hours I went through every one of those pages and highlighted for
my department members the ones I thought were relevant, because
they weren't even gathered together.

Having been involved in the process of developing computerized
comments, Alice questions the rationale behind comments as part of
the new report card and how misleading they are to parents:

ALICE: That was about two or three years ago, [name of superinten-
dent] held all kinds of sessions and gathered teams of math teachers,
history teachers, geography teachers. So I was ready to go to the
Moderns and I did and they had scads and scads of pages: 'Always
responds in the target language'; 'Generally responds in the target
language'; 'Usually responds in the target –' (trails off, in a hum-
drum tone of voice). And I said at the time, what does this say?
Imagine yourself as the parent, the person to whom it's addressed,
and you read 'usually [responds in the target language]' and you
don't know what the other adverbs are. So maybe you pat yourself
on the back and say 'This is fantastic, my kid is doing really well.'
But you don't know that it ['usually'] is about third from the top of
the possible list. And, you know what? This is really interesting!
Every person in the room (and there must have been about 20 of us,
and that was just the Moderns one) got $100 gift certificate from
Chapters. *Where is this coming from?* So I assume that also all the
geography teachers, the phys. ed. teachers, guidance people, got
$100 gift certificate from Chapters.

The availability of money for developing computerized comments in a
time of cutbacks is questioned and a private sector source (the book
chain, Chapters) is identified as having a vested interest in the development of computerized report card comments. The involvement of
private companies in the development of the new curriculum and the
new report card exposes corporate intrusion from the get-go in secondary education reform, influencing decisions and favouring corporate
imperatives over pedagogical considerations.

From focus group participants' accounts, teachers are the absorbing
group as front-line workers compensating for the inadequacies of the

system and protecting students from the negative consequences of ill-considered policies. Hastily implemented ministry policies driven by cost-cutting have delivered half-baked or non-existent curricula, inadequate or inaccurate textbooks, and copious meaningless report card comments for student evaluation. The 'newness' of reforms are called into question as discriminating against students who do not fit into the traditional academic mould. Considerable system disruption creates a false illusion of change, but without any real substantive positive transformation at the level of the classroom. As in healthcare, dynamics-without-change characterizes education reform in Ontario.

With centralization of power to the ministry and the emphasis on standardization across the province of school funding, curriculum, and evaluation, what has been orchestrated is a patent change in school governance. The relative autonomy and flexibility of school boards to respond to the specificities of local context is severely compromised. Historically, local school boards have constituted an intermediate level of educational governance between the province and individual schools. Predicated on the principle of democracy, school board operations are overseen by publicly elected trustees who have a say in policies, programs, and budget allocation, whereas the administrative functions of public education at the local level are performed by bureaucratic, hierarchically structured school boards. The responsibility of local boards to ensure and coordinate the distribution of local educational services and resources across districts was affirmed in the Royal Commission on Learning:

> That, while integration should be the norm, school boards continue to provide a continuum of services for students whose needs would, in the opinion of parents and educators, be best served in other settings. (Recommendation 39)

Even though school boards feature throughout the recommendations as instrumental in the administration of a 'continuum of services' in education (such as Special Education, French immersion, English as a Second Language), the intent to limit and phase out their powers is expressed not only in the shift toward centralization of funding to the provincial level but also in the amalgamation of boards:

That following the proposed shift to the provincial government of the responsibility for determining the funding of education, the two-tiered governance structure of the public schools in Metropolitan Toronto be phased out, with the Metropolitan Toronto School Board being replaced by an administrative consortium of school boards in the Metropolitan Toronto area. (Recommendation 156)

Under Bill 104 (Fewer School Boards Act, 1997), the number of school boards in Ontario was reduced from 129 to 66 (later 72), and school funding shifted to the province. The seven former school boards of Metropolitan Toronto were amalgamated in January 1998, under the new umbrella of the Toronto District School Board (TDSB), thus forming the largest school board in Canada. Significant upheaval caused by the immense task of 'harmonization' of staff, policies and procedures, and finances immobilized local governance at a crucial time during educational restructuring. The extent of disruption is demonstrated by the numbers involved in the amalgamation: 17,000 teachers, 9,000 support staff, 565 schools with combined enrolments of 272,000 full-time students. For the new consortium in the Toronto area, the former North York model of neoliberal local governance rose to prominence with the appointment of a former North Yorker, Marguerite Jackson, as director of education. Under threat of government takeover, the TDSB, like other local boards, complied with budgetary fiscal restraints within the confines of reduced funding imposed by the funding formula. Figures determined by average provincial costs in 1997 failed to take into account real costs in urban centres such as Toronto in 2002. While the provincial government cut funding, it was local communities that were left to determine which areas to cut. Whereas the degree of compliance varied somewhat from board to board, the TDSB took such a hard line that there have been school closures, retrenchment and staff layoffs, and reductions to programs and special services, while at the same time denying to the public the inevitable impact on students in the classroom.

Verging on bankruptcy, the TDSB became proactive belatedly in drawing public attention to the depth of the funding problem and acknowledging the inevitable impact of cuts on the classroom. The threat to the viability of public education is captured in no uncertain terms in the following statement issued by the Ontario Public School Boards Association:

Let me be clear, the school boards in this province are bankrupt or very close to being bankrupt. Our only source of revenue is the provincial government and with the money we are getting this year and expect to get next year, we will not have sufficient funding to meet our contractual or legal obligations ... School boards are legally responsible for developing a balanced budget, within the funding provided by the ministry. However, boards are also charged with the legal responsibility of conforming to: class size and workload requirements in the *Education Act*, Special Education legislation, the *Labour Relations Act*, the *Occupational Health and Safety Act*, and the *Pay Equity Act* to name but a few. School boards' question to the provincial government is rapidly becoming, 'Which law would you like us to break?' (Liz Sandals, 2002)[1]

The dilemma faced by school boards, with trustees at the helm, is whether to balance the budget or to satisfy education and labour legislation. Over the summer of 2002 school trustees in Toronto, Ottawa-Carleton, and Hamilton-Wentworth failed or refused to submit balanced budgets for the 2002–3 school year and government-appointed 'supervisors' took over those boards to enforce operations within existing fiscal constraints.

An analysis of school trustees explicates why it took so long for school boards to take a stand against the bankrupting of public education. In Toronto, 22 public school trustees are elected municipally to represent the public at the TDSB. With one seat vacant at the time of writing, the ratio of women to men is 18:3, only two of whom are from visible minorities. With honoraria to school trustees cut to a token amount of $5,000–$15,000 annually and given the amount of work and responsibility involved, who can afford to stand as a school trustee? It is not surprising that women of private means would be performing this public service 'charity work,' described by one trustee as the 'dirty work' of government. The imperative to meet the budgetary constraints under threat of government takeover rendered school boards vulnerable and in some cases (including the TDSB) overly zealous in following legislated mandates. Trustees at the TDSB were divided; those opposing budget cuts to programs and services (the so-called no cuts trustees) were outnumbered by those favouring compliance within government-imposed fiscal constraints. These disparate positions were divided roughly along urban-suburban lines, with the former Toronto Board of Education having historically supported more progressive and diverse programs to meet the local needs of the urban core.

Discordant relations internal to the TDSB is paralleled by adversarial labour relations with employee unions, including teacher unions, that have become strained and especially conflictual during collective bargaining. Despite adversarial labour relations that provoked withdrawal of voluntary services, a public relations pronouncement at the TDSB website characterizes teachers as follows:

> Our teachers are among the most qualified and most caring educators in the world. Our teachers come equipped with Education degrees, supplemented regularly with upgrading courses and professional development courses. Our teachers make a difference. They are dedicated to the task of helping our students be the best they can be and further enrich students' lives by volunteering their time for many activities beyond the regular school day. (http://www.tdsb.on.ca/educators/educators.htm)

The representation of teachers as 'qualified' and 'caring' in hyperbolic terms is contradicted by their actual treatment by the TDSB; it fails to translate into respect for decent working conditions or economic rewards. Teachers' salaries have not kept pace with inflation. Time in the school day for the essential backstage work of teaching (such as lesson preparation, marking, evaluation and reporting, consultation and committee work) has been eroded by the legislated definition of 'instructional time' as counting only time spent in the classroom teaching regular credited courses. Suppose lawyers were compensated only for time spent in court or politicians for time in parliament! The devaluation of teachers and their 'caring' work, while discounting the backstage work involved, is consistent with exploitative patriarchal relations that take for granted the reproductive functions in society performed largely by women teachers, whereas economic value accrues to the 'productive' work performed at the upper echelons of management.

Also posted at the TDSB website are school profiles that objectify schools, presumably to assist parents shopping for schools. General school information and program offerings are stated. Included are demographic data of students indicating percentages by sex and primary language not English, singling out students born outside Canada who are categorized according to length of time lived in Canada (two years or less and three to five years). This categorization feeds into biases of parents seeking the most homogenous, non-immigrant schools. Considerable weight in the school profile is accorded to EQAO assessment on Grade 9 mathematics results (two of four pages). Test results are broken down by stream (academic and applied) and graphs compare individual school results with those of others in the board and with the province of Ontario. The furor in Britain over the effects of league tables in negatively branding schools in underprivileged areas, impacting on student enrolment and threatening school closures (Woods et al., 1997), foreshadows similar trends in Toronto. Unrecognized are the potentially damaging consequences of school profiling according to the immigrant/non-immigrant status of students, with academic success measured along the single dimension of EQAO mathematics scores. These developments indicate the drift of the TDSB away from pedagogical considerations toward a competitive market-driven ideology of education.

A double standard regarding teachers as well as student equity and access is exhibited in contradictions between mission statements and actual practices. The TDSB's 'continuous improvement of schools' is purported to be achieved through 'relevant curriculum, equity and accountability.' Looking beneath the surface of these apparently benign terms, what do they mean in actual practice? Who determines 'relevance' and 'equity' for whom? Who is 'accountable' to whom for what? Without equitable representation and input at the decision-making level (such as on governing boards and in positions of responsibility), the definition of these terms is limited to the partial worldview and serves the interests of the dominant group in society.

At the decision-making levels of governance structures, focus group participants describe mismanagement in operation, not only at the ministry but at the board level as well. Whereas the curriculum (a theoretical document) is the responsibility of the ministry, in-servicing (sharing practical materials) is the responsibility of the board. Restructuring at the board level has impeded the effectiveness and availability of consultants and coordinators, leaving teachers as isolated individuals with 'nothing practical' that they can use in the classroom, and marginalizing them to the 'twilight zone':

ALICE: What's really interesting is that these [in-service] workshops are usually provided by board people, but the curriculum is coming from the ministry. I don't know in your subject areas but certainly in mine, the people at the board – the consultants and coordinators – have no clearer an idea of what the new curriculum is or how to implement it or providing materials, than we have. And more and more I just find it's all theory, it's all b.s. There is absolutely [nothing] practical; they don't know what to tell us. The people at the board are all being downsized left, right, and centre, so the consultants and coordinators are doing all kinds of other funny jobs, mostly moving their offices and being out of contact. You cannot get them by phone. So they are less help to you than they ever were.

JESSICA: I think we're in the twilight zone.

The disjuncture between teachers' sense of duty to fulfil their obligations to students and the vagueness of the new expectations leads to doubt and loss of faith in the consultative capacity of the TDSB. Jessica describes an experience at an in-service session that was haphazard, disorganized and a waste of time for teachers:

JESSICA: It's called Health for Life. It's health basically, it's not even phys. ed. really. And then we were invited to a workshop. And [a colleague] was dying to go because she's teaching this course, she had nothing [no course outline]! Plus [there is] another health [course], but you can't just give them the other health right? They [have to be] two different Grade 11 courses. So she got us released to go there and guess what? They went around and said 'Now how many people – even though it's down in the book – are actually teaching [Health for Life]?' Her hand went up. This poor woman, she was the only one! The whole thing, the whole day was a waste of time because [there was] nothing, nothing! It was supposed to be sharing resources. There were no resources to be shared! There was no outline! So it was an all-day 'bitch session.' In-service was 'in-bitching'! Nobody was there to share with her. And she was the only one in this whole room of people who was actually teaching it – or *trying* to.

Later, at this in-service workshop, as the ineptitude of designated curriculum leaders becomes apparent, the level of teacher discontent and frustration escalates from 'in-bitching' to 'civil disobedience':

JESSICA: But you know, these workshops, did you notice? I'm telling you, the civil disobedience! At the end, the guy up at the last hour, nobody was listening to him. He kept saying 'I'm having a real problem with this group' (Laughs) and everybody, they were blatantly rude. I mean I was trying not to talk. Oh my gosh, you looked around and people are teachers! You know what it's like when you can't command some attention.

From focus group accounts, the system within which teachers are working appears to be dysfunctional and in disarray. Lacking supports from the TDSB in terms of in-service workshops and subject consultants, they are left to their own devices, in some cases to invent a program for their students in the absence of a curriculum, most notably in non-academic courses. Yet this is not a demoralized group; when asked directly who is making the decisions, teacher-participants responded in a resounding chorus, 'We do!' At the classroom level, these experienced teachers are doing the best they can under the circumstances and drawing on their own accumulated resources, whereas at the upper levels of policy-making their input comes only as a stop-gap, with neither sanction as full-fledged participants in decision-making, nor legitimacy as professionals with expertise in education.

The professional identity of teachers was first vested in the Ontario Teachers' Federation (OTF) by the Teaching Profession Act of 1944. Established not as a union but as a professional organization for teachers in the province to enhance their professional standing, the OTF is largely invisible to practising teachers. Its main responsibilities are appointing representatives to various committees advising the other ruling structures, and overseeing the Ontario Teachers' Pension Plan in partnership with government. As managers of the largest private pension plan in Canada, the OTF is a well-endowed and significant player in the corporate investment world of Ontario.[2] The relevance of the OTF for teachers is its control over pension plan benefits that can influence performance, career path decisions, and the timing, terms, and conditions of retirement. In accordance with the Teaching Profession Act, OTF regulations and bylaws can be changed by ministerial command, suggesting that the OTF operates at the behest of government. Articles 13(2) and 13(3) of the Teaching Profession Act explicitly empower the minister 'to make, amend or revoke' any regulation or bylaw.

According to its bylaws, the OTF assigns each teacher to one of four affiliates: l'Association des enseignantes et des enseignants franco-ontariens, the Elementary Teachers' Federation of Ontario (ETFO), the Ontario English Catholic Teachers' Association (OECTA), or the Ontario Secondary School Teachers' Federation (OSSTF). These individually autonomous affiliations are closer to the everyday concerns of practising teachers. Originally founded as voluntary teacher organizations, most of the affiliates predate the formation of OTF; the exception is the ETFO that was formed in 1998 with the amalgamation of the Ontario Public School Teachers' Federation (OPSTF) and the Federation of Women Teachers' Association of Ontario (FWTAO). Between 1918 and 1998 the FWTAO represented elementary school teachers across Ontario by contesting discrimination in women teachers' salaries, and addressing broader issues concerning women and children in society. Under education reform, its assimilation into the mixed-gender ETFO marked the demise of one of the last remaining women teachers' unions in North America. Relations among the OTF, the various provincial affiliates, and their district offices are complex, with instances of fragmentation and sectarianism.[3] The Ontario Secondary School Teachers' Federation (OSSTF) and its Toronto chapter (District 12) will be focused on here, since the teacher-participants in this study are members of this particular affiliate.

Predating the OTF, the OSSTF was formed in 1919.[4] Its 50,000 members across Ontario include public high school teachers, occasional teachers, teaching assistants, and other education workers. The membership democratically elects executive representatives at both levels (provincial and local district). In the case of the District 12 executive, the ratio of women to men is 3:10, reflecting the dominance of men in senior positions as is typical of mixed-gender unions. Each school also elects school representatives who act as conduits between teachers on staff and the district executive. Whereas the provincial OSSTF establishes and coordinates province-wide strategies, it is the local district office that negotiates collective agreements with the local school board.[5] As a consequence of amalgamation of the TDSB, the OSSTF was forced to fold districts into a new District 12 chapter, thus forming a mega-union that encompasses the different and distinctive subcultures of the former progressive Toronto district and the more conservative suburban districts of the megacity.

Bestowed with the authority to bargain under the Ontario Labour Relations Act, the OSSTF is aligned with the labour union movement, and has been a politically active voice of opposition to externally imposed reforms and the erosion of public education. Within the original conception of a hybrid teachers' federation, socio-economic criticism, active participation in partisan politics, and collective bargaining co-existed with professional concerns, including overseeing professional development. Mobilizing its substantial membership in provincial elections, the OSSTF contributed to ousting the Liberal government of David Peterson (for putting money before people), bringing the NDP government of Bob Rae into power, and later ousting it (for the Social Contract) (see Martell, 1995). More recently, the OSSTF actively opposed the PC government of Harris/Eves for its Common Sense Revolution cutbacks to public education. In this respect, the OSSTF has taken a position different from the Alberta Teachers' Association (ATA) that adopts a nonpolitical stance in partisan politics (Bascia, 2001). Given its active involvement in partisan politics and close association with the labour movement, and consistent with the crackdown on unions characteristic of neoliberal governments, the OSSTF has been targeted to diminish its power. This has been accomplished by reducing the membership through the creation of the Ontario Principals' Council, marginalizing its role by delegating jurisdiction over professional matters to the newly formed Ontario College of Teachers and, as with the union movement in general, legislating restrictive labour laws.

From the perspective of teacher-participants, the OSSTF is perceived as the body that protects public education, represents teachers' interests, and supports their professional integrity:

HELENA: There is the body who protects us from all kinds of things that may happen to you [as a teacher]. And in my case I know, it happened to me. A very hard situation. Without OSSTF, I'd probably be in industry making more money! (Laughter) But I've never seen a magazine from OSSTF, where you have a list of people who were punished [like with the OCT]!

RACHEL: And I've had occasion to use their services as well. And I always felt they were helpful. I would never go to the College of Teachers for *anything*!

New Ruling Structures

The professional authority of the OTF and its affiliates was usurped by the establishment of the Ontario College of Teachers (OCT), with the passage of the Ontario College of Teachers Act (1996), thus creating a second professional organization for teachers over and above the OTF. The formation of such a new body with legislative authority over the professional association of teachers was envisaged by the Royal Commission on Learning:

> That a professional self-regulatory body for teaching, the Ontario College of Teachers, be established, with the powers, duties, and membership of the College set out in legislation. The College should be responsible for determining professional standards, certification, and accreditation of teacher education programs. Professional educators should form a majority of the membership of the College, with substantial representation of non-educators from the community at large. (Recommendation 58)

Like other professional registration bodies, the purpose of the OCT is to regulate teachers in the public interest. Modelled on the traditional construction of the professions, the OCT has worked on formulating standards of practice and an ethical code to control and standardize teaching practice. To the extent that the OCT's authority is delegated by the province to serve the province, a potential conflict of interest exists, since teachers' employers *are* public institutions. As a consequence, the value of professional autonomy is compromised. Although the OCT can be compared with the College of Physicians and Surgeons as protecting the public, differences in history, gender, and power of the medical profession has enabled it to maintain autonomy from government interference. Similarly, the College of Nurses, benefiting from the orbit of the powerful medical profession, has maintained a degree of autonomy from government interference. The OCT, on the other hand, operates closely with government and has been used as an instrument of control over teachers through certification. Compliance with government legislation (rather than with professional ethics and values) is enforced under threat of withdrawal of the professional licence to teach in Ontario.

Whereas the dual mandate of teachers' federations formerly encompassed both the professional function to protect the public interest and the union function to protect the rights of members, under restructuring these functions have been divided between the OCT and the OTF affiliates respectively. Professional functions that were previously the purview of the OSSTF became the designated responsibility of the

OCT, effectively diminishing the power of the teachers' union and marginalizing its role in professional matters. The OSSTF became restricted to the more traditional union function of collective bargaining through contract negotiations for salaries, benefits, and working conditions as well as establishing grievance procedures and strike action. Thus the OSSTF has been in a reactive position with respect to changes imposed by education reform. OSSTF and OCT positions on various issues are divergent and contradictory. For example, on the issue of teacher testing, the college collaborated with the ministry in putting forward recommendations; the OSSTF, on the other hand, while supporting professional development, is opposed to perpetual teacher testing. During labour unrest, including teacher strikes and withdrawal of voluntary services protesting legislation that threatens public education and discredits teachers' professional integrity, the OCT has remained conspicuously silent.

Bestowed with control over teacher training, accreditation, re-certification and mandatory perpetual re-education upon which continued registration is contingent, the OCT has seemed more an instrument of control and policing than an association of professionals furthering the profession. The fact that private-school teachers are exempt from obligatory membership of the OCT, and are not subject to the terms and conditions imposed on qualification and re-certification, exposes a double standard between increased regulation of the public sector and deregulation of the private sector, thus paving the way for privatization. According to the OCT website:

> The College maintains a register of teachers who are licensed to teach in Ontario's publicly funded schools. Information available to the public includes the names, qualifications, academic degrees and membership status of certified teachers.

Public posting on the OCT website of these digital profiles on teachers may infringe on rights to privacy. Furthermore, showcasing reports on disciplinary action taken against teachers both on the website and in the journal *Professionally Speaking*, discredits teachers as a group and the profession as a whole. Exacerbated by mandatory criminal background checks, the criminalization of teachers contributes to a negative construction of the teaching profession. This issue is particularly charged for teacher-participants in the focus group, as exemplified by their sense of indignation and outrage. *Professionally*

Speaking, published by the OCT, is considered an unprofessional 'rag newspaper' likened to the *National Enquirer*. The publication of teachers' transgressions is considered 'outrageous,' 'embarrassing,' 'ludicrous,' 'demeaning,' and analogous to technological public executions or witch-hunts:

ALICE: And you know the only thing that's changed as far as I'm concerned in that magazine, is you have a rag section in the middle. There are ten pages of all the people who were up on charges.
RACHEL: I agree! To me that is outrageous!
HELENA: It's like when everybody comes in the middle of the plaza with somebody who is going to be executed (Laughs). Well, everybody knows we are talking about different technologies nowadays, but [Rachel: And it's embarrassing! It's not nice], it's the same state of mind.
RACHEL: It's a very, um, unsavoury thing to do! We're *professionals* and there are those among us, yes, who do those things, but the way *this* is done. They go on to tell you what they [teachers] did and you know, what they were accused of. I keep thinking I don't want to know these things! Like, I read part of it and then I actually feel like a voyeur, you know.

Whereas teacher-participants strongly disapprove of unprofessional conduct, the OCT is perceived as a watchdog, performing a policing function that treats all teachers as if they were potential criminals. A recent case is cited where a teacher was 'caught' drinking a glass of wine in a restaurant at lunchtime. The negative profiling of teachers on trivial grounds leaves teachers feeling under panopticon-like surveillance:

RACHEL: You see what that does is says – it sends a message. The message I get is–oh–oh! – I'd better watch myself. I might be doing, you know, really *I* might be doing something wrong, that they're going to turn around and find me guilty of. Because if you can't drink a glass of wine at a restaurant, I mean who knows?

What teachers expect of a professional body is to promote a positive image of teachers and to provide professional material support:

RACHEL: If they really *cared*, they would perhaps write about all the *good* things teachers are doing. I don't need to see all that [reporting of disciplinary cases]!

HELENA: Maybe some lesson plans. Something useful for the classroom would be more useful than this!

Questions are raised about the compostion of the OCT and how many executive members are or have been teachers. Doubts emerge of the credibility of non-teachers purporting to represent teachers at the college. A Kafkaesque image of the teacher on trial, both professionally and in her everyday work is evoked:

RACHEL: That is who's telling us most things, unfortunately [non-teachers]! And we're the ones that are actually standing in front of them [OCT] – yes – *and* standing in front of the kids in the classroom.

An examination of the governing council of the OCT reveals that it comprises thirty-one members, of whom fourteen are appointed by government and seventeen are elected (similar to what was laid out in the Royal Commission on Learning). Despite the fact that women constitute the vast majority of practising teachers, the ratio of women to men is 12:19 and all except one of the council members are white. It would therefore appear that white male values dominate the OCT. The heavy proportion of government appointees to the board throws into question claims of being a self-regulating body. Closer examination of the seventeen elected members reveals that only thirteen are elected by public school teachers, the other four being elected by smaller constituencies: faculties of education, the Ontario Principals' Council, the Ontario Public Supervisory Officials' Association, and private-school teachers. Relegated to a minority position on the governing council, it is not surprising that an extremely low teacher voting rate of 4.4 per cent was reported by the OCT in the June 2003 election, even with prizes offered as an enticement to voters. Non-voting can be construed as a form of resistance and casts serious doubt on the OCT as a democratic institution. It suggests widespread opposition to token teacher representation at this new professional association which is legislated and controlled by government and has usurped the professional functions formerly carried out by the OTF. Without representation, consultation, or due democratic process, a unilateral deduction at source from teachers' pay finances the OCT in the form of an annual fee (in addition to OTF/OSSTF fees). The escalation of OCT fees by more than 54 per cent since its inception, while teachers' salaries during the same time period had not even kept pace with inflation, marks the operation of ruling relations. Teacher-participants in the focus group suspect that there was an ulterior motive behind the formation of the OCT – that it was intended as an arm of government set up to control and tax teachers:

RACHEL: I had a bad feeling about it since the beginning. I have just always felt that there may be – and I'm probably wrong – but I have always felt that the college is another arm of the government, and ... umm ... nothing to do with us. I guess especially since the extra courses [of the Professional Learning Program] have come up. But I don't have control over the College of Teachers.
HELEN: It's another way to take some money from us.
RACHEL: It's a money grab! They're watchdogs! Which makes me very uneasy.
HELENA: We had our own administration plus the union [already]. So this is one that we have on the top – the Teachers College. I don't know why they created this!

RACHEL: I think it [OCT] was designed partially to weaken the OSSTF.
HELENA: Exactly. Absolutely!
RACHEL: And I think it has weakened it.
HELENA: I think the OSSTF is losing money, because the principals are away, no?, from the same boat [with the formation of the Ontario Principals' Council]. The OSSTF is losing funds.

The underlying motive for the establishment of the OCT (like the Ontario Principals' Council) is suspected as having been set up to marginalize the OSSTF.

Whereas principals and vice-principals are members of the OCT, their removal from the teachers' union not only reduced the union membership but marks the orchestration of divisive ruling relations along management-labour lines. Established in 1997 by Bill 160, the Ontario Principals' Council (OPC) separated administrators (management)

from teachers (labour), through the restructuring of union and professional association. The formation of the OPC was not without contro-
versy; some administrators resisted until the legislated deadline of 1
April 1998 when principals and vice-principals could no longer retain
union membership by law. The OPC represents 5,000 elementary and
secondary public school principals and vice-principals. According to
its mission statement posted at its website:

> [The OPC] advocates for students; promotes publicly funded education;
> influences education decision making at all levels; fosters positive rela-
> tions among principals and vice-principals and the broader education
> community; works with government, district school boards, school
> councils and other members of the educational community to ensure
> exemplary schools for Ontario's students. (http://opc.inline.net/pacc/
> display_document.htm?opc_token=public user&id=7&isdoc=1)

By omission, this statement excludes and erases teachers from the
'education community,' even though the OPC declares that it is 'dedicated to exemplary teaching and learning.' How can this occur without
teachers?

The chain of command within a hierarchical educational structure
was spelled out in by the Royal Commission on Learning as follows:

> That the College of Teachers, the Ministry, and school boards emphasize
> that principals are accountable for satisfactory teacher performance in
> their schools, and that supervisory officers are responsible for ensuring
> that principals take appropriate action in dealing with teachers whose
> performance is not satisfactory. (Recommendation 80)

Since collegiality is held as a value in most professional associations,
this recommendation implicitly calls for a separate association for
principals. For members to besmirch the reputations of colleagues by
'dealing with' them via external mechanisms of control runs counter to
collegial relations. Under Professional Relationships, the Code of Ethics of the OTF states, that 'member(s) refrain from personal depreca-
tion of other member(s).' However, the code does not preclude
disciplinary action for misconduct exercised through internal mechanisms prescribed by due processes, such as the Judicial Council.
Within the ruling structure, principals emerged as a managerial class,

with enhanced control over teachers, who are relegated to the rank of 'intellectual workers.' The formation of the OPC thus drove a wedge between teachers and administrators.

The enhanced power invested in principals under education restructuring is exemplified by Bill 74, which endows them with absolute authority over teacher time; principals can assign teachers duties anytime, twenty-four hours a day, seven days a week during the school year, analogous to military service. Having no right of refusal, this bill arguably infringes on the labour rights of teachers and raises questions of the threat to democracy posed by centralized government control over education. Principals are also responsible for evaluating teachers through the Teacher Performance Appraisal process of top-down accountability. Whereas the practice of the former Toronto School Board for promotion of principals by committee included teacher representation, under the TDSB teachers are excluded from the process, thus imposing a top-down hierarchical structure not only on directives and accountability, but also on promotions so as to ensure the 'right' ideological mindset will advance into the upper ranks.

Operating under the motto 'Quality – Our Principal Product,' the OPC subscribes to the corporate-managerial discourse of 'total quality management' promoted by the management system standards of the International Organization for Standardization (ISO 9001). The norms and values adhered to by this new ruling structure thus determine what constitutes 'quality' in education according to accountability measures derived from the manufacturing industry rather than from sound pedagogical research. It is explicitly declared at the OPC website that:

> [the] OPC is now registered as an ISO 9001 compliant organization. This means that we have achieved the internationally-recognized standard for quality management in 'the design and delivery of training and professional development programs and the provision of association support services to members.' (http://opc.inline.net/pacc/display_document .htm?opc_token=public user&id=2&isdoc=1)

At the OCP website, access to non-members is denied at various links calling for login and password. Information available to the public is limited to glib promotion of the office of principalship couched in corporate-managerial language: standards, quality, delivery of services,

Table 4.1. Full-time teachers in schools 1998–99

	Elementary	Secondary	Total
Public school boards			
Male	12,759	16,201	28,960
Female	37,114	15,318	52,432
Roman Catholic school boards			
Male	5,292	5,878	11,170
Female	18,241	5,659	23,900
Total	73,406	43,056	116,462
Positions held			
Principals and vice-principals	5,498	1,897	7,395
Percentage female	54.9%	39.6%	50.9%
Department heads-	8,991	8,991	
Percentage female	–	45.1%	45.1%
Classroom and other teachers	67,336	32,740	100,076
Percentage female	77.2%	50.6%	68.5%
Median years of teaching experience	13.3	14.5	13.7
Average age of teachers	42.5	43.3	42.8
Median age of teachers	44.3	44.4	44.3

Source: Ministry of Education, Ministry of Training, Colleges and Universities at http://
www.edu.gov.on.ca/eng/general/elemsec/quickfacts/1998-99/#fulltime

excellence, leadership, and so on. Blatant commercialism is evident in
offering on-line shopping at the OPC website as a distracting substi-
tute for access to meaningful information. The motto of 'Exemplary
Leadership in Public Education' begs the question: Where is the leadership of the OPC in public education?

The board of the OPC consists of an executive director and a president, one man and one woman. Who gets promoted to leadership positions in schools would seem not only to be predicated on allegiance to
corporate values, but demographic analysis confirms the glass ceiling;
women are under-represented with only 39.6 per cent being principals
or vice-principals in the secondary panel, even though teaching is
largely a feminized profession (see table 4.1). These figures suggest
that male values dominate secondary schools governed by apparently
powerful principals backed by legislative authority. The gulf between
teachers and principals is confirmed by the fact that few teachers are

applying to be principals, indicating that teachers may be unwilling to adopt the requisite paradigm or to perform the work of corporate-style managers. Even if not all individual principals are biased toward androcentric corporate-managerial values, given the hierarchical construction of the chain of command and given the construction of the office of principalship by the OPC, there is no evidence to suggest that the initiative for a more equitable system of public education with alternative models of leadership will emanate from these 'middle managers' in the bureaucracy of educational governance.

Principals are subject to the dictates of senior managers above them in the hierarchy of educational governance. Supervisory officers, superintendents, and directors of public school boards are not necessarily teachers, but all are affiliated under the Ontario Public Supervisory Officials' Association (OPSOA). Superintendents are employed by public school boards but answerable to the ministry, thus performing functions reminiscent of the dreaded school inspectors of the past. In its mission statement posted at the website, 'OPSOA must be a full partner in the cooperative planning of educational law, policy and practice.' With the emphasis on 'the business of education' comes the language of leadership, excellence, effectiveness, efficiency, and accountability. OPSOA's board of directors is comprised of thirteen members, with a ratio of women to men of 4:9, reiterating the glass ceiling in senior management positions. The changed role of principals since the formation of the OPC is more closely aligned with the business administration mindset of senior managers above them than with teachers. For upwardly mobile principals, emulation of this mindset is a prerequisite for personal career advancement.

From the perspective of focus group participants, the decline in collegial relations in schools is attributed to the new role of principals as administrators rather than as head teachers. Administrators are perceived as under pressure and preoccupied with management duties, so that they abdicate responsibility on pedagogical issues:

ALICE: I think the administration has been unhinged by the whole thing, because they're operating on a very different mindset – they're management – [preoccupied with] how's the academic year going to go, particularly in a school like ours where the parents have to be informed well in advance; this block of time is going to be set aside for January exams, this – (trails off).
JESSICA: But also it puts the administration on the line too. Because

with these new courses [of the new curriculum], literally the administration says – and I've heard this – [when teachers ask] 'What
should I do with this course?' [administrators respond] 'Teach whatever you like.'

ALICE: It needs time to stabilize, particularly when in the old Toronto
system you've got teachers who are the admin. team, who *have* been
in the classroom. So they – principals – still want to have the inter-
personal relationships with us [Rachel: I think we still want it too!]
and we still want it. We don't want to let go of what we have a certain comfort level with, and yet we want more input with the administration. And I certainly see a time when a principal will not be a
principal teacher. He/she will be somebody who is paid to oversee a
budget, to watch the little bit of waste over here – (trails off).

Alice foresees a time when principals will no longer be teachers at all
but trained business managers, with teachers shut out of decision-
making altogether. Falling in line with some jurisdictions in the United
States where schools are run as businesses, Ontario seems to be drift-
ing away from pedagogical values towards bottom-line budget
management and fear of litigious customers/parents in educational
governance.

The move towards a consumer-driven model of education is corrobo-
rated by the establishment of the Ontario Parent Council as a network
of local parent councils. The enhanced powers of parents operate
mainly at the level of the local school, where the parent council operates in an advisory capacity to the school principal on matters such as
staffing, curriculum, and procedures. The mandate for each school to
set up a parent council was the first recommendation of the royal commission to be implemented, and took effect in 1995 under the NDP
government of Bob Rae. Membership of parent councils as outlined by
the royal commission was broad and designed to promote 'school-
community' links, including the business community:

> That the Ministry of Education and Training mandate that each school in
> Ontario establish a school-community council, with membership drawn
> from the following sectors:
> • parents
> • students (from Grade 7 on)
> • teachers

- representatives from local religious and ethnic communities
- service providers (government and non-government)
- municipal government(s)
- service clubs and organizations
- business sectors. (Recommendation 108)

Providing a forum for parental input into decisions affecting the school conceals the underlying changed relations of decision-making towards a consumer-oriented approach that opens the door to business intrusion into policy-making in schools. A major problem with parent councils is limited representation on the part of parents. Few parents have the time to volunteer, with the result that the burden falls on a few committed ones who tend to represent the interests of a small segment of the school population – typically the privileged white middle/upper-middle class. Parents tend to emphasize the needs of their own children over those of the student body at large. The interests of non-dominant groups (such as immigrants, single-parent families, lower socio-economic groups), for whom systemic barriers to participation exist (such as language, shift work, double jobs, or lack of daycare) are rendered invisible in school decision-making. The skewed values and priorities of parent councils threatens to further tailor schools to the dominant group at the expense of less vocal groups within the diverse population of Toronto. The composition of parent councils as implemented by the Rae government was explicitly exclusionary towards teachers within the school at which they teach (limited to one teacher representative). Teachers were also barred from parent councils at the schools their own children attend (*Toronto Star*, 26 September 1998). The marginalization of teachers from school policy decision-making and the disregard for teachers' professional expertise constituted a foretaste of the changed relations of ruling envisioned by the royal commission. Moreover, the diminishment of the community liaison function of local school boards through bestowing increased powers on parent councils paved the way for downsizing local boards and marks a step towards the eradication of this local level of school governance.

In day-to-day relations, teacher-participants take the responsibility of acting 'in loco parentis' seriously. They regard themselves as accountable to and on the same side as parents in striving for what is best for their students – that is, students with names and faces, rather than students as a nebulous, disembodied group. However, as frontline representatives of the school system, teachers are in a difficult position in having to explain and justify education reform to parents:

ALICE: It makes me feel very insecure and inadequate, particularly in a head's role, if you're the one that's expected to show up at the parent information night, which happens around this time of year, and explain to parents what the difference is between academic and applied [courses] and how important a decision that is for them to be making with their children.

Rachel refers to a recent newspaper article on the amount of homework students have to do to keep pace with the new curriculum:

RACHEL: Homework – you know this article about homework in the paper the other day. It was made very clear in that article that parents are very resentful when *they* have to help their kids do homework. Very resentful. [Alice: Oh yes!] [Helena: Kids have to do their homework, not the parents.] One of them even made the comment, 'Well, that's what we pay *you teachers* for.'

The assumption that parents are willing and able to help with homework is called into question. But it is teachers who get the blame and admonishment, not curriculum policy. Media reports such as this pit parents against teachers, driving a wedge between them. In addition, parent councils use parents as leverage to open the door to the 'business sectors,' thus violating the age-old struggle to protect education from interference by outside vested interests and marking the turn towards a competitive, consumer-driven model of education.

The infiltration into education of business principles derived from the manufacturing industry is epitomized in the operations of the Education Quality and Accountability Office (EQAO). Established by Bill 30 in 1995 with an annual budget of approximately $15 million, the EQAO oversees and reports on province-wide standardized testing of students – the 'products' of education. The fact that the EQAO was the only new body to receive an influx of government funds suggests that it constitutes the cornerstone of educational restructuring. The inherent contradiction between funding cuts made to schools while millions have been poured into student testing marks this body as pivotal to the ruling apparatus. The formation of an agency to monitor accountability through student testing was laid out by the Royal Commission on Learning as follows:

> That the construction, administration, scoring, and reporting of the two assessments be the responsibility of a small agency, independent of the Ministry of Education and Training, and operating at a very senior level, to be called the Office of Learning Assessment and Accountability. (Recommendation 51)

Whereas the EQAO was originally established to test grades 3 and 6 only, its increased mandate over time has been supported by annual budget escalations, reaching $47.5 million by 2001–2 and still rising. Tests include Grades 3 and 6 Assessments of Reading, Writing, and Mathematics; and at the secondary level, the Grade 9 Assessment of Mathematics and the Ontario Secondary School Literacy Test. In the design stage at the time of writing, is the Ministry of Education's Core Testing Program.

As far as teacher-participants are concerned, the EQAO tests are of negligible value, an 'unbelievable' waste of money, and denigrate teachers' broader in-depth contextual knowledge of students' capabilities. Aside from the cost of maintaining the EQAO and compiling the various tests, Alice recounts her experience in marking the Literacy Test and itemizes the 'hidden' expenses associated with the practice at the time of bringing markers from across the province to Toronto to mark anonymous tests in an assembly-line operation:

ALICE: Unbelievable hidden cost, to what end? To tell us what the grade 10 English teacher already knows and tells students and parents on the report card! By 'hidden cost' I mean, have people from all over the province [and] have to pay for hotel, airfare, meals, stipend, gas, mileage, food. And technical support – hundreds of techies – because it's marked on palm-pilots, with administrators checking productivity and accuracy.

The standardized testing machine of the EQAO claims to be 'an independent agency of the government of Ontario' that 'conducts provincial assessments and coordinates Ontario's participation in national and international assessments' (EQAO press release, 2 November 2001). The Provincial Report on Achievement produced by the EQAO reports the results of student tests directly to the minister. The validity of EQAO results has been contested by teachers' unions on the basis of flaws in data capture, calibration, errors in reporting, overuse of multiple choice questions, and the lack of contextual information.[6] Despite these flaws, published computer-generated graphs and charts of EQAO test results assume an authority and continue to exert a powerful influence on the construction of knowledge about education in Ontario that is disseminated system-wide and to the public through the media. Could lack of transparency about the problems associated with test results be due to the questionable arms length relationship between the EQAO and the ministry, whose curriculum the EQAO tests assess? Questions are raised of a potential conflict of interest between these closely connected structures.

Lengthy delays between EQAO test administration and availability of results renders them useless pedagogically at the level of the classroom, contradicting the EQAO claim of 'improving student learning.' The results of the Grade 9 Mathematics test is a single page bar graph that is filed in the student's Ontario Student Record (OSR). The Literacy Test is also a single sheet indicating only pass/fail on each component (reading/writing) that is also filed in the student's OSR; a check mark in the box for the Literacy Test on the student transcript makes the difference between graduating or not graduating from high school. The high stakes associated with this single test pose the danger of teaching to the test. Since publication of EQAO test results impacts on student enrolment, there is a tendency for school administrators to defer students deemed unlikely to pass the test to the next year, whereas practice is particularly necessary for those at risk of failure. The competitive, market-driven approach to education promulgated by the EQAO emphasizes school reputations over student welfare, contradicting the ministry claim of putting students first. The emphasis on standards of English literacy and mathematical numeracy – in testing and in the new curriculum – disadvantages students whose strengths lie elsewhere, and denies the range and complexity of the student population that an accessible and equitable public education system serves in a heterogeneous society such as Canada.

Purportedly testing the success of the new curriculum, improvements in test performance proved negligible for Grades 3 and 6, when EQAO comparisons were first available. Rather than critical evaluation of standardized tests or of the new curriculum, the EQAO shifted the

blame for lack of improvement onto teachers, as reflected in the following recommendations:

- That the *Ministry of Education, the Ontario College of Teachers, the teachers'
  federations and all faculties of education* help teachers develop and expand
  their assessment-related knowledge and skills.
- That *school boards* carefully review their action plans in relation to the
  board data they have accumulated over the past four years and take
  additional measures to address those areas of the language and mathematics curriculum that are not showing improvement.
- That *principals and teachers* act on the subject-specific recommendations
  and the comments from markers about student achievement in reading,
  writing and mathematics. (EQAO press release, 2 November 2001,
  emphasis in the original)

Student test results are thus turned against teachers, who are por-
trayed as deficient in the knowledge and skills of assessment, and the
entire power structure is mobilized to manage teachers to 'expand' in
these areas – the ministry, the OCT, teachers' federations, faculties of
education, school boards, and principals.

Emanating from the EQAO is a systemically entrenched corporate-
capitalist modus operandi. An analysis of the eight-member board of
directors appointed by the ministry corroborates the prevalence of
business people, career bureaucrats, and former politicians with a
track record of supporting education reform; singularly lacking in this
group is teaching experience in the classroom. How can the EQAO
claim to be independent of government when its board is appointed by
the ministry? The ratio of women to men representatives on the board
is 3:5 and all are white.[7] As the designated custodian of 'quality' and
'accountability' in public schools, the EQAO, like the OPC, operates
within the parameters of the discourse of scientific management and is
consistent with the management system standards of the ISO 9001
derived from the corporate sector. It is outside the purview of this discourse to question assumptions such as: What constitutes quality in
public education? How can it be measured? Who is accountable to
whom for what? Who has the power to set standards? Within this paradigm, education is reduced to measurable skills and reiteration of
content (outcomes) that belie broader, more progressive notions of the
meaning and purpose of education.

Other Extralocal Ruling Structures

More inclusive conceptions of education to contest those espoused by the EQAO may be expected to emanate from faculties of education in universities, such as the Ontario Institute for Studies in Education (OISE/UT). However, universities are also the beneficiaries of calls for increased training of teachers and entire academic careers are constructed around research into student and teacher testing. Founded in 1965 as a centre for graduate studies and research, OISE is renowned for contributions to critical theory and feminist studies in education. In 1996, with the amalgamation of OISE and the Faculty of Education of the University of Toronto (FEUT), OISE/UT was restructured as a new professional faculty under the governing council of the older, more 'traditional' University of Toronto, to form the largest faculty of education in Ontario. Initiated by the minister of education and training in answer to funding problems at OISE, integration entailed combining two distinct faculties into a single entity, under the direction of the former dean of FEUT, Michael Fullan. Given the unequal power relations surrounding the circumstances of the merger and the dominance of former FEUT faculty through the appointment of the dean, critical/feminist theorist/activists at OISE became marginalized. Why, for instance, was there not a shared appointment from each of the former faculties to ease the transition?

The influence of universities on education is exerted in two major ways: first, directly through teacher training (what is taught), gatekeeping (who gets accepted) and credentialing (who graduates); and second, as a primary site of knowledge production where educational discourses are generated. The Royal Commission on Learning proposed major changes to teacher education. The recommendation of increasing credentialization by extending teacher pre-service training to two years (Recommendations 68 and 69) has not been implemented, although a pilot program was offered at OISE/UT for the 1995 to 1997 period, in response to a call from the Ministry of Education and Training. OISE/UT continues to offer the option of a two-year program (masters in teaching) to a small contingent of teacher-candidates, as an alternative to the B.Ed. Although this extended teacher training is not yet a requirement to qualify as a teacher in Ontario, it creates a two-tiered system of graduates, that gives an advantage to those who can afford the extra year for promotion in the system. What purpose is served by extending the time and financial debt incurred in pre-service training? What is the impact on recruitment and promotion of teachers from underprivileged groups already under-represented in the teaching profession?

Extending teacher pre-training and increasing credentialization arguably exacerbate what Livingstone (1999) refers to as the 'education-jobs gap,' producing an 'overqualified' workforce whose skills and knowledge are under-utilized in the workplace. Livingstone's analysis subverts the 'common sense' assumption that lack of education is the problem. The extent to which tacit knowledge is acquired through reflection-in-action (Schön, 1987) is overlooked when the traditional 'banking model' of education (Freire, 1972)[8] is valued over learning in and through actual practice, or acquired on a voluntary basis outside formal structures through informal learning (Livingstone, 2000). The trend towards increasing credentialization through formal education is both a cooptation of professional education by universities and a quest for legitimacy by the professions. In the case of teacher training, the OCT and faculties of education such as OISE/UT operate in concert to regulate pre-service and in-service training of teachers. By legislation, control over teacher professional training was bestowed on the OCT, including accreditation of pre-service programs and approval of in-service courses, thus impacting on cherished university principles of institutional autonomy and academic freedom. The implementation of mandatory perpetual in-service training under the auspices of the OCT's Professional Learning Program, following the royal commission's Recommendation 75, is a particularly contentious issue for teachers (and is discussed further in chapter 5).

Universities also exert influence over teachers, since educational discourses are formulated through their research function. The proximity of academics to the real world of the classroom is often remote, such that in the vernacular of teachers, theory is considered 'edubabble' – in other words, it has little relevance to their day–to-day work or it states the obvious. The objectification of teachers is exemplified in the interconnected discourses of teacher testing and teacher competencies. These discourses emanate from research conducted in faculties of education, in close collaboration with the OCT. Idealized conceptions of education, to which practice aspires and by which it is measured, often lead to contradictions, discrepancies, and shortfalls that belie the complexity of actual teaching practice, thus highlighting the importance of integrating theory with practice. Discourses formulated in universities not only influence teachers-in-training, but also the public at large through 'expert' opinions expressed in the media and by government agencies. The promotion of university-business partnerships and the consequent corporatization of the university is accompanied by the emergence of the 'academic entrepreneur,' the lucrative 'consulting' business, and spinoff companies benefiting from academic research (Newson and Buchbinder, 1988; Tudiver, 1999; Turk, 2000). An example of local education academics benefiting from consulting are the educational change 'experts,' Fullan and Hargreaves (1991, 1998). Their research is consistent with educational reform while arguably performing a disservice to teachers. Is it coincidence that Michael Fullan was appointed to the position of dean of education for the newly merged OISE/UT?

During teacher protests across the province in recent years over declining conditions in public education, OISE/UT refrained from official public comment (apparently under directives from upper administration), although there were a few isolated public events in support of public education. The university administration's claim of political neutrality to justify its silence implicitly condones the ideological position and socio-political consequences of education reform. It would seem that adherents to neoliberal policies among academic staff dominate, rather than social critics and activists in the public interest. Newson and Buchbinder (1988) attribute lack of resistance on the part of the professoriate to three possible reasons: lack of awareness, a sense of powerlessness, or support for university-business links. The importance of the university as a key site where counter-discourses and alternative discourses are formulated seemed peripheral in the public debate throughout the PCs' reign. Although it is beyond the scope of this inquiry, universities themselves are affected by education reform and have been sites of labour unrest by faculty, student assistants and staff. In these relations, protest has arisen from the gulf in perspective and values between administration/management and intellectual workers at universities, echoing what is being experienced in schools.

Aside from universities, the business lobby also exerts a powerful influence over education policy and public opinion through right-wing think-tanks, such as the Fraser Institute and the C.D. Howe Institute. Supported by abundant corporate funding, these think-tanks conduct ideologically motivated research under the guise of objectivity. The Fraser Institute produced the *Report Card on Ontario's Secondary Schools* (Cowley and Shahabi-Azad, 2001), in which schools were rated on a scale of 1 to 10 and ranked in order, according to questionable, limited criteria biased in favour of schools in privileged locations. Not surprisingly, given socio-economic benefit and criteria that reflect privilege, sixteen private schools occupy the first rank, with a top rating of 10. Rating and ranking the effectiveness of schools serves no pedagogical purpose, but the timing of the release of this report to the media immediately prior to the announcement of Bill 45, suggests it was instrumental in priming the public to believe that private education equals better education. Despite temporary withdrawal of the report when serious research flaws were exposed by critics (including biased criteria and inaccurate data), this report was re-released. It remains on public record as representing the true state of education in Ontario, having achieved the goal of skewing public policy in the direction of privatizing education. Is it mere coincidence that following his resignation as premier of Ontario, Mike Harris was rewarded with an appointment as senior fellow at the Fraser Institute, joining Preston Manning, founder of the former ultra-conservative federal Reform Party?

Also operating at the national level, the Conference Board of Canada's Corporate Council on Education has exerted pressure through its *Employability Skills Profile*, which is intended to guide educational policy. It has shaped the 'learning outcomes' of the new curriculum according to skills considered desirable to businesses, emphasizing skills training for the workplace over critical thinking as the mission of education. In particular, employability skills are central to the new careers half-course that is a compulsory credit for graduation from high school in Ontario. At the international level, through international testing of students and ranking of countries, OECD is instrumental in determining 'indicators' that inform policy decisions in Canada, exercised via the Canadian Education Statistics Council (CESC), a joint initiative of the Council of Ministers of Education, Canada, and Statistics Canada. Through national and international organizations such as these, the business lobby exerts a powerful influence on government, affecting legislation and public policy decisions in ways that serve the corporate agenda.

In alignment with this agenda and with the emphasis on partnerships by the royal commission, power and legitimacy was lent and the way paved for renewed corporate sector involvement in education:

That the provincial government review legislative and related impediments, and that they develop a policy framework for collaboration to facilitate partnerships between community and schools. (Recommendation 113)

Community-school partnerships here refers primarily to, and is overwhelmingly represented by, the business community, whose self-interested encroachment into public education may be concealed as charitable donations to a cash-strapped system. Public-private partnerships (P3s) that influence education policy include the Toronto Learning Partnership and the Ontario Knowledge Network for Learning. Both fund research on 'best practices' and engage in policy discussions to mould education in the image of the corporate sector.

The Toronto Learning Partnership (TLP, formed in 1993) is supported by both the federal and provincial levels of government, together with businesses and community organizations, educational institutions, and boards of education. According to their 2003 report tellingly entitled *Return on Investment* (2003),[9] Greater Toronto area school boards invested $150000 in the TLP at a time when school boards were virtually bankrupt. Of the program partners, the largest category by far is the corporate sector, which includes banks and companies invested in insurance, technology, oil, and utilities.[10] What these large companies share is a scale of operation well beyond small businesses in local communities. Promises of a return on investment suggest that private sponsors not only benefit from this form of advertising, but also from the TLP power base as a group lobby. Yet, according to its mission statement, the TLP asserts it is a 'not-for-profit organization dedicated to bringing together business, education, government, labour, policy makers and the community to develop partnerships and strengthen public education in Canada' (http://www.thelearningpartnership.ca/ROI_2003.pdf).

The fact that funds may be designated for specific programs affords corporate sponsors influence over the curriculum. Among the twelve programs coordinated by the TLP are the Principal for a Day program, and the Take Our Kids to Work program. The first program is an exchange in which business/community leaders work alongside a principal or vice-principal at the workplace, or vice versa, with the stated purpose of sharing ideas on organizational leadership and management techniques. The second program is the TLP's trademarked 'signature program,' in which Grade 9 students job-shadow a parent/guardian for a day; the underlying assumption is that all parents/guardians are in the privileged position of being able to accommodate their children safely in the workplace. Trademarking and copyrighting these programs not only has a hollow ring but has disconcerting associations with the privatization of 'intellectual property' so antithetical to the free exchange of knowledge and ideas as a value held by educators.

As a community partner of the Toronto Board of Trade, the TLP operates as a conduit between the public and private sectors to promote corporate interests and corporate citizenship. Among the list of stakeholders, private-sector sponsors are construed as 'good corporate citizens,' playing a leadership role in 'positively impacting Canada's education system.' Consistent with corporate-speak, the TLP asserts its allegiance with parents (customers) who are regarded as possessing 'reliable and credible expertise on educational issues,' as compared with teachers who are implicitly disregarded as needing improvement through 'professional training and development, exposure to best practices and access to materials' at the behest of corporate 'experts' (http://www.thelearningpartnership.ca/ROI_2003.pdf, p.3). Analysis of the board of directors of the TLP exhibits a particularly homogenous group of senior management officials, including presidents of companies, deans of education and directors of school boards. A ratio of women to men of 10:14 reflects the glass ceiling at the upper management level and suggests a boardroom bias in favour of corporate executives trained as tough, masculinist, 'cutting-edge' decision-makers.

In a similar vein, the Ontario Knowledge Network for Learning (OKNL) claims to be a partnership between government, education, and business with a commitment to improve student achievement through the use of the latest information technology. According to the OKNL website, 'Stakeholders are working together to develop and implement a provincial approach to using ICT to enhance learning, improve student achievement and increase opportunities for parents to be involved in their children's education' (http://oknl.edu .gov.on.ca/eng/about_us/).

This office of the ministry operates in collaboration with faculties and boards of education, the Conference Board of Canada, and the IT industry to promote school-business partnerships. It provides funding for research that contributes towards a 'best practices ideas bank' to inform policies and standards. The OKNL funds projects in fifteen 'demonstration' schools with input from its private sector partners: Apple Canada Inc., Dell Canada, Hewlett Packard, IBM Canada, Microsoft Canada, Sun Microsystems, and Telesat Canada. Analysis of its board of directors reveals the dominance of IT industry people and the senior manager heralds from the federal government Department of Industry, with prior experience in the IT sector.[11] Being a partner/ stakeholder of Industry Canada, whose mission is developing the economy, the operations of the OKNL raises the question of which contingency is driving education policy reform – educators or economists?

Public-private partnerships, such as the OKNL and the TLP, not only afford the corporate sector a powerful lobby base with direct access to the highest levels of public policy development in government, but they also serve to disseminate the corporate ethos throughout the institution of public education via the projects and programs they chose to fund. Dependency on corporate sponsorships for supplementary funding forces schools into ceding advertising rights and promoting the ideology of free-market capitalism. Corporate goods and logos appear insidiously; corporate values and 'visions' of the future come to inform education policy and insinuate their way into the curriculum. Agreements between Pepsi, the Youth News Network, and Rogers Cable with the former Toronto School Board exemplify abuses of community partnerships in business-school relations (Barlow and Robertson, 1994; Klein, 2000). This marks a fundamental shift away from the philosophy of secular progressive child-centred education, which was intended to be autonomous from vested outside interference by state, religious, or business interests. Public-private partnerships highlight the dangers of naïvely responding to the overtures of the 'captains of industry' (Veblen, 1979, first published 1918) without examining the educational implications: Whose interests are served by these arrangements? Are schools trading students' attention as impressionable captive audiences of future consumers and workers, in exchange for money or technology? Are public funds invested in education effectively subsidizing the agendas of private corporations?

Interlocking Ruling Relations

In summary, this overview of the major power-brokers affecting secondary education in Ontario elucidates how teachers' work is regulated and controlled by an extensive array of extralocal ruling structures; some are newly established under restructuring, while others that predate restructuring have had their mandates changed so as to reduce or enhance their relative powers (see figure 4.1). These include newly created institutional structures (OCT, OPC, Ontario Parent Council, and EQAO); previously existing structures reorganized through amalgamation and downsizing (the ministry, school boards such as the TDSB); and structures purportedly not under direct government control affected through changing their mandates or funding base (OTF and affiliates, OISE/UT). Input into education from the corporate sector has been enhanced through school-business partnerships, parent councils, and think-tanks, influencing policy-making up to the highest level. Analysis of the composition of boards of governors, or executive level decision-makers of new ruling structures, indicates the dominance of white male values (at the OCT) and white corporatist values (at the EQAO). Singularly lacking is recent teaching experience on the boards of any of the ruling structures, demonstrating that decision-making is vested in non-teachers or public officials remote from teaching practice. The prevalence of ministry appointments on the executive boards of the new ruling structures (OCT and EQAO) suggests where the power lies; these government appointees guarantee tight governmental control over educational decision-making. Since teaching is largely a feminized profession, this analysis focuses on gender, although it is apparent that inequities exist along other axes of difference. The changed relations of ruling that have been orchestrated through restructuring the institution of public education, as laid out by the Royal Commission on Learning, exhibits signs of an intensification of the same old power relations executed through new or different structures.

Through analysis of the ruling relations that operate within and between the various structures, it becomes clear that educational restructuring has ensured centralization of power to the province and increased government control over teachers. The creation of the new superministry of education, amalgamation of school boards, and the integration of OISE/UT, combined with downsizing, suggest significant upheaval and destabilization of educational structures and social relations system-wide. Together with the creation of new structures, increased bureaucratic control over teachers is coordinated from 'command central' at the ministry. Complex interlocking relations between the ruling structures become evident by examining links through money flows, text flows, and mobility of high-ranking personnel across the various structures.

Under education reform, centralization of provincial government control over education policy and school funding marks a shift in power relations from the earlier emphasis on flexibility according to local context, as exercised through the intermediate level of local

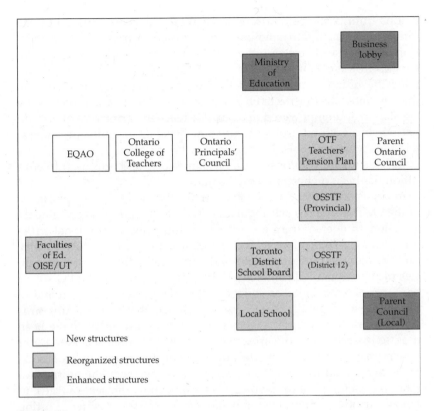

Figure 4.1
Ruling educational structures in Ontario

school boards. Reduction in salaries for publicly elected school trustees not only devalues democracy, but could have the effect of squashing opposition by weighting boards in the direction of compliant candidates. As pointed out by Chandra Mohanty, the 'lady charity' mentality of performing discretionary 'good' works in the community actually reinforces the status quo. The beneficiaries of privilege are unlikely to challenge the hegemony, nor to lead opposition at the local level.

The coordination of these new structures, backed by full legislative authority, undermines democratic processes. Democratically elected representatives (whether trustees at local school boards or representatives of teachers' unions) are thus neutralized. The marginalization of unions from participation in policy-making has been achieved by the formation of the OCT (removing jurisdiction over professional matters from the OTF affiliates) and the OPC (removing principals from membership in the OTF); together, the OCT and the OPC serve to undermine the union of teachers by limiting their mandate and reducing their membership respectively. Legitimized as 'education leaders' by legislation and empowered to discipline teachers, principals operate in partnership with advisory parent councils so as to undercut collegial relations within schools. Through restructuring, divisive hierarchically structured social relations and a consumer-oriented approach to education has been orchestrated by the ministry.

Analysis of links at the ministry website throws into question claims of the OCT as being a self-regulating body and the EQAO as being an arms-length agency from government. These new institutional structures actually share close relations and, to a great extent, the ministry exercises control over operations and imposes deadlines on these agencies of government. Technology flows emanating from the EQAO, in the form of test results, are disseminated across the institution and to the public at large, dictating how knowledge about the institution is constructed. My analysis suggests that EQAO test results have been used to discredit the education system and to blame teachers in order to manufacture consent for education reform, and to rank schools so as to instill competition for customers/students. The negative profiling of schools through publication of EQAO test results represents a threat to schools in lower SES areas and has led to school closures. Posting results in graphic form on the TDSB website affects student enrolment and hence funding to low-ranked schools under the terms of the new funding formula. Moreover, increases in realty property prices in areas of high-ranked schools (reported in the *Realty News*) indicates who the beneficiaries are within the larger political economy. The fact that the EQAO was the only new body financed by government funds (with an annual budget that more than tripled in six years) at the same time as cutbacks to education were executed, connotes the priority placed on standardized testing and centres this office as the cornerstone of ruling relations. The other new bodies are funded largely through membership fees (OCT and OPC) or through volunteers (parent councils). The fact that the OCT is applying for government money to fund its Professional Learning Program provides additional confirmation of close ties with the ministry. Similarly, the Ontario Parent Council's website is maintained by government funds.

Mobility of personnel across structures at the upper echelons of governance is evidenced by the appointment of Marguerite Jackson to run the EQAO. The public announcement of the appointment by the minister (in *Ministry of Education News Release*, 12 September 2001) contradicts the arm's length relationship between the ministry and the EQAO. According to media reports, Jackson received a $360,000 severance package upon her voluntary resignation as the high-paid director of the TDSB, even though she attained another high-profile position within education governance. The applicability of corporate practices such as generous severance packages to public servants must be viewed critically and in context. Where is this money coming from? Meanwhile, the TDSB was on the verge of bankruptcy and teachers lacked textbooks for the new curriculum. In her speech to the Canadian Club (November 9, 1998), addressed to 'community leaders' (that is, business leaders) and later 'shared' with teachers, Jackson's mix of economic rationalization and new-age guruism is typical of CEO-talk. The emphasis on her achievements 'streamlining' the TDSB masks the impact on the everyday 'streamlining' of students. Placed on a par with Albert Einstein and Marshall McLuhan (who are also briefly quoted) is Bill Gates, upon whom Jackson bestows prophetic insight:

> As our nation moves to the end of one century – and the beginning of a new millennium – it's time for us to decide about the legacies we want to leave for future generations. We must be clear in our goals and definite in our purposes. We must seek improvements, recognizing as Bill Gates said in his autobiography, 'Even if you are on the right track, if you just stand there, you will still be run over.' (Marguerite Jackson, *Exchange*, December 1998)

Corporate greed and monopoly as epitomized by Bill Gates (and Microsoft) are proffered to guide the goals and purposes of education. The stampede to the top – ever fearful of a moment of stillness lest the dust should settle – is the legacy Jackson would leave to the next generation; she now arguably holds the most powerful position in the institution of education in Ontario.

Not only mobility upward, but also mobility across the divide between union and professional associations at the upper echelons is indicated by tracing the career path of Margaret Wilson. Wilson had previously served as president of the OSSTF at both district and provincial levels, and also as president of the OTF before being appointed first registrar of the OCT. The shift to an elitist perspective is high-lighted in *D12 Voice*, where Wilson is quoted using the derogatory term of 'brownshirts' to characterize union members.[12] Among the dedications delivered upon her resignation as registrar is that of Dave Cooke, former NDP minister of education who set up the Royal Commission on Learning and who was subsequently appointed by the PC government as co-chair of the Education Improvement Commission. In his dedication, Cooke declared that he had known the Wilson family since childhood (*Professionally Speaking*, December 2000), suggesting the operation of cronyism at the upper levels of the ruling structures. Former ministers of education benefit from patronage appointments to commissions and senior positions at the various ruling structures, thus ensuring tight control by an educational elite that begins to read like a list of usual suspects. Another former minister of education, Bette Stephenson, has been a longstanding official at the EQAO. Having served on the advisory board from 1995 to 1996 that was instrumental in formulating the mandate of the EQAO, she was thereafter appointed to its board of directors. As minister of education in the prior conservative government of Bill Davis, Stephenson is on record as an early proponent of a new professional body for teachers (like the OCT), although legislation was not passed at that time. Similarly, the former deputy minister of education under Harris and director of education for the North York Board of Education, Veronica Lacey, was appointed president and CEO of the TLP. As a senior fellow at OISE/UT, Lacey co-chaired the Curriculum Implementation Plan with Michael Fullan, who in turn serves on the board of directors of the corporate-friendly TLP. Clearly, ideological congruence exists across the upper ranks of educational structures, and who you know counts for senior appointments.

OISE/UT is implicated in the interlocking ruling relations among ruling structures. Another example is Lorna Earl, director of assessment for the EQAO, who also held a part-time faculty position at OISE/UT. Commissioned to prepare a paper on accountability for the ministry's Royal Commission on Learning, Earl is quoted striking a cautionary note:

> Unfortunately, it is rarely clear what is meant by accountability. It is an emotionally charged term that implies such things as striving for success, confidence, trust, communication and responsiveness, but does not define actual behaviours or practices. (vol. 4, p. 137)

Notwithstanding these apparent reservations, Earl has been involved since the beginning at the EQAO and has been instrumental in formulating accountability measures that have been orchestrated across Ontario. Her mobility across ruling structures between the ministry, OISE/UT, and EQAO suggests ideological links between them. The royal commission's call on universities to assist in educational restructuring named OISE in particular,[13] and expressed the hope that 'OISE and other Ontario graduate schools of education would respond enthusiastically to the call for proposals, as would measurement experts in departments of psychology or elsewhere' (vol. 4, p. 141). This was a promise to open career opportunities in academia for assessment and evaluation, but using a competitive contract process involving public calls for proposals. Who decides which proposals are accepted? Who benefits from these proposals? How are standardized tests helpful in actual teaching practice?

And who gets promoted or 'appointed'? The cases cited of Marguerite Jackson, Margaret Wilson, Bette Stevenson, Veronica Lacey, and Lorna Earl suggest that positions of power are transmutable across ruling structures including the EQAO, OCT, ministry, school boards, faculties of education, the business lobby, and even unions. The point here is not to single out individuals, but to identify how power works systemically. These individual women in positions of power who managed to break through the glass ceiling into senior management may be considered 'male-identified' women who are ideologically aligned with education reform. Like Margaret Thatcher who spearheaded neoliberal policies in the United Kingdom, they achieve their personal ambitions by subscribing to the dominant ethos rather than taking a stand to alter the destructive course of education reform, as perceived by teachers. It seems that more gender balance at the top of hierarchical structures, or more women in positions of power, is not a guarantee. Social transformation is unlikely to occur without critical analysis of the construction of 'leadership' in education, and without more equitable representation and participation (by gender and other axes of difference) at all stages and levels of decision-making.

The centralization of decision-making to the ministry, with close links to the key new ruling structures of the EQAO and OCT, enables the coordination of mandates and accountability: whereas the EQAO operates as a watchdog over system performance, the OCT operates as a watchdog over teachers. The OPC and Ontario Parent Council, through their members, serve as watchdogs over schools. In each case, the Royal Commission on Learning has constituted the blueprint for government legislation that has orchestrated ruling relations across these ruling structures under education reform. An analysis of relations that pertain to secondary education in Ontario suggests a ruling apparatus that enmeshes teachers in an interlocking complex of structures. Moreover, mobility across ruling structures of high-ranking officials suggests ideological congruence at the upper levels of hierarchies, and of 'academic entrepreneurs' at universities, who share similar salaries, status, and worldviews. Among the educational elite, it appears that the mindset converges on adherence to corporate managerial systems analysis, standardization, and policy control.

But this is a far cry from the everyday world of classroom teachers.

5 Teachers in Texts and Text-Mediated Relations

Beginning with teacher-participants' experiences as expressed in the focus group, three specific texts emerged as problematic to them. Teacher-participants' reactions constitute markers of ruling relations and a starting point for mapping text-mediated relations across the institution of public education. The three texts are a letter from the OCT (appendix I-A) announcing the commencement of the Professional Learning Program that two teacher-participants 'threw in the garbage'; a letter from the TDSB (appendix I-B), deducting a day's pay for an alleged breach of legal duties that precipitated a group grievance; and the Remedial Support Program–Teacher Log (appendix I-C) recording extra help provided to students that putatively places teachers in the position of 'lying.' Teacher-participants' objections to these three documents mark discrepancies between the subjective experience of teaching practice and the objectifying textually-mediated policies intrinsic to the ruling relations. Analysis of these three documents provides access to the operation of ruling relations and the tensions between compliance and defiance experienced by teachers under education reform. Textual analysis reveals how ruling relations are mediated across the public education system through texts. These documents (and/or related texts) not only occupy a particular location on file, but also enter the realm of permanent records held by the institution about teachers and/or their work. How teachers are constructed in texts (whether printed or electronic) and how their work is regulated is made visible through comparing teachers' experiences with textual analyses of these official documents.

Each of the three documents is analysed by locating it within the context of events unfolding in Ontario at the time, by chronicling focus group reactions to it, and by undertaking a textual analysis of the document itself, as well as an intertextual analysis of related texts. Tracing the flow of documents and mapping textual links show how ruling relations operate across the institution of public education. What is brought to the foreground through the analysis is the ideological code constitutive of educational reform that subjects teachers to objectifying surveillance and control by extralocal structures far removed from the everyday experience of the classroom.

OCT Letter: The Creation of a Privatized 'Teacher Training Industry'

The OCT letter was mailed to those teachers singled out for the first phase of the Professional Learning Program (PLP), commencing in the fall of 2001. The second phase draws in all remaining teachers who are members of the OCT, effective in the fall of 2002. Derived from the discourse of teacher-testing and managed by the OCT, the PLP program imposes mandatory ongoing professional development on teachers, as legislated by Bill 80. According to this program, teachers are required to take fourteen courses every five years in order to maintain their Certificate of Qualification that is issued by the OCT annually. This certificate constitutes the licence to practice in a public school in the province of Ontario.

Teacher-participants in the focus group at first reacted to the letter with confusion; as the dialogue unfolds, objections were voiced strongly with anger and defiance, thus constituting markers of ruling relations. The dialogue as recorded on the transcript shows how teacher-participants attempt to make sense of the letter in the moment-to-moment interaction of the focus group:

JESSICA: I didn't get a letter, did you?
RACHEL: I don't know. I got a letter that *may* have been – (tentatively, trails off).
JESSICA: Did you open it?
RACHEL: I did open it. It made me so *angry* I ripped it up and threw it in the garbage because I thought it might have been for that and I have no intention whatever of doing it!
JESSICA: Oh Rachel, so you're one who got 'selected'!
RACHEL: I don't know because – (trails off).
JESSICA: She didn't quite finish reading it but – (trails off).
RACHEL: It *sounded* like I was one.

JESSICA: Was it the same time frame as everyone else got the letter?

RACHEL: It was.

JESSICA: There you go!

RACHEL: I'm not positive (tentatively). But the point is I don't *care*! (emphatically).

HELENA: Well, probably I was also chosen, but taking into consideration that I took, just three years ago, another one of those special exams, I don't really *care*.

JESSICA: But you'd know if you were chosen.

HELENA: No, I know. I got a letter at home.

ALICE: Saying that your number was up?

RACHEL: What did the letter say?

JESSICA: I don't know, I never saw it. I didn't get one.

HELENA: I got a letter. They said something that you have to take – blah blah – all the courses and – (trails off).

JESSICA: You have to begin! That's the letter!

HELENA: That's the letter? Well, I threw it in the garbage!

JESSICA: Oh, good, well! (Laughs).

RACHEL: I guess that must have been what it was too. I – (trails off).

JESSICA: The real joke of it is I love taking courses!

RACHEL: Yuh!

JESSICA: I LOVE TAKING COURSES! (noise – all talking at once).

RACHEL: Not from them!

JESSICA: Some of my phys. ed. qualification courses, I had a ball. It was great. I want to do Part 2 [of the Additional Qualification courses]. I don't know if that *counts*. I haven't looked into it. Who *cares*! (slaps her leg).

RACHEL: *That's* the point! You do it because *you* want to do it.

JESSICA: Yeah, exactly! And I mean I've taken about sixteen ministry courses since I graduated.

HELENA: Me too!

JESSICA: And I've enjoyed it.

HELENA: Two honours specialist [qualifications], never mind part 1, part 2, part 3. All the others and very recent[ly]. Why do I have to take other courses? I don't understand!

JESSICA: From the receipt of the letter, your clocks are ticking! (Laughs).

ALICE: Not mine!

Two of the four participants (Rachel and Helena) received the letter indicating that they had been 'selected' to start the PLP program. Both recipients threw it in the garbage without reading it, indicating defiance of mandatory courses, even though teacher-participants insist that they enjoy taking courses voluntarily. This contradiction is a marker of ruling relations at work. Intense emotion and mockery suggest a breach of trust (Garfinkel, 1967) in relations between teachers and their professional organization, the OCT. 'Clockwork' imposed externally by an arbitrary timeframe begins, as 'clocks are ticking' for these two teachers. Which courses count is questioned, as are restrictions on teachers' control over their own professional development. The emphasis and frequency of statements such as 'I don't care' are unusual for teachers. It suggests that these teachers are reassessing what they care about in their own terms and that they are willing to risk the personal/professional consequences for non-compliance. Noncompliance with the particular formulation of professional development imposed by the OCT represents no harm to students, and thus does not run counter to the ethic of care for their charges that is a central value for teachers.

In this situation, where lack of transparency is coupled with a power play between the OCT and teachers, rumours are generated:

JESSICA: And you know, I heard that most people, also, that got these letters, they just put 'Return to Sender'!

RACHEL: Ooo! Good for them! I should have done that!

JESSICA: Yuh, all the people I know in Ottawa, they just sent them back. And so then they want – the government [sic OCT] – was wondering whether they should send them a registered letter. I mean – *excuse me* – we're just caught in a pissing contest! (Laughter). It *is*! I mean how silly is that? Oh yeah, 'Wait a second, we can get around that!'(mimicking an officious machismo voice and gesture). That's crazy though.

The rumour that Ottawa teachers had returned the letters was verified in a personal communiqué with an inside source at the OCT. Interlocking power structures are suspected in Jessica's slip of the tongue, conflating the OCT with 'the government.' The power struggle between teachers and the OCT/government is characterized as a 'pissing contest.' Language usage deploying a male metaphor for power issues and confrontation denotes gender relations in operation. It draws attention to the gendered construction of professional development inherent in the PLP program that is clearly a charged flashpoint for teachers.

Textual analysis identifies this lengthy four–page letter on OCT letterhead, as dated 15 October 2001 and co-signed by the chair and registrar of the college. The purpose of letter is to announce the commencement of the PLP program. Personally addressed to the 40,000 teachers in the first phase ('about 30 per cent of the college membership'), the letter was mailed to their residences. The inclusion of the teacher's 'Registration #' in the top right corner signifies impersonal and objectifying accounting logic that reduces the teacher/person to a number. Dehumanization is further reflected in the fact that no contact person is mentioned anywhere in the letter, thus denying person-to-person contact. Various links at the OCT website utilize technology to buffer the college from questions, requests for clarification or objections, thus shutting teachers out of any dialogue.

It is stated that this is 'your official notice' to recipients who must complete their first PLP cycle by the deadline of 31 December 2006, officiously emphasizing the unequivocal imperative in bold type. By contrast, the informality of a P.S. seems incongruous with a formally served official notification. The postscript that contains the web site address for regular updates presumes a familiarity and mutuality at being 'together' on the exciting edge of fast-paced change, a sentiment clearly not shared by teachers in the focus group. The logo of the OCT at the bottom of the letterhead page – 'Together We're Shaping the Future' – begs the question: Who's shaping whose future? Who are 'we'?

Relying heavily on legislation for its authority, the letter refers to Bill 80 and makes stipulations as 'required by law.' The frequency of the imperative 'must' forecloses negotiation: in accordance with Bill 80, recipients must complete '14 courses – seven core and seven elective – every five years.' Business language abounds: providers, delivery, outcomes, learning opportunities, etc. The rhetoric of choice in the statement, 'You will be able to choose courses offered by many providers' conflates liberty with consumer choice. It belies restrictions not only in what counts for credit, and conditions that pertain to the overall categorization into prescribed core areas, but overrules the freedom to construct professional development in entirely different terms. Consumer choice, as determined by the OCT's pre-selection of approved courses and approved providers according to rigid criteria and categories, amounts to forcing teachers to select pre-packaged educational products as if from the supermarket shelf. Choice is also limited by time: *'You can complete your Professional Learning course credits at your own pace*, as long as you accumulate 14 credits by December 31, 2006' (emphasis in the original). An average of three courses per year to be taken outside school hours leaves little flexibility for teachers to construct the pacing of professional development. The pretence of choice is thus contradicted by strict controls not only over course content but also over pacing. The OCT's claim of 'commitment to equity' reflects a limited understanding of equity, where equity of access is reduced to offering courses in the two dominant official languages. Adherence to the principle of individualism purports to meet 'your' (individual teacher) needs. Choice over 'your professional learning,' 'your professional growth' and 'your professional needs' reserves the privilege of prescribing what 'professional' means, and simultaneously discounts that personal learning, growth, and needs may actually contribute positively toward professional performance, as well as general well-being.

As required by Bill 80, the first group of teachers were 'randomly selected from the College register' or 'were first certified to teach in Ontario in 2001.' New teachers not only have the task of adjusting to teaching practice, but also to building their resources (such as lesson plans, support materials, supplementary references, overheads, worksheets), the compilation of which requires extensive overtime. Yet new teachers are expected to make time for additional courses and to incur additional expenses over and above recently accumulated student debt. If the motivation is to keep teachers current and up to date, then why would recent graduates be explicitly selected for the first phase?

Only courses approved by the college and 'delivered by providers approved by the College' qualify for credit. Providers include not only traditional institutions (such as faculties of education, school boards, teacher federations, independent schools, and professional associations), but also private businesses. The list of approved providers is 'growing by the week' and expected to be in the 'hundreds' by the end of the year. With approximately 180,000 teachers across the province (with the inclusion of the rest of teachers in the second phase) obliged to take an average of three courses per year, a massive influx of money into the economy has been orchestrated. It seems that what is being set up is a new partly privatized 'teacher training industry' to serve the economy at teachers' expense. Teachers are expected to attend courses without release or lieu time, compensation for expenses, or increase in salary. The creation of an artificial niche market in the private sector for educational courses supposedly stimulates the economy by creating money flows that register as a positive on standard economic measures of national accounts (Marilyn Waring in Nash, 1995), thus bolstering government claims of economic growth. Links to the wider political economy and job creation, tinged with suspicions of vindictiveness to lower teacher salaries, was identified in the focus group:

HELENA: You know it's another way to create jobs. And they [course providers] practically are subsidized by us, because we pay. It's another way to lower our salaries. We create jobs, government says more jobs are created, and who pays? *Us!*

In keeping with this comment, the PLP program may be characterized as a 'tax to teach.' Here, PLP course fees arguably constitute enforced subsidies to the private sector.

The negative incentive of avoiding being struck off the college register is the strategy to 'discipline and punish' (Foucault, 1979) non-compliant teachers. Consequences for failure to comply include suspension of the teaching certificate and the threat of public exposure: 'However, as required by law, any teacher whose teaching certificate is suspended for failure to complete the required 14 courses in five years will have the suspension and reasons recorded on the College's public register.' 'Teaching certificate' refers not to university credentials, but to the Certificate of Qualification issued by the OCT; its suspension is therefore tantamount to loss of employment. Perpetual learning is imposed by a (re)certification process, that under the auspices of the PLP program, is dependent upon compliance with on-going formal courses and backed by the full force of the law. The threat of suspending licences to teach (and hence teachers' jobs) places teachers in a perpetually provisional status, and destabilizes job security. A comparable situation applies in universities with threats to abolish tenure, and the increasing use of casualized sessional instructors.

The PLP committee at the OCT is responsible for approving providers and courses, establishing procedures for approval, and conducting regular reviews. Requirements include: courses must be a minimum of five hours long, and at least one course must be completed in each of the seven specified core areas, emphasizing management, technology, and assessment. Imagine the deliberations to arrive at these categories, according to which each approved course must be classified for single or multiple credits! The remaining seven electives must also have been pre-approved, leaving no latitude for alternative courses. The proliferation of private providers (who may advertise by other means), leaves teachers with the responsibility of locating courses and providers that 'count,' determining the terms and conditions in order to gain credit, applying for pre-approval of courses and multiple or retroactive credits, and satisfying the overall five-year package requirements in order to maintain registration. The bureaucratization of professional development proposed by the PLP program enmeshes teachers in a quagmire of red tape.

Exemptions ('actually extensions to the timelines') are to be laid out by forthcoming government regulation, anticipated to be 'quite limited' to extensions for 'long term medical leaves' only. Illness legitimized by the medical profession is presented as the only acceptable excuse for extensions.

According to the minimum requirement of five hours of instruction, day-long seminars, as in the business sector, are eligible. Three conditions for establishing approval are spelled out:

All courses must:
- support the *Standards of Practice for the Teaching Profession* and the *Ethical Standards for the Teaching Profession* (available on the College website)
- have outcomes that include improving student achievement
- contain a formal assessment mechanism.

The first criterion refers to two OCT documents that constitute reference points for the college, indicating the intertextuality of documents within the OCT and forming a closed loop of internal discourse.[1] These documents constitute the foundation for decision-making regarding not only approval of in-service courses, but also accreditation of pre-service teacher training, and disciplinary action against teachers. The second and third criteria for course approval operate within the discourse of quality control management derived from the manufacturing sector, emphasizing quantification and measurement as guaranteeing efficiency, effectiveness, and accountability. How can the contribution of course outcomes to student achievement be assessed or measured? Which outcomes? Which students? How can this be accomplished – in advance – for all courses offered by the hundreds of course providers? The third criterion emphasis on a formal assessment mechanism rules out personal learning and informal learning as legitimate professional development, owing to their immeasurability in objective terms. Teacher retraining is thus reduced to a limited view of the whole person/teacher, and of what constitutes learning and how learning is assessed. The criteria for courses suggest that policies have been formulated from economics discourse, rather than pedagogical discourse, rendering teachers as learners invisible in the PLP construction of professional development.

A premature, externally imposed deadline has been set, before the full extent of the requirements have been clarified, awaiting binding legislation as indicated in the phrases: 'We now expect to receive this [exemption] legislation within the next few months'; and 'we are not able to answer all your questions yet'; and 'the process [of confirmation of retroactive credits] ... will not be completed for several months'; and 'guidelines for multiple course credits [will be decided] in mid-November and early December.' Regardless of lack of clarity, the PLP program was started in October 2001, and as pointed out by Jessica, 'clocks are ticking' for those teachers in the first phase. As with the new curriculum and the new report card, it seems that the PLP program has been implemented before the details and consequences have been fully worked out.

Forewarning is given of the inception of a separate document referred to as the 'annual statement' to record each teacher's credits, effective in 2003. As part of the permanent record, it constitutes yet another document that inscribes teachers in textually mediated relations. This annual statement is linked to and will be mailed with the Certificate of Qualification that the OCT sends to teachers' home addresses annually. The bureaucratization of professional development through the PLP program clearly entails increased paperwork for policies, rules, and regulations that necessarily require maintenance. Record-keeping systems will require additional personnel, computer technology, and office space. Associated rising costs will likely be passed on to teachers in the form of membership fee increases.[2] Although the OCT states that the PLP program is not intended for 'ongoing performance appraisal' (which is covered under the Education Act), the effect is similar in that power is exerted over teachers through linking the program with the licence to practise in Ontario.

Intertextual analysis of the OCT letter announcing the PLP program reveals an interlocking network of text-mediated print and electronic relations that extends to extralocal ruling structures (see figure 5.1 on

p. 111). Ultimate authority rests with government legislation: Bill 80 (Stability and Excellence Act) and Schedule B (Teacher Professional Learning Requirements). Non-compliance is tantamount to breaking the law. Coercive control over teachers' professional and personal lives through legislation is indicative of the authoritarian practices of the PC government. Like other education reform measures, the PLP program can be traced back to the Royal Commission on Learning:

> That mandatory professional development be required for all educators in the publicly funded school system, with continuing certification every five years, dependent on both satisfactory performance and participation in professional development recognized by the College of Teachers. (Recommendation 75)

Within the OCT are various committees (such as the PLP Committee, Discipline Committee, Fitness to Practise Committee) responsible for managing texts (such the Certificate of Qualification, the annual statement, the college register, Standards of Practice and Ethical Standards, and approved PLP providers and courses). During its time in effect, the Professional Learning Committee, set up to oversee the PLP program, is composed of four members of the OCT, three appointees of the minister of education, and two college members at large. Of a total of nine members, only two are teachers, one of whom is a school principal. These two members at large were both appointed by the college, and only after the commencement of the PLP program and after the date of the OCT letter. Given the close relations between OCT and the ministry, teachers are overwhelmingly outnumbered by pro-government members and thus had negligible input into the PLP program.

The Certificate of Qualification specifies teaching qualifications, school system divisions in which a teacher is qualified to teach (primary, junior, intermediate, and senior) and additional qualifications completed after pre-service training. According to recent policy, the certificate must be presented annually to the administration of the school where the teacher works, to be photocopied and placed in the teacher's personal file at the school and reported to the board. Needless paperwork and bureaucratic control is questioned by Alice, who describes the enactment of this annual ritual:

ALICE: The fact that every year they send out on parchment paper with cardboard and an envelope, all of which [HELENA: It costs money!] adds to postage, a copy of our certificate. Why won't one certificate do? And if we're applying for a new job somewhere else or if our status changes, then we can get another copy. And the [school] principal is on our case because she wants copies of our updated certificate. So then we're running to the machine and photocopying for her, once a year – for a document you only need once a lifetime!

This ritual of control (Foucault in Rabinow, 1984)[3] must now be performed every year: teachers are responsible for following the prescribed routine of relaying the document within which they are inscribed, or risk the consequences of loss of pay. The ritual is thus a perennial reminder of the interlocking power structures and the chain of command. The documentary trail of the Certificate (and the TDSB letter analysed below) constitutes a strategy for destabilizing job and financial security to enforce compliance.

The OCT website posts in electronic form a public register[4] that contains records of every teacher for public scrutiny, declaring full name and registration number, listing qualifications (including institutions/places where qualifications were attained) by date, and giving the current status of the teacher. It is noted that 'membership is mandatory only for those employed in Ontario's publicly funded schools,' thus exempting private school teachers from public scrutiny, and raising questions as to why differential treatment should apply. Screens are available for each of the following categories of member information: name history, status history, qualifications, letter of approval, academic history, and employment history. The register also contains a record of findings from the Discipline or Fitness to Practise committees, if a finding of professional misconduct or incompetence has been made.

Under the category of 'letter of approval,' teachers in the focus group (as well as myself) with more than ten years experience have a 'temporary letter of approval.' What does this mean? To the lay public, it may cast doubt on the professional integrity of the teacher. Relegation to preliminary status that is embedded in these publicly available electronic documents about individual teachers reflects power relations at the OCT. This relatively recent institution can thus bestow not only the professional qualification to teach, but also professional status contingent on attaining PLP credits. The question also arises of a potential violation of the right to privacy in disclosing information about individual teachers without their consent. First, women, for a variety of reasons, including those escaping abusive relationships, may not wish information disclosed that could reveal their whereabouts. Second, teacher immigrants from war-torn countries or where ethnic strife prevails may have grounds not to make information publicly available that could set them up for reprisals. Just as important are serious questions raised in the focus group about the accuracy of these public records. Inaccuracies were reported by Helena on her Certificate of Qualification that are also electronically-posted on the public register, and that she was unable to get corrected by the OCT:

HELENA: From a bureaucracy point of view, they are not very accurate. On my transcript, in one year I took four courses, from their point of view (Laughs). I took Special Ed., Computers, and the same summer I took Honours Specialist Mathematics, twice – twice in that year! And, I took another course, which was Specialist in Reading in elementary school, that I don't have the qualification for! (Laughter) And I called them, I couldn't reach anybody and [when I did], they said to me 'Write on your response paper.' Okay, I wrote on the response paper. Next year, it came back with the same mistake! Oh, I had to pay $17 in order to correct it. And the second year when it wasn't correct, I said, I'm not going to pay another $17, because *you* [OCT] made the mistake. I can live with the [courses].

I checked the public register, freely accessible to any member of the public. Not only is Helena's account borne out and the mistakes remain, but I checked my own record and found mistakes there too. This suggests poor accuracy in the reporting practices of the OCT. Not only does the public register contain permanent records of individual teachers, but it constitutes a research source from which knowledge about the institution of public education is compiled.

The traditional 'trait theory' of the professions considers the existence of a registering body as a defining characteristic of professions. Two other essential aspects of a profession include established standards of practice and a code of ethics. In the case of the teaching profession, five statements encompass the OCT *Standards of Practice* for teaching: commitment to students and student learning, professional knowledge, teaching practice, leadership and community, and ongoing professional learning. These standards were developed in answer to the fundamental question, 'What does it mean to be a teacher?' The solipsistic definition derived is that 'in the College of Teachers Act, Regulations under the Act, and, in this statement of standards of practice 'teacher' means a member of the Ontario College of Teachers.'

The OCT therefore claims authority not only over who qualifies as a teacher and what constitutes competent teaching practice, but also over how a teacher is defined and links this definition to government legislation. It follows under this definition that non-members are not entitled to call themselves 'teachers,' thus excluding teachers in private schools who are not required to be members of the OCT. Derived from this definition of a teacher are somewhat vague standards of practice. Not only is this one of the two documents used to accredit courses, but also based upon these standards and interpretations thereof, teachers are judged by the Discipline Committee and the Fitness to Practise Committee. Whereas obvious acts of misconduct are easily identifiable as reprehensible, the problem lies in finer distinctions in the grey zone of interpretation.

The second document defining the profession and forming the cornerstone of public accountability is *Ethical Standards for the Teaching Profession*. It consists of twelve items based on general criteria of respect for values, confidentiality, collaboration, and impartiality. Whereas few would argue against these criteria in principle, in practice the latter two entries conflict in certain instances, thus posing an ethical dilemma for practitioners (a specific instance of which is discussed below in the context of the Remedial Support Program–Teacher Log).

According to government legislation (the College of Teachers Act and Regulations under the Act), the OCT is bestowed with the authority of accreditation of pre-service programs, in-service, and additional qualification courses, as well as qualifying courses of principals and supervisory officers, including those offered by universities. The college's claim of being a self-regulatory body (Standards of Practice, OCT website, p. 4), is contradicted by the heavy weighting of government appointees to its board (as demonstrated in chapter 4) and the extent to which legislation governs its mandate, as exemplified in the PLP program imposed by Bill 80.

Comparing across professional groups, no self-regulated profession is subjected to this type of formalized continual mandatory re-education in order to retain registration such as has been imposed on teachers through the PLP program. Alternative constructions of professional development used by other professions, including nursing and law, permit negotiation of individual 'growth plans' that afford flexibility and value informal, personal learning as well as formal courses. Growth plans was the model of professional development under the former Toronto School Board and is the one favoured by the OSSTF.[5] The mandate of continual professional development through course attendance outside work hours enforced by the PLP program is predicated on an androcentric model of professional development that infringes on personal time after school or on weekends, and assumes no obligations and commitments to families (or children), despite the fact that the majority of teachers are women. The construction of teachers/women as deficient and in need of constant improvement to conform to the norms and standards of patriarchal structures suggests oppressive gender relations at work.

Under the auspices of the PLP program, privatization is favoured by approving an array of private providers for a burgeoning in-service teacher training industry. The impact on education faculties at universities is to move teacher retraining outside the university, with consequent loss of funding for faculties of education from teacher tuition fees.[6] OCT power over accreditation of faculties of education may translate into loss of autonomy over curriculum for the university. If the thousands of teachers across the province comply and opt for five-hour crash courses, universities will likely be forced to conform with one-shot courses in order to be 'competitive.' The longer-term question arises as to where all this will lead: Could it previsage privatization of teacher pre-service training as well? Could these arrangements indicate a return to the past when a two-tier system existed, where teachers attended normal schools and nurses attended hospital schools, while students of the dominant professions of medicine and dentistry (mostly male) attended university?

Social relations depicting alliances and tensions between various ruling structures over the PLP program are evident in a letter from OISE/UT (see appendix I-D) that I located at the OTF website.[7] Signed by Michael Fullan, the dean of OISE/UT and dated February 12, 2002, this letter is addressed to Janet Ecker, minister of education, and copied to the deputy minister, secretary treasurer of the OTF, and registrar of the OCT – heads of the major ruling structures in public education. The letter is a response to protest action taken by the Ontario English Catholic Teachers' Association (OECTA) advising its membership not to volunteer as teacher-associates for practicums with faculties that have registered as PLP course providers. The fear of the Elementary Teach-

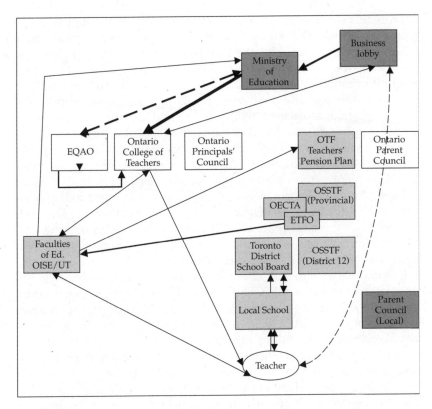

Figure 5.1
Text-mediated relations: OCT letter – Professional Learning program

ers' Federation of Ontario (ETFO) following suit is stated. Such a boycott of OISE/UT for being a PLP course provider would have the effect
of depriving teacher-candidates of placements in Catholic (and possibly elementary) schools.[8] In the letter, this union action is blamed for
forcing OISE/UT to 'seriously consider deregistering as a provider of
the Professional Learning Program, an action we [OISE/UT] would
find difficult.' The dean's declared support for the PLP program and
call on the minister to sort the matter out isolates the teacher unions
involved as the outsiders in these relations: 'Essentially we see this as a
matter to be resolved by the Ministry and the teacher associations. We
are also very much committed to contributing to the continuous development of teachers through the Professional Learning Program.'

From this statement, it seems that there is a shared ideology with the ruling apparatus vis-à-vis teacher-testing policies implemented under education reform, of which the PLP program is an integral part. The other contentious teacher-testing instrument referred to in this letter without questioning it is the 'new Initial Teacher Qualifying Test'[9] for teacher graduates. The discourse of teacher testing that includes the PLP program, the Teacher Qualifying Test and also the Teacher Performance Appraisal (introduced in September 2002) together lock teachers into a system of evaluation that not only strictly controls entry into the profession but perpetually controls who retains the right to practice. Divergent perspectives on the issue of teacher testing is evident between teachers' locally elected representatives to union affiliates (in this case OECTA and ETFO) and senior administration at OISE/UT, aligned with the ministry, the OCT, and the OTF. Recall that the OTF was the former professional body for teachers according to legislation passed in 1944 and is therefore arguably more closely aligned with ruling structures than the affiliates are. The teacher affiliates identified as oppositional in this letter (OECTA and ETFO) have been bypassed by copying the letter to the higher level of the OTF, capitalizing on internal divisions within the teachers' federation; the higher in the hierarchy the closer to the ruling apparatus. As within the OSSTF affiliate, conflict occurs between 'business unionism' operating at the provincial level and a more radical grassroots 'social justice unionism' at the local district level closer to actual teaching practice.[10] Operating from different ideological mindsets, the opposition of OECTA to the issue of privatization promoted by the PLP program seems to elude the highest authority at OISE/UT; the letter not only exhibits a non-critical position towards privatizing teacher professional development but seems unaware of the potentially negative implications for faculties of education themselves. How different might the outcome have been had OISE/UT joined forces with the teacher affiliates to oppose the PLP program at this critical juncture?

To gain a sense of the organization behind the fracas and to investigate what personal information they hold on teachers, I visited the college in downtown Toronto. The spacious offices are located on several floors of a prime location at Yonge and Bloor Streets, slickly renovated in blond wood and glass. From one of the computer stations behind the counter, an attendant fields inquiries with her eyes glued to the monitor. After explaining the purpose of my visit as to rectify my OCT record and to view my file as part of my research into education restructuring, I am directed to wait. In the empty waiting area, a few potential teachers requesting information come and go. While waiting, I browse through the glossy pamphlets on display. Still waiting, I wander into the Margaret Wilson Library. There is not a soul in sight. A bank of state-of-the-art flat-screened computers flanks the left wall. The shelves of books are in perfect order, as if unused. In the disconcerting silence, I feel like an intruder. From the inner sanctum, peels of laughter echo through the emptiness. A librarian emerges, looking startled at my presence, as if unaccustomed to 'customers.' She explains how borrowing works; the library is only open when teachers are in school. The library tour is cut short when a youthful, stylishly suited and moussed representative strides towards me, looking more like a corporate CEO than a teacher. He has the demeanour of a public relations front, not a real person. The thought enters my mind that if I extend my hand, it will pass right through the apparition, the v-actor. Having paid the fee to correct the error, I again request to view my personal record. I'm told that the only information the OCT has on me is in the public register that is accessible on-line. Knowing that OCT records include at least my address and social insurance number that are not on-line, I persist. I'm told I have to submit a request in writing. In this high-tech computerized organization, handwriting on paper seems curiously anachronistic; nevertheless I comply. Later, I received an e-mail stating that I had received the information required. Stonewalled, but having no desire to re-enter that alienating environment, I did not pursue it further – I'd seen enough.

Teacher-participants revile the OCT for vilifying teachers and for orchestrating the PLP program. The wedge issue of the PLP program surfaces as spelling the demise not only of that program, but also of the college as a primary instrument of government control in education reform, if the unequivocal and outright defiance expressed by teacher-participants is representative of teachers at large, and if decisive collective action in the form of a boycott succeeds. This form of protest against coercive control over their professional and personal lives does not risk harm to students, and hence is in keeping with an ethic of care. But what will happen when clocks stop ticking for thousands of teachers across the province? Will all lose their licence to practice? Who then will pay OCT fees? Who then will teach students in Ontario public schools? (See Afterword for subsequent events.)

TDSB Letter: The Brave New World of Surveillance

During March–April 2001, CUPE 4400 support workers were on strike in Toronto. Schools were kept open without secretarial, custodial or janitorial workers. Picket lines were in place at entrances to schools and a protocol was established whereby teachers reported to the CUPE site-captain, who recorded names and times of arrival. Teachers were permitted to cross the picket line at intervals. Upon entry to the school, there was a second sign-in sheet in the main office, recording the time of entry into the school building. Classes continued until conditions in school had deteriorated to the point that they were declared unsafe for students; however, teachers were required to continue to be in school. On 5 April 2001, certain school superintendents visited schools and ordered teachers to cross the picket line. By collective action, most teachers observed picket lines and followed the protocol established with CUPE 4400, rather than following the superintendents' orders. Almost three months later, the day before schools closed for the summer holidays, approximately 290 teachers across the TDSB received a letter informing them of a retroactive pay deduction for April 5.

During the focus group discussion, reaction to the issue surrounding this letter was characterized as 'confrontational' and as 'alienating' for teachers, marking the operation of ruling relations. Following receipt of the letter in June, Alice recounts an exchange that took place during a visit to Beaconsfield Collegiate by the superintendent that shows how resistance to the allegations was stonewalled. Collegial relations between teaching staff and the principal are questioned in Alice's account:

ALICE: The whole issue was nothing but confrontational [All: Yes!], and it served no purpose but to alienate us. [It] was the superintendent, I understand, who initiated the whole thing at Beaconsfield Collegiate and it happened at [another school] as well. [The superintendent] was in the school one day – the last two or three days before the end of school – and I just happened to be walking through the foyer. [Some colleagues] were there talking to [the superintendent] – but just trying to explain – you know, the letter says 'It's come to our attention that you were not in the workplace on such and such a date,' and [a colleague] very calmly, always reasonable, said, 'I was! I was prevented from coming in. I in fact came into the school at 9 –

whatever – 25 [approximately 9:25 a.m.].' [The superintendent's response was] 'I don't know about that. I can't speak to that. When I came into the school at – whatever it was, 9:15–9:20 – I saw, according to the list provided by the principal – '(trails off).

[The principal] also seemed to appear to absolutely alienate you. Not only from the administration at the board level, but from the administration from your own school! Who gave them the list that showed who was in and who wasn't there? Your own darn principal! And we just finished saying we would like to think that they are colleagues – um – well, you know what? Somebody's squealing somewhere along the line.

The act of the school principal in passing on the list (the school sign-in sheet in the main office) to the superintendent, while teachers were delayed at the picket line according to the established protocol, is construed as a betrayal of collegial relations. This partial list was later utilized to misconstrue the day's events and teacher attendance, such that only teachers who had signed into the school by approximately 9:20 a.m. were paid for that day.

During the CUPE strike, Alice reports that her car tires were slashed. She questions misrepresentation by the TDSB in the media of schools as a 'safe environment' in order to keep them open, and the devaluation of teachers' safety. According to Alice, the principal abdicated responsibility:

ALICE: The day previous to the day – the Thursday – when everybody got docked [pay], I had driven my car to school and not parked over in the community centre parking lot. I had opted to park on the street, out to left of the school and when I came out from the school that day, I had four slashed tires. (Gasps from the group). I called [the principal]. I said to her on the phone around 6 o'clock at night, 'I think you have some responsibility here. We advertise in the paper that we are keeping our schools open, that they are safe learning environments for our children. But you know what? The board isn't providing a safe environment for me.' And she was totally unwilling to enter [this discussion]. 'Well, that has nothing to do with me' [she said]. Yeah.

The onus was placed on teachers to follow up on the letter with paperwork according to a deadline, just as they were winding up at school and dispersing for the summer holidays:

HELENA: Because again, I was extremely busy and by the time I had
[the time] to take the paper and follow the paper[work], it was too
late.

Because of the busy time of year, Helena missed the deadline for submission of the paperwork. The OSSTF is perceived as representing
teachers' interests in rectifying the wrong done to them:

ALICE: And then again, the onus is placed on us to go to the OSSTF to
try to make this right.

The precedent of using pay as a means to discipline and punish has
registered on teacher-participants' consciousness, as evidenced by reit-
erations in comments that refer to other situations:

RACHEL: It's all designed for one reason: to provoke – that's what it is
all about – it's to provoke and to not pay you!
JESSICA: I'd love for them to come back and say, 'Oh, I'm sorry, you
don't get your pay cheque!'

The disjuncture between teachers-participant' accounts of events
that day and the official story leaves teachers breached (Garfinkel,
1967) regarding the rules by which the TDSB operates. Suspicion
about motives leads to speculation that the TDSB used the CUPE
strike as an excuse for non-payment in order to save money to offset
cutbacks. Wariness of provocation and fear of the punitive consequence of loss of pay may be influencing teachers' actions. Could
other acts construed as non-compliant similarly be framed and punished by pay deduction?

Textual analysis of the TDSB letter reveals adversarial labour relations between the teachers and their employer. The single-page form
letter on TDSB letterhead (appendix I-B), dated 22 June 2001,
announces the deduction of a day's pay retroactively for an 'unauthorized absence' on 5 April 2001. It is signed by the superintendent of
human resources, and copied to the school principal, school superintendent, and personnel file. Addressed to individual teachers by full
name, the letter was delivered to the school and distributed to each
singled-out teacher at school on the day before school closed for the
summer holidays, on 27 June 2002.

Opening with formal, depersonalized language, the letter makes a false accusation: 'It has come to our attention that you were not present at your work site as required on Apr. 5/01 and have not delivered a medical certificate explaining your absence.' Nowhere in the letter is the CUPE 4400 support workers' strike mentioned. Stripped of the context of that strike taking place at the time, and ignoring circumstances that caused delays at the picket line of between one and two hours, the letter thus misrepresents teachers' 'unauthorized absence' as either due to illness requiring a medical certificate, or later as illegal strike action on the part of the teacher. The obfuscating language of 'It has come to our attention ...' raises such questions as: Who informed? On what evidence is the claim based? Why the delay between the event (5 April) and the action taken (late June) by the TDSB? Was the timing to dispel dissidence since teachers disperse for the summer? Was there an assumption that the issue would be forgotten over the interim of the summer? Was it to obtain watertight legal interpretations of the legislation?

Not only the legal profession but also the medical profession emerge as integral to the ruling relations. In this case, a medical certificate constitutes the only legitimate document to explain an absence caused by delays at the CUPE picket lines. Recall that a medical note is required by the OCT for extensions to the PLP program and by the TDSB in the case of snowstorms. The consequence of the TDSB letter is that teachers are penalized financially for events beyond their control.

The letter ignores documentary evidence that accounts for the absence, in the form of two sign-in sheets for that day: one that records the time of arrival at the worksite taken by the CUPE site captain, and the other that records the time teachers signed in at school, having been permitted to cross the picket line. According to this evidence (as reported in a personal communiqué from the school representative of the OSSTF), all teachers at Beaconsfield Collegiate had arrived at the picket line before 9 a.m., had signed into the school by 10:55 a.m., and remained on duty for the remainder of the school day. That this evidence was available but ignored and that the penalty meted out was in excess of actual work time lost, suggests either miscommunication, incompetence, coercion, and/or deliberate use of the event to set an example of the consequences for any affiliation with the labour movement. Even when teachers challenged the school superintendent on the decision (as reported by Alice above), insisting that teachers had been blocked by the picket line of CUPE workers, the TDSB did not retract its position. It seems likely, therefore, that the TDSB action was based on full knowledge of the evidence and was a coercive tactic consistent with the crackdown on unions characteristic of corporate-capitalist relations.

Legal discourse is used in the letter to paint certain teachers as 'law-breakers.' It is stated in the letter that teachers were not in a 'legal strike position' and that events on that day constituted a 'breach of your legal duties, including those under the Education Act and its Regulations.' According to the terms of the collective agreement, teachers may not strike for the duration of the contract:

> There shall be no strike or lock-out during the term of this Agreement or of any renewal of this Agreement. The terms 'strike' and 'lock-out' shall bear the same meaning given by the *Ontario Labour Relations Act*, R.S.O. 1990, as amended and the *Education Act* R.S.O. 1990, as amended. (Collective Agreement 2000–2002, Clause 1.2.3.0.0)[11]

The eliding of who was actually on strike creates a misapprehension: teachers were not on strike; CUPE 4400 workers, including caretaking, secretarial and support staff were. Violation of the collective agreement is used to frame a false accusation made in the letter, backed up by the authority of legislation contained in the Education Act and its Regulations, but stripped of the contextual events within which the alleged infraction occurred. The threat that 'this letter will be placed in your Personnel File' points to the negative 'profiling' of teachers in the permanent records held at the TDSB. Such a punitive measure could have implications for teachers' careers, impacting on promotion or letters of recommendation, when viewed in isolation in individual files. Stripped of context, these teachers are framed by legal documents incriminating them as illegal strikers in contravention of the collective agreement, and guilty of unprofessional conduct according to the Education Act. Bad faith in labour relations is epitomized by the TDSB letter, not only in the content and language, but also in the form and the timing. Addressed personally, individual teachers are singled out from the collective to set an example, just prior to the summer break – isolated, bewildered, infuriated, or too busy to care, after a particularly hard year in teaching. Indeed, this was the year that precipitated Alice's decision to take early retirement, even though she was 'at the top of [her] game plan professionally.'

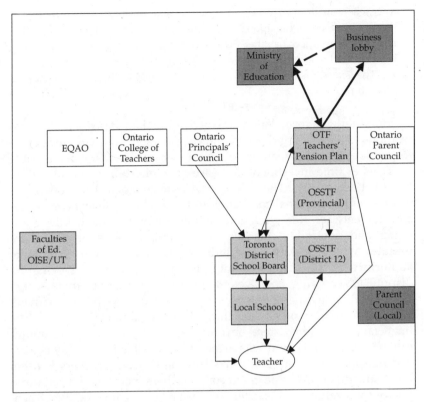

Figure 5.2
Text-mediated relations: TDSB letter

Intertextual analysis of the TDSB letter makes visible the power relations mapped across sites that prevail through the intertextuality of
government legislation, the collective agreement, payroll records, and
the teachers personnel file (see figure 5.2). The letter itself also constitutes a methodological field of knowledge (Barthes, 1977) about the
teacher, as it becomes embedded in permanent records held by the
institution. Aside from salary and benefits information, two locations
where permanent records of teachers are kept by their employers are
the personnel file in the Department of Human Resources for Secondary Teaching Records and in the personal file in the main office at the
local school. Teachers have access to their records according to the collective agreement:

A Teacher shall have access during normal business hours to that Teacher's personnel file upon prior written request and in the presence of a supervisory officer or other person(s) designated by the Director. The Teacher shall also have access to the Teacher's personal in-school data file. The Teacher may copy any material contained in these files. (Clause 3.5.1.0.0.)

Computerized form letters merged with data bases standardizes relations while lending the appearance of personal individualized correspondence to mass mailings. Paper flows are also made manageable in terms of time investment and ease of 'replicability and iterability' (Smith, 1999, p. 134). The dehumanizing technological process of the form letter has personal consequences for teachers; the text constitutes a bridge between ruling relations and everyday local actualities regulating and controlling teachers. Extralocal relations of ruling are revealed when legislative and judicial systems are used as ultimate authorities, in this case for framing the accusation and resolving the dispute. Objectifying, coercive employer power relations thus emerge as controlling teacher-employees through the pay cheque, with no recourse to redress other than through the legal-judicial system. The financial implications extend beyond the loss of a day's pay: communication between the payroll department responsible for the pay cheque and pension administration (linked to the Ontario Teachers Pension Plan) suggests ramifications affecting teachers' pensions for the duration of their retirement; teachers on special leaves, for example, teachers in the '4 over 5 Plan,' received a separate follow-up letter dated 28 November 2001, stating the implications.[12] From the event of the CUPE strike, a complex trail of text-mediated relations has ensued, between various departments internally within the TDSB and extending externally to other agencies.

The punitive action of the TDSB conveys the message that these 'professionals' can be managed and controlled through timesheets linked to pay cheques, thus constructing teachers as 'workers.' The antagonism towards labour unions assumes a broad interpretation of what constitutes strike action (any association with or support for the labour movement, or resistance to scabbing), and adopts a zero tolerance position that misrepresents the actual events of that day so as to incriminate teachers. Linked to the discourse of mandatory criminal background checks for teachers, the repudiation of labour rights of teachers and the criminalization of teachers are connected in new labour relations that prevail between teachers and their employers at the TDSB.

The OSSTF took up a collective grievance on the events of 5 April 2001. At first a strong counter-stance was taken by the OSSTF, holding the TDSB accountable for intimidation and/or harassment in accordance with the Charter of Rights and Freedoms and of the Ontario Labour Relations Act. After legal consultation and consideration of costs and delays associated with a court challenge, they backed down on compensation to seeking only full reimbursement of pay.[13] Following due procedures for collective grievances, a negotiated settlement was denied by the TDSB, claiming that teachers were not in 'physical danger' (contradicted by Alice's account of slashed tires above) and desiring 'retribution' for defiance of superintendents' orders to cross picket lines; an alternate possible reason for superintendents' desire for retribution could be to punish teachers by other means for collective action in withdrawing voluntary services during that year when teachers were required to teach an extra half-course.

The presence of lawyers and lengthy negotiations between the TDSB and the OSSTF denotes the advent of increasingly litigious adversarial relations and costly legal bills. Who benefits from these disputes? The insertion of another layer of legalistic text-mediated flows illustrates the complexity of legislation that regulates teachers' work and actions, where interpretations hinge on single words or phrases in legal documents. Through a litany of new legislation, government controls teachers' work and lives, it also interfers in labour relations by threatening to introduce further restrictive legislation, such as to declare extra-curricular activities mandatory and to classify teachers as 'essential service workers,' thus eroding labour rights and relegating teachers to the role of babysitters, or 'governesses.'

Because I was one of the 290 teachers who received the TDSB letter, what follows is an autoethnographic account tracing the TDSB letter through my private teacher records, in my personnel file at the TDSB offices and my personal file at the school. To gain access to my personnel file, I was required to submit a request in writing and arrange an appointment in advance with the supervisor of human resources for secondary teaching records at the TDSB. One week later, I viewed my file in the presence of the supervisor, according to whom approximately ten teachers a year view their files, usually in the presence of a representative.

Indeed, the TDSB letter is contained in my personnel file, but not my rebuttal sent by e-mail to the superintendent in which I specifically requested its attachment to the letter in my file. Since my e-mail response was submitted according to instructions and before the deadline, its absence confirms lack of teacher control over file contents. Other information in the personnel file includes general salary and payroll information, and board confirmations of leaves of absence. Most of the information is in numerical form. Looking through the record, I was reminded of a previous pay deduction (for 25 October 1996) relating to collective action during a day of protest. As I stopped on this one-line record, the thought crossed my mind: this has been a long struggle. However, this previous instance of a pay deduction was not contested.

During the appointment, I informed the supervisor of human resources that the reason for my request was as part of my research into educational reform and how teachers are documented in the official records. The following information is compiled from the informal conversation that transpired. With the amalgamation of school boards in September 2000, the new TDSB following the North York model, merged various systems into the computerized EIS (Employment Information System). The former Toronto Board of Education had only yellow-coloured filing cards with general personal information (e.g., address, school history) and microfilm records referred to by roll number, containing scattered information, whereas Scarborough had reams of paper records containing redundant information. Each former board had its own system and all the data had to be collected and entered into the new integrated system. In the move to computerizing records, another new record system, SAP, referred to as the 'paperless world' of electronic record keeping, is in the works. This accounting program for financing and budgeting was used by all boards prior to amalgamation, but will be expanded to include human resources as well. All information will be merged into a single data base (similar to a smart card): pay, leaves, sick days, seniority, and human resources information. This data base is cross-referenced across various departments at the TDSB, including payroll, purchasing, and so on, so that information will automatically be forwarded to the relevant department. Under the new SAP system, principals and office managers will have some limited access, but teachers will have no access to their computerized records. The system of computerized record-keeping described by the supervisor of human resources raises a number of issues regarding control, privacy, and access to information. This invisible textual world in which teachers are embedded is transmitted through technologically automated cyber-links across various sites, virtually removing human agency. Through the advent of technology and consistent with accounting logic, a system of surveillance is being set up of top-down graduated access to electronic records, with teachers at the bottom of the hierarchy shut out entirely. How will teachers check for errors, omissions, or incriminating records that they may wish to contest? Who will have access to what information?

Visiting the school to view my personal file was less formal. The office manager gave me immediate access. According to the office manager, the personal file follows teachers as they change schools. This permanent record of teachers' work history is also implicitly a history of personal lives. I was surprised by the comprehensiveness of the documentation: the approximately ¾ inch-thick manila folder contains every piece of correspondence, including letters of reference I submitted when first hired by the board and my employment letter of acceptance. There are evaluations of my out-of-country teaching qualifications and recommendation for placement on the salary grid. Letters requesting leaves of absence (maternity, the year and a half in Rome, illness and death in the family) and the board's responses are all there. One could construct a biography from these records! Included is a copy of my Certificate of Qualification from the OCT. A copy of the TDSB letter is not in my personal file, but is located in a separate file kept by the principal, according to the office manager.

The office manager left me alone to view my file, and afterwards asked if I wanted anything 'purged.' I wonder, what would have happened had I requested the TDSB letter purged? As I stepped out of the school into the sunlit parking lot, I experienced mixed feelings of nostalgia, having glimpsed my life represented in the official records, like looking through an old photograph album, but also exposed and slightly unnerved at how much information the institution has stockpiled about me. Could any of this be used against me in the brave new world of technological surveillance?

RSP–Teacher Log: The Ethical Dilemma of 'Accounting Logic'

The Remedial Support Program (RSP) pertains more directly to teachers' daily work. It was implemented suddenly in September 2001 following the passage of Bill 80 over the summer. This program substituted for the former contentious policy of timetabling 6.5 courses out of 8 that had been mandated by the ministry during the previous academic year (2000–1), rather than the customary 6 out of 8. In opposition to the intensification of work imposed by teaching an extra half-course, teachers had taken collective action in the form of withdrawal of voluntary extra-curricular activities. Under the RSP program, teachers were timetabled instead for 6.25 courses out of 8, amounting to an extra ninety minutes a week timetabled outside school hours for teachers to offer extra-help to students. Teacher timetables had to be reworked when schools opened in September, leading to considerable disruption in the school and protracted negotiations between the TDSB and OSSTF (District 12) to figure out the legislation.

For the focus group, the RSP program constitutes a marker of ruling relations by the extent to which participants are breached in complying with a policy that contradicts their experience of how extra-help works in practice. These teachers think the RSP program is 'stupid' and 'the most ridiculous thing' that has been dumped on them. They feel that it is demeaning to operationalize extra-help that teachers do voluntarily anyway on an as-needed basis, such that one participant states 'I'm just going to make a mockery of it.'

As the dialogue unfolds, teachers' struggle with making extra-help outside class time fit into the reporting requirements of the teacher log exemplifies the dilemma between 'caring' and 'counting:' students must be currently registered in the teacher's classes and receive extra-help during designated times for which the teacher is timetabled outside regular school hours. A log sheet must be submitted to the office, specifying the details. Extra-help that does not satisfy the parameters does not officially count:

RACHEL: You have to have a set time and if the kids don't come at that set time it doesn't *count*, even though you're sitting there waiting. And if you help a kid for three hours, at any other time, it doesn't *count*. What I have is all the kids show up on the day before a test. That's not the correct time – it *counts* [to me] but I mean – but it *counts* so I put it down. I put it down because the administration has given us the idea, 'Just put them down!'

What counts in practice as extra-help does not officially *count* if it falls outside the designated time. Extra-help by 'clockwork' does not fit the reality of student needs. So:

JESSICA: I'm having nil reports.

RACHEL: I don't make up names but what I do do is – I can't help everyone at the time that I'm supposed to, but I do help them [at other times] and as long as I help them, their names do go down, in the time that they weren't there [i.e. the designated remedial period]. But I won't make up anything. I won't, I won't – (trails off).

In some subjects, out-of-class time spent with students does not fit the category of 'remediation' as defined by the TDSB, posing a dilemma for how to satisfy the reporting requirements:

JESSICA: In phys. ed, it can't be coaching, it can't be any clubs or teams or anything. Well, do you think the kids will come for remedial? And they're supposed to be the kids you teach. I had some kids that were doing a movie for our English class so I put down their names, because I came in, you know, 5 to 7 [p.m.] for a couple of nights just to help be a staff person. So I put that [down] – at least it helps. I said, I don't *care*, let them come back.

Some teachers have been assigned other duties during the remedial period that they have been doing voluntarily all along. The difference is the time it takes to fill out the paperwork:

HELENA: You see, in my case they gave me the [computer] lab, which means I have to write what I do in the lab. Well, fortunately I can bullshit anything I want! (Laughs) Because who is going to check if I am going to fix a floppy drive, if I am going to fix a machine? Anyhow, I fix it. I don't know when – it's all kinds of things. But what happens right now, I have to take the time to log everything.

Helena has the double duty of lab maintenance, but her students still need extra-help, yet her log sheet only records the former category. The accounting logic of the teacher log constitutes a surveillance strategy of accountability that belies the complexity of teachers' backstage work in practice. The paperwork that has to be filled out is expressed in particularly strong language as 'bullshit.' According to these teachers, administration abdicates responsibility (they 'don't want to know') by enforcing compliance to paperwork and implicitly encouraging rule-breaking, in ways that teachers construe as putting them in the position of lying:

RACHEL: Well, we've been given the idea from everyone that that's what we do: we help them, we fill it in. They [administration] don't want to know anything else and they don't – (trails off).

JESSICA: They're [teachers] just handing them in. But you know [the office manager]? I got a reminder in my box saying the December list wasn't there. So I sent one and said '[office manager],' – she just like, I could tell that she didn't want [to know] – I said, '[office manager], this is not my kid, these are not my kids, I put this down, I *was* there at that time.' They don't want you to even *talk* about it, they just want the sheet [teacher log]. But now, I refuse. I'm not going to just make up people that weren't there. I mean swim team practice, you know if that doesn't *count*, and you're there huge hours a day, you know what, skiing or whatever – (trails off).

RACHEL: That's what you put down, no matter. You don't mention that it's not the exact time. You helped them [even if] it was outside of the regular time. That's all they *care* about. They don't want to know. You're put in the position of *lying* (confirmation from the group). It's a horrible feeling!

Teachers use humour or the 'mockery mode' (Bakhtin in Holquist, 1981), in the unofficial sphere to dispel the tension of hierarchical control from above, as a strategy for coping with the 'monologic' of the official discourse. As a teacher of physical education who supervises various extra-curricular sports that don't count, Jessica's dilemma is that students do not come in for extra-help:

JESSICA: And they say what activity did you do? – on the thing [teacher log]. What did you do? I'm going to say, 'We did stretches, to improve calf muscles' (Laughter, as Jessica physically demonstrates stretches). You know what? I'm just going to make a mockery of it! Because I don't want to make a mockery of everything else in the whole school, but when you get this stuff dumped on you – (trails off).

Why are teachers complying with an irrational system (or a hyper-rational system) by lying to satisfy the reporting requirement? Fear of the consequences of pay deduction (for which a precedent exists in the form of the TDSB letter) seems have entered teachers' consciousness and to constitute a mechanism of control to enforce teacher compliance:

RACHEL: No one *says* anything.

JESSICA: I don't know but I didn't *care*. But I certainly don't lose sleep over it, and I'd love for them to come back and say, 'Oh, I'm sorry, you don't get your pay cheque because you don't have all your kids here. You didn't see all these kids.' I mean, ohh (drop in tone), wouldn't that be – (trails off).

According to these teachers, by disowning knowledge of falsification of records while implicitly encouraging it, and by abdicating responsibility for opposing the workability of the RSP with their 'superiors' in the hierarchy, school administrators distance themselves and download responsibility onto individual teachers for the consequences.

What is the purpose of this apparently meaningless reporting exercise? Alice connects the rationale for the RSP program with earlier events, following the CUPE strike, when the newly amalgamated TDSB 'commanded' heads of department to a meeting that turned out to be a 'propaganda session.' The use of militaristic language suggests unease about being controlled and suspicions about political motives:

ALICE: Something very much like this type of thing happened in the springtime too. The heads of department were all commanded to go to various centres throughout the city in late May–early June. And we thought, Oh this is terrific! I thought it was going to be because we had all these former boards getting together and now being one TDSB, so we needed to share stuff so we would be consistent, all the way from Etobicoke out to Scarborough. It wasn't that at all! It was a propaganda session! You had to read very carefully between the lines [to realize they wanted us] to come up with strategies to help the kids who were at risk. Well, what does this mean? It was following the [CUPE] strike, the lockout, and I think they [the board] were getting really panicky that at the end of June the public was going to be screaming their heads off, saying my kid is not getting a credit [because of the strike]. They were looking for us to provide strategies so that we were providing a net for the kids who were at risk in case there was a huge hue-and-cry at the end of the year. And so they could publish something, so that they could say, 'Here are things that are actually happening in the schools.' (All talking at once).

Alice pinpoints the incipient concern for so-called at-risk students who are falling behind in credits under the new curriculum. Rather than addressing barriers to learning inflicted by education reform, teachers are called upon to compensate for systemic inadequacies through the RSP program.

Textual analysis of the RSP–Teacher Log (appendix I–C) reveals a one-page grid comprising five columns and twenty-seven rows. The form is to be filled out by teachers recording extra-help offered to students during the designated remedial period. The make-shift quality of the graphics of this first version suggests the haste with which it was devised. Blanks to be filled in include 'Teacher name' at the top and 'Total Time Logged' at the bottom of the page, the latter in bold capitals, indicating quantification of time as the primary concern. Five columns must be completed, specifying the details of remediation: Date, Time, Student Name, Homeform and Topic/Activity. Instructions at the bottom of the form spell out that it must be returned to the office manager in the main office, on the last Friday of each month, underlined in bold to emphasize the imperative. The office manager is designated as overseer of the paperwork, thus not only acting as the custodian of records, but also as a formal gatekeeper, distancing and buffering the principal from teaching staff, as in hierarchically structured corporate offices.

As a mechanism of accountability, submission of the teacher log constitutes monthly surveillance over teachers through the enactment of the ritual (Foucault in Rabinow, 1984), similar to the annual submission of the OCT Certificate of Qualification. The teacher log brings to the forefront one aspect of teachers' backstage work for routine accountability. With the implementation of the RSP program, timetabling a remedial period for extra-help by 'clockwork' imposes a framework that belies how extra-help works in actual practice, and devalues teacher and student time and schedules. Whether or not students show, teachers are required to clock-in and clock-out at their designated locations, and to quantify total time logged (in terms of actual minutes spent with students) to the satisfaction of their employers. Analogous to scientific management of factory workers, if teachers adhered strictly to the designated time slot for extra-help, student needs would be ignored, in the interests of official records. What would happen to a student who needs help with tonight's homework in preparation for tomorrow's class if the next remediation period is not until another day? What about the student who has other commitments during the scheduled period? Not only is the format of the RSP–Teacher Log unworkable for how extra-help actually works in practice, but it is time-consuming to fill out sheets, logging details and specific activities, thus adding to the paperwork required of teachers without adding to student learning or student/parent feedback.

Completed teacher logs are kept in a three-ring binder in the main office, in case of an 'audit by the board or ministry' (according to a personal communiqué with the office manager). This document constitutes the institutionalization of teacher accountability and bureaucratic management of teachers work for the purpose of top-down surveillance. It is an account of time spent outside the regular school day on an activity (extra-help) that previously was offered voluntarily and informally on an as-needed basis. According to teachers in the focus group, the accounts as entered constitute a fabrication that distorts reality. Teachers are required to satisfy the requirements, for which administrators abdicate responsibility. Yet these sheets constitute the factual permanent record of teachers' work in writing, and become part of the accountability process to monitor teachers and schools, assessed formally and officially by 'auditors' from higher levels of the hierarchy. Furthermore, students are inscribed in these records by name and the 'service delivered' to them under the category Topic/ Activity.

In most cases, the RSP–Teacher Log routinizes extra-help that teachers do anyway in the course of their daily work. The construction of teachers as 'lazy' is inherent in the imperative to enforce this through documentation, surveillance, and accountability mechanisms. Since some teachers are given other duties to perform during the remedial period (even though they teach classes), the RSP program can be utilized to assign additional non-teaching duties, thus adding to work intensification and setting the conditions to exploit teachers under the guise of serving student needs.

Analysis of the intertextuality of the RSP–Teacher Log reveals direct ties to government legislation mediated through boards of education (figure 5.3). What counts as extra-help is connected to the government's definition of 'instructional time' that arose with regard to the mandatory addition of an extra half-course to teacher timetables in 2000–1. Only a course that qualifies for student credit counts as teaching-time. The definition was intended to ensure that school boards and principals did not use the period for 'soft' duties. Ironically, remedial help was explicitly excluded as valid teaching-time under those regulations. What counts under the RSP program, however, remains tied to

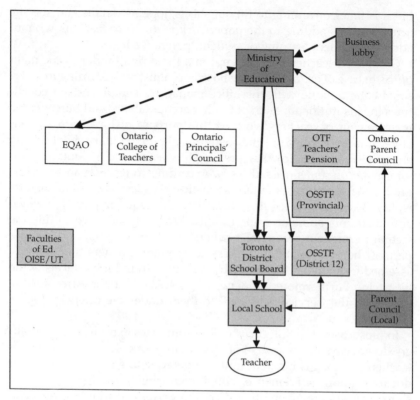

Figure 5.3
Text-mediated relations: Remedial Support Program – Teacher Log

course content. It discounts the myriad of student-teacher interactions that contribute to holistic education, for example, as mentors through extra-curricular activities, or as confidants not only of students currently being taught but also past students with whom a relationship has been established. The narrow view of student-teacher relations and of what constitutes remediation, delimited by the categories established in RSP policies, reduces education to direct teaching of content, and restricts teachers to technocratic 'deliverers' or 'implementers' of curriculum. This instrumental view dehumanizes schools as mechanistic organizations, rather than as communities of people engaged in relationships and in learning in the broad holistic sense.

The terms and conditions for the RSP program are specified in government legislation under Bill 80 with befuddling accounting logic that rejuggles numbers so as to create a misleading impression of 'improvement,' but that holds to a predetermined arbitrary standard. It's all in the optics. Bill 80 permits boards of education to reduce teacher 'instructional time' from 6.5 to 6.25, substituting 0.25 for the RSP program for the extra half-course, but increasing the average class size from twenty-one to twenty-two students. However, when the additional 0.42 for TAP (Teacher Advisory Program), remediation, and on-calls/supervision is added on top of the 6.25, the total aggregate is 6.67 periods. In terms of time, this is no different from what was in effect during the previous year. The intricacies of this bill are not as much of a concession to teacher workload issues as may appear on the surface. Whereas teachers are relieved of the preparation, marking and reporting associated with teaching an extra half-course, increasing class sizes and adding on non-classroom duties means that teachers' workload remains higher than prior to education reform, when teachers taught six out of eight classes.[14] Thus less is given back than was taken away in the first place.

As an entry on the official teacher timetable outside regular school hours, the remedial period actually extends the school day for teachers (and students). Not only is 'clockwork' imposed, but extra-help is instrumentalized in ways that are a disservice to students, according to teacher-participants. Was the imposition of the remedial period a government face-saving measure to manipulate teachers into ending their withdrawal of voluntary extra-curricular activities, without appearing to back down? Was it a public relations measure to cover anticipated parent complaints about the new curriculum (as suspected by Alice)? Lack of transparency for policy directives – and sudden shifts in those directives – leads to speculation and suspicion about motives.

Whereas other documents, such as daily student attendance sheets and quarterly student report cards, indirectly record teachers work, the teacher log ironically constitutes the only official record of actual work performed by teachers in the course of duty, thus elevating its importance as an instrument of accountability in excess of its pedagogical value. Students too are inscribed in the log by name. What are the implications? In the case of parent complaints, the teacher log could be used as evidence: if a student did not avail him/herself of the extra-help offered, then he/she can be blamed for failure in the new curriculum, thus shifting blame onto students (or teachers) for the inadequacies of the system. As part of the school's official records, these documents may be sequestered by the courts, contributing 'false' evidence to the judicial system; for instance, as testimony regarding a student's whereabouts at a particular time. The illusion of factual authority vested in official records according to accountability policies is revealed through textual analysis of the RSP–Teacher Log; the existence of the document is sufficient in itself, assuming an importance and authenticity within the institution regardless of its meaninglessness in actual practice, inaccuracy of information, or consequences in the larger scheme of things.

As part of the larger reform strategy, could the RSP program be setting in place a mechanism to phase out Special Education by substituting a program that downloads responsibility for remediation onto classroom teachers, just as the TAP program introduced earlier could serve to phase out Guidance? Both programs are good public relations ploys for governments to manufacture public consent and distract attention from budget and staffing cuts to Special Education and Guidance. In principle, both of these programs are difficult to contest for teachers, since both carry positive associations with 'motherhood' so easily assimilable into a caring profession, but neither works in practice despite good intentions. Just as women's work of mothering is devalued and unpaid, so does the downloading of further responsibility onto teachers under the auspices of the RSP and TAP programs add to teachers' workload without recognition or compensation, while conceivably jeopardizing important educational support services in schools, especially for 'students-at-risk.'

The ethical dilemma for teachers attempting to mediate legislated policy directives like the RSP program lies in the inherent conflict between two contradictory principles in the OCT's *Ethical Standards for the Teaching Profession*: 'comply with acts and regulations' and 'advise the appropriate people in a professional manner when policies or practices exist that should be reviewed or revised.' According to focus group accounts, teachers who attempted to advise the administration that their logs were not entirely accurate in terms of the reporting policy received the message that 'they [the administration] don't want to know.' As members of the OCT, administrators (principals and vice-principals) are equally bound by the ethical code. In their new role as middle management in the education system, and buffered by the office manager, the administration's primary concern seems to be ensuring completed teacher logs exist on file. Stonewalled by the administration, these teachers rely on their professional discretion in justifying to themselves how to complete the forms so as to comply with the regulations. With senior administrators washing their hands of the responsibility to advise on policies that should be reviewed, it is teachers who risk recrimination in the case of an audit.

The effect of monitoring and surveillance of teachers by a system of reporting in writing is to enforce compliance with new mandates. Increased red tape has been identified as a key factor in teacher burnout (Burke, Greenglass, and Schwarzer, 1996). The teacher log adds to bureaucratized reporting procedures, consuming teachers' time in more paperwork, just as the new report card does, without contributing to student learning. On the contrary, wasting teachers' scarce time for backstage work with senseless paperwork detracts from actual time available for students. The RSP–Teacher Log exemplifies an objectifying accountability instrument derived from scientific management principles that has little to do with everyday pedagogical practice, according to teacher-participants.

What are teachers' options? If they were to submit 'nil reports,' would they be timetabled for alternative duties? Or required to teach an extra half-course? Would they have pay deducted? Fear of possible punishments through the timetable and/or pay cheque is not ill-founded, given precedents under education reform. In mediating a reporting requirement that does not fit with the realities of everyday extra-help and that devalues the range and complexity of backstage work performed by teachers, deliberating over what counts in their own terms – that is, what matters in their daily relations with students – constitutes the reference point for resolving the ethical dilemma posed by new mandates, such as the RSP program.

Accessing the Ideological Code

Carried in texts that coordinate the activities of individuals across multiple sites is the ideological code constitutive of the public education system. Mapping text flows pertaining to each of the three documents that raised the concern of teachers and then overlaying these mappings illustrates a dense interlocking net of text-mediated relations across the ruling apparatus that operates to govern and regulate teachers (figure 5.4). Not only teachers but colonies of administrative staff across the ruling apparatus are coordinated to devise and maintain the record-keeping enterprise. Textual analysis reveals the extent to which teachers are embedded in texts and enmeshed in text-mediated relations that serve to control their work and their personal lives. Under reform,

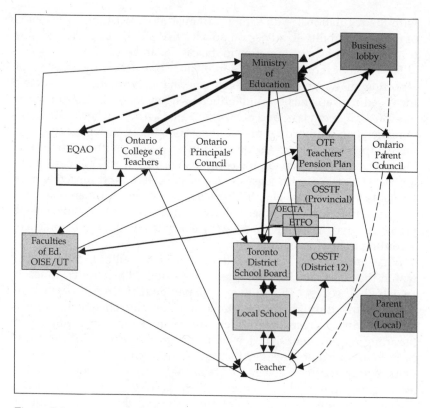

Figure 5.4
Text-mediated relations superimposed

changes to how teachers' work and professional lives are prescribed, measured, and evaluated run counter to teacher-participants' experience of what matters in education. Regardless of accuracy or meaningfulness in actual practice, the objective 'facts' inscribed in these texts enter the permanent records held by the institution of public education. Extracting recurrent themes running through these documents brings to the foreground the code that is not only the interpretive paradigm for the policies of the institution, but also has a political force that is reinforced in and through the actual practices of the institution.

Texts such as these come to assume an authority and authenticity within the system that is belied by the subjective experience of the teacher-participants in the focus group. The disjuncture between the lived experience of teachers and the official discourse of reform policy is marked by two words that occurred with particular frequency in the transcript of the focus group: caring and counting. The tension between compliance, resistance, and defiance for teachers revolves around contested constructions of these guiding principles. Teacher-participants' deliberations over what counts – as professional development, collegial relations in the workplace, or remediation for students – highlights the discrepancy between the different discourses of critical/progressive pedagogy for practitioners and neoliberal economics for policy-makers. Imbued with an ethic of care as intrinsic to teaching practice and central to teacher-student relations, statements such as 'I don't care' are particularly poignant as markers, and as acts of resistance to the burden of care imposed on predominantly women teachers working under financial constraints. However, what teacher-participants declare they don't care about is explicitly limited to policy mandates that could have negative consequences only for themselves, such as non-compliance with the PLP program, or pseudo-compliance with the RSP program. Downloading onto the classroom teacher through the RSP program (like the TAP program) has contributed to an intensification of work and extended the school day. The construction of instructional time as limited to course content discounts the invisible backstage work that extends into hours of homework or overtime for teachers. These constraints preclude time for critical reflection, let alone for mandatory professional development. As observed by Gramsci (in Buttigieg and Callari, 1975), if hegemony can keep the people busy with no time to reflect, then the people can be controlled.

Control is exercised through imposing standardization and accountability mechanisms that deny diversity, promote homogenization, and inculcate assimilation of the norms and values of the predominantly white-colonial policy-makers. Patriarchal constructions of teaching as boundless caring work and corporate-capitalist constructions of accounting logic that govern the workplace must be viewed with a critical lens. Herein lies the key to the ideological code.

6 Counteracting Despair with Hope

Through analysis of texts of the institution of public education and mapping relations across ruling structures, it becomes apparent how teachers' lives and work are governed extralocally. What emerges is evidence
of an ideological code of patriarchal corporate-capitalist neo-colonialist
norms and values as constitutive of the institution of public education
under reform in Ontario. Acceptance of and adherence to the code
extends across the particular gender, class, or race/ethinicity of individuals or groups; it becomes internalized as a mindset and entrenched as
the dominant worldview that is assumed to be 'normal' and 'natural.'
The beneficiaries of (or aspirants to) privilege are among the most likely
to be blind to the ideological code and its effects, that is to 'false consciousness.' As teacher-educators, we are as much part of the ruling
relations as we are affected by them. But, as primary agents of socializa-
tion within the ruling apparatus, teacher-educators are also crucially
positioned to challenge the dominant mindset and to disrupt taken-for-
granted assumptions through the practice of critical pedagogy.

The ideological code that pervades the policies and practices of the
institution of public education is not new, nor is it unique to Ontario.
Rather, it is an intensification of old hegemonic power relations and a
backlash against progressive social change. Comparisons with other
provinces and countries suggest it is coextensive with neoliberal political economies colonized into the globalization agenda. Corporate-capitalist organizational structures predicated on economic principles
emphasize scientific management and quality control. The crackdown
on unions that is characteristic of corporate-capitalist relations frees
employers to maximize profits by keeping wages down and enforcing
compliance through fear of loss of income or job security. Public insti-

tutions modelled after private for-profit organizations that are motivated by getting more for less assessed in reductionist monetarist
terms disregard the effects on the lives of real people. Teachers (and
students) become reduced to numbers, enumerated, measured, represented as statistics in databases, charts and bar graphs, like workers
(and widgets). Under the pretext of striving for efficiency, effectiveness
and excellence, corporate-managerial principles of accountability
(enforced by the OCT) and standardization (monitored by the EQAO)
intercede in mechanistic, dehumanizing ways to override collegial
and/or equitable social relations across the institution. With the ascendancy of a managerial layer in educational governance (orchestrated
through the OPC), a numerophiliac obsession with accounting logic
has risen to dominance as the ruling principle by which system performance is measured. A consumer-driven model of education (abetted
by the Ontario Parent Council) has replaced the former progressive
child-centred approach; this marks a fundamental gulf between policy-
makers and teacher-practitioners. The new structures of the OCT,
EQAO, OPC, and the Ontario Parent Council must be contested as primary instruments of control through which education reform has been
coordinated.

As structural analysis of the executive boards of educational ruling
structures reveals, decision-making is dominated by white male corporatist norms and values. Gender relations characteristic of systemic
patriarchy operate to control the feminized profession of teaching.
Masked as protecting the public interest and having student (children's) needs at heart, gender relations coordinated across the ruling
apparatus devalue and denigrate women/teachers. Disregard for
women/teachers' personal life commitments and the utilization of
essentializing rhetoric of caring, cooperation, collaboration, and self-
sacrifice, while simultaneously devaluing women/teachers' work, is
symptomatic of the operation of patriarchal relations. Blaming teachers
for the ills of the education system serves to portray teachers as deficient, lazy, incompetent, and even latent criminals. In the face of such a
'threat,' how are parents likely to react? The interrelated discourses of
teacher testing and teacher competencies (emanating from the universities, in collaboration with the OCT and EQAO) fabricate the need for
surveillance and constant improvement of teachers, subjugating them
to increased regulation and control to measure up to the 'standards'
established by a corporatist male-dominated hierarchy. Education policies (such as the PLP and RSP programs) perpetuate systemic gender

bias that marginalizes women/teachers from policy-making and precludes them from exercising agency in their daily work and lives. Systematic attacks on women/teachers have functioned as a strategy to manufacture consent for education reform, while deflecting public attention away from the negative consequences of funding cuts on the classroom – that is, on students.

Neoliberal policies of austerity measures through cutbacks, outsourcing and privatization of public services, advocate a competitive hyper-individualism, marking a turn away from the social democratic values of the Keynesian welfare state. The imperative to lower income taxes by eroding public institutions and stimulating the economy by clearing the way for private enterprise constitute the premise of neoliberal public policy. The fundamental belief is in the invisible hand of the market. Despite an OISE/UT survey (by Livingstone, Hart, and Davie, 1999) indicating that the public in Ontario favours increased spending to education, the PC regime proceeded with cutbacks to public education. The casualization of labour and curtailment of labour unions constitute key aspects of neoliberal policies internationally; these same intentions are explicit in punitive threats enunciated in the OCT letter (threatening job security) and the TDSB letter (deducting pay for respecting union picket lines). The privatization of education is evident in the creation of a partly privatized 'teacher training industry,' orchestrated under the auspices of the PLP program. Increased regulation of the public sector coupled with deregulation of the private sector under educational restructuring highlights the contradictory double standard inherent in neoliberalism. The pervasiveness of these trends internationally points to globalization operating at the supra-national level as influencing the public policies of national/provincial governments vying for competitive advantage in the global marketplace. The international exploitation of women workers as a casualized, flexible labour force reverberates in the PLP program for teachers in Ontario. Governments colonized into following neoliberal economic policies enact policies similar to SAP conditionalities that restrict the public sector to liberate trade and investment for the private sector. In some countries in Africa, teachers' salaries have been frozen or they have not been paid for months, schools fall into disrepair and lack resources, and there are not enough textbooks to go around.[1] For teachers in Ontario, does this ring a bell?

The apparent pervasiveness of ruling relations can lead to a debilitating sense of hopelessness, powerlessness, or despair. Critical analysis needs to be balanced with hope for alternative futures; not a passive naïve hope, but hope-in-action that is grounded in the socio-political realities of our lives. Moving beyond 'awfulizing' (to use Ursula Franklin's term) to empowerment and political activism is crucial to turn the tide of change dominated by neoliberal policy reform and its underpinning ideology. Active participation can have an impact in resisting the ruling relations by withdrawing complicity in our own coercion and conscientiously engaging in 'creative non-compliance' (to reclaim a phrase from a former minister of education, Janet Ecker).

Altering the course of education reform necessitates a paradigm shift in order to recognize the ideological code carried in texts that govern the everyday policies and practices in the workplace. As demonstrated by analysis of the public education system in Ontario, ruling relations are often remote, invisible and so embedded as to be assumed natural and normal by people whose everyday lives and work are regulated and controlled by them. The assumed authority of textually mediated materials (policies, procedures, reports, records, data bases) conceals the sources that preserve power and privilege, while actual practices in the workplace reproduce inequality and contribute to the subjugation and disempowerment of disadvantaged groups in society. It is the organization of power as dispersed over different locations and multiple sites that renders the structures and mechanisms of power relations largely invisible. Shifting the paradigm to critical/feminist pedagogy highlights the importance of opening dialogue across educational sites and advocating self-reflexive praxis to better understand how the dominant ideology is systemically embedded in extralocal enclosures, such as the university and the professions, so as to enforce complicity with the ruling apparatus. The beliefs, norms and values inherent in dominant discourses not only determine public policy but are perpetuated in practices orchestrated across the institution, including the classroom. Changing the political party in power is necessary but not sufficient to alter the course of education reform; all three official political parties in Canada (as elsewhere) have to a greater or lesser degree shifted to the right and bought into the political economy of globalization once ensconced in power, as brought to the fore by tracing educational reforms to the NDP's Royal Commission on Learning. What is necessary is a proactive critical stance against hegemonic control orchestrated through homogenizing neo-colonialist constructions of standardization, reductionist corporate-capitalist constructions of scientific managerialism, and essentialist patriarchal constructions of women/teachers' work. It is the ideology itself that must be contested on an ongoing basis, at local sites and through education.

Foucault's (in Gordon, 1972) radical reconceptualization of power posits that power/knowledge is dispersed throughout hierarchical structures, rather than concentrated in the upper echelons, and is inextricably entwined with constructed 'knowledge' and discursive practices that pertain within those structures. This suggests that if hierarchical structures rely on the active cooperation of participating subjects at all levels, then making power relations visible affords a means to identify how unintended cooperation is enlisted; and if all participating subjects are implicated in maintaining power structures, then withdrawal of complicity from oppressive hierarchical structures by participating subjects – at any level – undermines the entire enterprise. This different conception of power, as dispersed rather than located in certain omnipotent individuals, constitutes a potent source of empowerment; it also offers an alternative to the paralysis response of those conspiracy theorists who overemphasize the overwhelming magnitude and intentionality of power, inducing a sense of powerlessness in overcoming it. Like Foucault, Smith's methodology of mapping ruling relations affords not only an understanding of how power works as a dispersed coercive force, but also entails self-reflexive analysis of how we are complicit in our own coercion and in sustaining the ruling apparatus through our everyday practices as teacher-educators.

The manufacturing of consent by culling 'expert' knowledge from the text-mediated relations between universities, think-tanks, foundations, and pollsters all feed into and become embedded in societal institutions, including public education. The establishment and maintenance of hegemonic ideologies and inequitable power relations is contingent on controlling public discourse, dismissing counter-discourses, and marginalizing alternative discourses. Dominant discourses disseminated by the mass media mould public opinion and determine public policy. As primary sites of knowledge construction, the universities are key locations for the management of discourses. According to Smith (1999), universities are integral to the ruling apparatus through the texts generated at universities (as well as other settings) that 'are coordinated conceptually, producing an internally consistent picture of the world and providing the terms of policy talk and decisions' (p. 157), and universities themselves 'are being increasingly pulled into direct subservience to the requirements of a global capitalism' (p. 27). It is faculties of education that determine what academic work is sanctioned, published, funded, and rewarded through hiring and promotion practices. This in turn determines how educational discourse is framed, whether within academia, the professions, or the public media. In particular, the interconnected discourses of school renewal/school improvement (e.g., D.H. Hargreaves, 1994; Fullan and Hargreaves, 1991, 1998) and teacher development (e.g., Nias, 1989; Noddings, 1992) are in accord with educational reform mandates in Ontario and elsewhere. Confluence occurs on the strategy of eliciting teachers' essential cooperation and flexibility as passive 'implementers' of educational policy.

Writing within the contemporary context of educational reform in Ontario at OISE/UT, Andy Hargreaves and Michael Fullan have achieved considerable international recognition as educational 'change experts.' A scan of the research literature on educational change shows the frequency with which these names appear as authors or co-authors of books, articles, and audio-visual materials; as editors of compilations and journals; as citations in other sources and as presenters at education conferences. This marks their work as significant in the academic discourse of education reform. Recall that Fullan was the dean of education at OISE/UT who wrote a letter to the minister regarding the PLP program and who was proclaimed by the Royal Commission on Learning as an early ally for the proposed changes. Andy Hargreaves held the position of director of the International Centre for Educational Change at OISE/UT. How is it that these authors have achieved their acclaim?[2] Hargreaves (1994) professes that, 'The rules of the world are changing. It is time for the rules of teaching and teachers' work to change with them' (p. 262). According to whose rules of change are teachers expected to adapt? A non-critical embrace of change for its own sake leaves unquestioned the larger socio-political context of education reform. It also disregards critical/feminist critiques of the negative consequences of change driven ideologically by techno-science and corporate-consumerism whether locally or globally.

In the Fullan-Hargreaves model (explicated over several volumes and various media under the catchy title *What's Worth Fighting For?*), principals are vested with authority as 'change agents' and as 'leaders' in the schools, who (condescend to) 'listen' to teachers. Disguised beneath the rhetoric of orchestrating 'collaborative cultures' in schools and 'menus of choice,' is change controlled in a top-down direction, wherein teachers' work is prescribed by the power relations of the structural hierarchy of school management. Similar in tone to new age inspirational/motivational workshops, these materials appeal to essentialist notions of 'women's ways,' emphasizing relationships, collaboration, responsibility and dialoguing, without questioning how these qualities can be capitalized on to exacerbate exploitation of women/teachers, and how they can be used to manipulate adaptation to external conditions that are accepted as beyond teachers' control.

The cornerstone of the Hargreaves-Fullan model is the formation of 'collaborative cultures' within school communities, through dialoguing and configuring 'leadership teams.' Promotion of a static notion of culture disregards the dynamic quality of active participation by subjects engaged on an ongoing basis in constructing an emergent collective identity for themselves. Teachers are persuaded to make time to dialogue with their colleagues by giving up their lunchtime, by having colleagues cover a class to allow release time, or by the principal/vice-principal offering to take a class. These proposals put forward in *What's Worth Fighting For?* assume that no systemic change is required to allow time in teachers' timetables for dialoguing. Another proposal is for principals to add an extra five minutes of teaching time on to each day so that a half-day can be accumulated to dedicate to 'collaborative culture' building. The exploitative tendencies inherent in extolling the virtue of self-sacrifice, or in arbitrarily extending the work day, goes unnoticed; so does the contradiction of reform policies that impose change while simultaneously cutting back on time for preparation, in-service training, and PD days for teachers. Localized initiatives that ignore the broader socio-political context of education policy manipulate teachers to adapt to externally mandated change. Promotion of educational reform is expressed as follows: 'We want teachers to believe that they're in the business of scientific breakthroughs ... Then we will see a profession that has come of age' (Fullan, in Fullan and Hargreaves, 1998, program 1, videotape 1).

This quote conveys the double message running through this work that purports to respect teachers and declares that change cannot occur without them, whereas there is a discernable attitude of paternalistic condescension: first, the authors assume the role of expert harbingers of change; second, the authority of business and science are evoked to bring teachers on board with change; third, the professionalism of teachers is thrown into doubt as not yet having 'come of age.' Rather than overt teacher-bashing and coercion perpetrated by the PC regime, teachers are cajoled covertly by new-age feel-good 'hope' ('We want teachers to believe') and by appeals to the aspiration for professional status. Glossed over is the power differential inherent in collaboration that subjugates teacher agency to 'leaders' in the administrative hierarchy and that denigrates teachers' work as out of step according to the change experts. The solution to the problems schools face is to persuade teachers to redouble their efforts at a time when legislated changes downloading responsibility onto the classroom teacher have contributed to significant intensification of work.

The mixed message of purporting to value teachers' work and to embrace teacher empowerment, while simultaneously seeking to control it is captured in the following statement:

> The future of restructuring is, in this sense, one which embraces the principles of teacher empowerment, without necessarily accepting or endorsing many teachers' existing conceptions of it. Collaboration and empowerment will mean more discretion for teachers in some domains, but, as they work more closely with students and parents as partners in the learning process, considerably less discretion in others. (Hargreaves, 1994, p. 261)

Embedded in Hargreaves's notion of strictly constrained teacher empowerment is a strong element of control by external partners. Who gets to determine which aspects of teacher empowerment are endorsed and which are not? Within this conception, not only principals, but parents and students are enlisted as controlling agents over teachers' lives and work. The use of the word empowerment in this context is a misleading and manipulative misnomer for 'teamwork' promoted by corporations. Stripped of critical/political consciousness, it is reminiscent of the 'non-negotiable collaboration' proposed by the royal commission (vol. 4, p. 123). While on the one hand acknowledging the 'overload, intensification, guilt, uncertainty, cynicism and burnout' (Hargreaves, 1994, p. 261) experienced by teachers, there is no cognizance of the necessity to transform the oppressive socio-political context within which teachers work. Rather than empowerment, Fullan and Hargreaves's proposals for collaborative cultures can be characterized as encouraging a *culture of compliance* among teachers, thus turning equity on its ear. Anti-essentialist feminist scholars (such as Chandra Mohanty and Judith Butler) propose that oppressed or marginalized groups (such as women, racial/ethnic minorities, homosexuals) tend towards collective collaboration as a compensation for their lack of individual personal power, deriving strength and solace in numbers, rather than being inherently more caring and cooperative by nature. To capitalize on sentiments of marginalization by depoliticizing the collective is to exacerbate the disempowerment of teachers and to perpetuate exclusion from participation in real decision-making that affects their daily work.

Benefiting from the emerging education economy of 'academic entrepreneurs' (Newson and Buchbinder, 1988), Fullan and Hargreaves run the risk of compromising academic autonomy to commercial self-interest. On the lecture circuit and hired as consultants by school boards, they persuade teachers to opt for 'hope,' to push themselves harder to 'take ownership' of change within their own schools, and to aspire towards professional status through self-sacrifice. The school renewal project, as exemplified by Fullan and Hargreaves, places the emphasis on schools creating their own 'spaces' and conditions for change, as if schools existed in a vacuum unimpinged upon by external conditions, thus diverting attention away from important socio-economic issues. Behind the emphasis on collaborative cultures in schools, is a model of educational change that is consistent with corporate organizational change and management of change orchestrated at a distance. The burden of making change work is predicated on the efforts and sacrifices of teams of teachers working under a contrived sense of professional collegiality and collaboration.[3] Meanwhile, imbued with the authority of leadership as change agents, principals act as conduits for experts who inform education policy. Teacher perspectives, however diverse, are neutralized in favour of a professed consensus of corporate-driven change. Specifying a finite set of goals/outcomes prescribed by the single-minded, short-term vision of corporate interests hypothetically geared towards serving economic growth in the global arena conflates education with training. As pointed out by Woods et al. (1997), persuading teachers to adjust to the technical-rationalist age in education reduces stress but at the cost of 'narrow-minded, conformist and uncreative' education (p. 165).

The construction of teachers as 'resistant to change' (Hargreaves, 1994) disregards the need to balance continual change with some sense of stability or a still point that allows for reflective practice. This construction feeds into and fuels media reports that influence public opinion of teachers as incompetent, lazy, and recalcitrant. What if teacher resistance actually reflects *conscientious objection* to changes perceived as destructive to students or to public education, but without resorting to outright confrontation or defiance? The fundamental disconnect is such that meaning is clearly not shared across the ideological divide between the official discourse of education reform and the discourse of teachers who subscribe to progressive pedagogy. During the focus group, 'breaches of interpretive trust' occurred when policy directives derived from the economic/corporatist paradigm ran counter to teacher-participants' frame of reference. On one hand, Fullan and Hargreaves do admit to teachers' sense of overexposure to perpetual change and their resistance to pedagogically questionable fads; however, teachers' objections are ultimately overruled by enlisting docile cooperation with the ruling relations of education reform.

Idealized and abstract notions of school community construed through the framework of organizational change ignore the diversity, instability and flux of people within schools. In actuality, students pass through and graduate, parents' commitments pass on with their children, and principals and vice-principals were recycled through the system every four to five years (under what was referred to as the 'Christmas package').[4] Students may not graduate from the same school they entered in Grade 9, transferring to other schools that better meet their needs, or taking credits outside the home school. These migrations suggest that school loyalty (like corporate loyalty) is less valued in contemporary society. Given the ebb and flow of people, teachers often constitute the most stable contingent, remaining in the same school longer than the four-to-five-year commitment of other members of the school community. Moreover, the rapid pace of change imposed by educational reforms leaves teachers as the absorbing group, mediating between policy directives and students in the classroom. Given ever-changing constituents, and the upheaval of education reform, the question raised by teachers is how to maintain a sense of equilibrium and continuity in school communities that are in constant flux.

Critical/feminist pedagogues (such as Freire, Giroux, hooks, and Mohanty) subscribe to a different notion of empowerment than that suggested by the school renewal pundits. For Freire (1972), empowerment is a process of 'conscientization' and praxis for oppressed peoples, defining their struggle collectively for themselves (not by leaders) according to the realities of the local context; the aim is social transformation, not conformity to the status quo. Similarly, for Smith (1999), *agency* involves active participants constructing social reality in and through their everyday work activities, conscious of their agency, responsible for their actions, and considerate of the consequences. As counter-hegemonic praxis, critical/feminist pedagogy integrates theory with practice and the academy with the everyday world so as to empower people on their own terms. Within the ruling structures and relations orchestrated by education reform, the challenge lies in 'reconciling agency and structure' (Acker, 1994a, p.110). To disrupt power differentials that determine who or what is legitimized and to prevent assimilation into the dominant ethos requires creating spaces for 'cultures of dissent' (Mohanty, 1997a). Not only do these spaces offer a counterpoint to conformist collaborative cultures, but they are vital to a functioning democracy. Spaces for participation and empowerment of non-dominant groups (whether by identity and/or ideology) provide a context for developing tools of critical analysis to challenge the dominant discourses of the ruling apparatus.

Whereas a professional ethic of care poses a counterpoint to the dominant discourse of accounting logic, it is important to detect where the attributions are coming from and when they are being abused to enlist complicity with the ruling apparatus in ways that disempower women/teachers. The centrality of an ethic of care in feminist praxis can be traced to the early work of Carol Gilligan (1982), which identified a distinctive morality for women as compared with men; specifically, women tend towards an emphasis on relationships and contextualized responsibility and care, as opposed to universal notions of individual rights and abstract principles of justice. The application of an ethic of care to teaching practice is articulated by Nel Noddings (1992) whose writings have exerted a significant influence on the project of constructing schools as 'caring communities,' particularly elementary schools.[5] Based on a biological argument that constructs a 'feminine' identity for women from the idealized mother-child relationship, this feeds into 'essentialist' representations of women. First, it induces women to conform to the male-determined passive, acquiescent 'femininity,' and ignores the diverse locations of women brought to light by the third wave of feminism. The third wave expands beyond the mothering role in the west to include other vantage points, such as childless women, lesbians, women of colur, and third world women; it draws attention to the social construction of women as historically, geographically and culturally contingent. Second, Noddings's simplistic version of relational feminism based on 'women's ways' downplays the political aspect of women's positioning in the larger socio-political context. Failure to explore the interconnectedness of personal and public space, and the complex web of social relations that operate internally and externally, limits the focus on the microcosm to the exclusion of the macrocosm.

The subjugation, devaluation and blaming of the mother in patriarchal society, which is carried over into the caring script of the feminized professions, renders teachers susceptible to being manipulated into neglecting their own needs by complying with a service ethic appropriated by neoliberal governments. In the absence of power-sharing and reciprocity, a service ethic or ethic of care comes to resemble the Hegelian master-slave relationship. Under the guise of being student-centred, patriarchal relations inherent in educational reform institutionalize the subservience of women/teachers as reproducers of the next generation. Valorization of a culture of care construed as a culture of compliance elevates subservience and self-sacrifice to a ruling ethical principle that lays the conditions for exploitative relations. An ethic of care must therefore be expanded beyond individualized dyadic relations and/or familial relations, and balanced with an ethic of justice that takes into account principles of socio-economic equity and responsibility to the broader collective. If a morality does not integrate both caring relations and universal principles of social justice, the important element of agency is missing. An overemphasis on relational communities runs the risk of precluding women from acting in their own interests and can serve to enlist complicity in the dominant ruling relations.

The construction of the teaching profession (like nursing and social work) around an ethic of care regarded as an extension of mothering attributes value to the 'feminine' qualities of caring, nurturing, and connectedness. Acker's (1999) ethnographies expose the emotion of 'doing good and feeling bad' as commonly experienced by women teachers in elementary schools and in academia. This contradiction of living out the caring script but conscious that something is wrong marks a fault-line that reveals the operation of ruling relations. Consciousness that something is wrong was expressed by teacher-participants as 'I don't care' in response to the enforcement of the PLP and RSP programs. The burden of care imposed by education reform arouses an emotional response of internal conflict in certain aspects of teaching practice that seem incompatible with the caring script, such as the standardization of the new curriculum and the objectification of student evaluation in the new report card. The invisibility and lack of appreciation or rewards for the emotional work of caring that typify the 'contradictions of caring' (Acker, 1999) is demonstrated by adversarial employer relations with the TDSB. As feminists have pointed out, the unbounded open-endedness of caring in women's professional and personal lives gives rise to the double-duty of responsibility for the reproductive functions of society, not only in the biological sense but also in terms of sustaining societies.

For the feminized caring professions, reclaiming an ethic of care entails shaping the form it takes in practice, insisting on value both in moral and economic terms, and setting limits (Neysmith, 2000; Clement, 1996). It is important to differentiate between private caregiving in the domestic sphere and public service work, in which employer-employee relations intercede between the caregiver and the recipient of care. For Clement, the balance between an ethic of care and an ethic of justice hinges on reconciling autonomy with caring; an ethic of care without valuing autonomy tends to result in distorted forms of caring that are oppressive. Clement defines autonomy as 'requiring the capacity for critical thought' rather than following bureaucratic orders, as for example in challenging the social structures that create/perpetuate dependency relations (1996, p. 44).[6] Empowering teachers to exercise control over their work and lives requires critical awareness of social justice for students as well as for themselves, and is contingent upon possessing some measure of autonomy as a professional group.

Rather than empowering teachers with professional autonomy, the OCT enacts policies designed to control teachers through enforcing conformity with the ruling apparatus. The prerogative of occupational definition, reflection, and self-regulation by the occupational group itself – in this case teachers – is denied by pre-emptive legislation and overruled by the preponderance of government appointees to the board at the OCT. According to Smith (1999), the professions are integral to the ruling apparatus as 'an institutionalized form of standardizing skills, knowledge and practices in the many actual local sites of professional practice' (p. 32). Being consistent with standardization, calls for the professionalization of teachers in education restructuring constitute a means to regulate teaching practice across the institution. D.H. Hargreaves (1994) purports to identify an emerging trend among teachers towards a 'new professionalism' that is characterized as the integration of professional and institutional development. Repackaged as cutting-edge change, old traditional notions of professionalism associated with individualism, hierarchies, and supervision are ostensibly replaced by new notions of mentoring, professional development, and (again) a collaborative culture of teams. What is hailed as the new professionalism by D.H. Hargreaves represents capitulation to the power relations of corporate organizational change. Accumulated knowledge and experience is devalued:

> Older teachers who found the changes too stressful took early retirement; those remaining now divide into those who increase stress by trying to persist with the old structures and culture and those who are, sometimes reluctantly and painfully, generating a more collaborative culture built on new social structures (1994, p. 426)

The reluctance and pain of teachers forced into compliance with the new social structures seems to be condoned as an inevitable side effect of education reform. Typical of new-right spin, a facile polarization prevails in which 'old' is out/bad/obsolete and 'new' is in/good/innovative, regardless of the human consequences. Veneration of the new for its own sake could be described as a *neophilia* that displays amnesia of the past, devalues experience acquired over time, and endows neophiliac 'leaders' with prescient power to determine the future and to lead the charge of change towards that future. What is hailed as new to educational reform pundits is contested as such by teacher-participants with an institutional memory. A somewhat more critical stance towards change than that of D.H. Hargreaves is taken by Woods et al. (1997) in their description of new professionals as teachers 'willing to countenance change, though not uncritically' (p. 38), and who engage in informal and more genuine collaboration as distinct from contrived collaboration orchestrated at the formal policy-making level.

Ideologically consistent with education reform, professionalism as an occupational strategy has been contested by Witz (1992) on the grounds of being inherently patriarchal (about control) and capitalist (about power), and as motivated to maintain monopoly over practice by closure achieved through university credentialism and government legalization. Historically, the traditional professions have restricted entry to women (as well as other marginalized groups), thus excluding them from practice. Unlike the older, established male-dominated professions, the feminized professions of teaching, nursing, and social work are sometimes derogatorily referred to as 'semi-professions.' This gendered division of labour has been sanctioned on professional grounds, for instance in the historical relative power and control of doctors over nurses. The professional dominance of physicians is preserved and reinforced through university credentials, and by reserving an exclusive monopoly over diagnosis and drug prescription. Maintenance of differential status and prestige for physicians is integrally linked to the powerful professional association of the Ontario College of Physicians and Surgeons (and its equivalents elsewhere). Whereas medicine is often considered the oldest and dominant profession, the professions as an occupational category are historically and geographically contingent. In *Professional Gentlemen*, Gidney and Millar (1994) trace the history of the professions in Ontario. Based on the European model with androcentric and aristocratic biases, as the title suggests, professional status was conferred on 'learned gentlemen' from the upper classes educated in the university. During the late 1800s and early 1900s, when the professions were becoming established in Ontario, physicians and lawyers attained professional status by lobbying for government legislation. At this critical window of legislative opportunity, according to Gidney and Millar, the pursuit of professional status for teachers was hampered by transience, with few committed to a life-long career; factors cited as mitigating against organizing as a group lobby include the high percentage of women (especially in elementary schools) for whom teaching was a precursor or adjunct to raising a family, combined with the aspirations of some men for whom teaching was a stepping stone for advancement to enter the university and the 'higher' professions of medicine or law. Ironically, it is government that has pushed for teacher professionalism under education reform, not teachers lobbying for it themselves. Embedded in the constitution of the government-controlled OCT, both in the composition of its board and its policies, is the endemic androcentric bias characteristic of the traditional professions. With practising public school teachers in a marginal position on the OCT board, this systemic bias is unlikely to change, and a bogus election of token teacher representatives to the board only serves to create the illusion of democratic participation and self-regulation.

Attainment of professional status thus entails complex and contested relations between government, professional associations and the university and as such can be viewed as a quest for power and prestige through assimilation into the ruling apparatus. Paradoxically, teachers are stymied between two contradictory trends that have been structurally orchestrated in education reform: one pushing *for* professionalization (through the OCT), and the other *against* it, and in favour of deprofessionalization and proletarianization. *Deprofessionalization* devalues professional knowledge and expertise in favour of consumer relations, with a more informed public exercising consumer choice (Freidson, 1985). The establishment of the Ontario Parent Council that endows parents with increased influence over how the local school is run exemplifies the shift towards consumer choice and consumer power in education, where parents (not students) are the consumers. *Proletarianization* draws on neo-Marxist analyses of management-labour relations, whereby professionals are increasingly treated like the working class exploited by managers (Freidson, 1985). The divisive strategy of separating teachers and administrators through the establishment of the OPC effectively inserts a management layer of principals who are legislatively bestowed with extraordinary powers over teachers. The enhanced powers of principals and parents working together exclude teachers from decision-making, devalue their professional expertise and curtail their professional autonomy. Teachers are not alone in the experience of loss of professional autonomy and discretion. Utilizing the framework of proletarianization theory, Broadbent, Dietrich, and Roberts (1997) attribute loss of autonomy and the general sense of demoralization experienced across professional groups to being relegated to technicians at the bottom of the hierarchy, and thus removed from the upper levels of management where decisions are made. The rise to dominance of management in professional practice and the subordination of professional ethics to the economic rationalization of accounting logic is certainly evident in teaching, as exemplified by the PLP and RSP programs.

Without a strong historically established self-regulated professional association, teaching is vulnerable to co-optation by the state or by corporate interests and to the low status and remuneration associated with being at the bottom of a gendered division of labour. As a second, new professional body purportedly established to enhance the professional status of teachers, the OCT displaced the OTF and has foregone self-regulation and autonomy as central tenets of professional association; it has collaborated with government regulations controlling teachers externally, contributed to teacher testing that feeds into teacher-blaming, and orchestrated the privatization of teacher in-service training. Rethinking the decline of the professions within the larger contemporary context, Broadbent, Dietrich, and Roberts (1997) argue that professionals should settle for partial autonomy and multiple identities, which will be necessary for the survival and regeneration of the established professions. For teachers, whose standing within the hierarchy of the professions is less established, professionalization seems an outmoded and counter-productive project. The challenge is to create a different occupational strategy, along with the other feminized occupations, so that we can 'come of age' (to use Fullan's phrase) on our own terms.

In constructing an alternative occupational identity to professionalism, unionism proffers a particularly pertinent counter-weight to the advance of global capitalism. However, unions modelled on traditional trade unionism have also been characterized as 'male-dominated projects' (Casey, 1993) with the emphasis on combative, adversarial relations. Hierarchically structured leadership, in which executive positions are overwhelmingly occupied by men and where entrenched leaders form alliances with management, has a propensity to lose touch with the rank-and-file membership. Indeed, there are indications of business unionism operating at the upper levels of the provincial OSSTF. The 'new unionism' identified by Bascia (1994) as emerging in teachers' unions in the United States and in Alberta substitutes cooperative relations for adversarial labour relations; unions become the locus of teachers' professional community based on social collective values, opening 'spaces' for teachers to formulate alternatives and to participate actively in decision-making. In this new unionism, teachers participate in policy decision-making by cooperating on reform with district administrators through their unions. Whereas in Alberta, the attempt to withdraw principals and vice-principals from the Alberta Teachers' Association failed when they voted to remain affiliated with their teacher union, relations between teachers and school administrators are different in Ontario. The separation of principals into the OPC and their alignment with education reform presents an impediment to genuine cooperative relations in schools. Bridging the 'us-and-them' divide between teachers and administrators is tantamount to reaching across an ideological divide and reconciling different paradigms. Within the hierarchical organizational structures and inequitable power relations orchestrated under education reform in Ontario, new unionism runs the risk of bordering on business unionism in promoting cooperation with management where the power resides.

The polarization of labour and management orchestrated through the strategic restructuring of education has induced adversarial relations between teachers and employers (school boards), such that teachers deemed it necessary to engage in job sanctions and strike action to gain a voice at the table in Ontario. The move towards more radical union activism is not taken lightly and is received differently by teachers, whose political views cover the political spectrum; it runs counter to the sense of professional duty and caring for students' education and well-being. The deep-rooted notion of teaching as 'caring' public service work is in conflict with actions that are construed as self-serving, such as demands for wage increases. Linking teachers' work locally with the preponderance of part-time, casualized, and piecemeal jobs for women internationally (Mohanty, 1997b) draws attention to how control operates through OCT re-certification processes to impose a perpetually provisional status on teachers and to disrupt job security. This suggests that union affiliation is especially crucial under advanced capitalism. In the absence of unions, the strategy of dividing workers as isolated individuals is a means to dissipate and control collective opposition, thus paving the way to keeping wages down, intensifying work demands, and permitting the deterioration of working conditions. The drift towards teaching as part-time, casualized work is already evident in the province of Alberta (Harrison and Kachur, 1999).[7] As evidenced by the outbreak of teachers' strikes all across Alberta in 2002, cooperation in policy formation alone cannot turn the tide of authoritarian regimes. What is needed is active political participation to oppose legislation that negatively affects teachers' daily work and lives, undermines public education, and threatens democracy. The slippage between cooperation and co-optation can occur virtually indistinguishably in the absence of a collective location attuned to the bigger picture to frame action.

During the brunt of education restructuring in Ontario, when policy decisions were being passed down faster than they could be accommodated, teachers and their unions were caught off-guard, and forced into a reactive rather than a proactive modus operandi:

> Too often, we have set our tactics to fit their events, 'participating' in their consultations, budget statements and elections. While these official events can offer opportunities for popular mobilization, more often they co-opt and diffuse resistance. Instead, we need to organize in terms of our own priorities and pace and create our own creative initiatives outside of 'official' channels of complaint which draw the links between who is winning and who is losing from the cuts. (Diana Ralph, 1997, in Ralph, Régimbald, and St-Amand, pp. 182–3)

To organize in terms of our own priorities requires a location outside the official structures of education reform. Just as collaborative cultures within school communities are pivotal to educational change to elicit teachers' cooperation in reform (Fullan and Hargreaves, 1991, 1998), collaboration and cooperation constitute cornerstones of both the new unionism (Bascia, 1994) and the new professionalism (D.H. Hargreaves, 1994). To counteract teachers' complicity in educational reform that serves neither the interests of teachers nor students, and foreshadows the demise of public education, simple versions of collaboration-cooperation must be called into question. Cooperation is predicated upon equitable relations and willingness of those with power to relinquish some in order to share power with teachers in the interests of democratizing relations at the local level. Within the existing socio-political context of Ontario, the question arises as to who is in a position to grant power-sharing with teachers? If cooperative relations depend upon mutual respect, trust, goodwill, and transparency on all sides, then without such reciprocity, calls for cooperation can too easily be confused with co-optation. As long as the reference point of visions and goals lies with economic rather than social values, and the locus of control of policy formulation is vested in actors and agencies far removed from pedagogical concerns and the everyday experience of the classroom, cooperation is a misnomer for coercion. Pseudo-collaboration, based on inequitable power relations and lack of reciprocity, insidiously utilizes peer pressure to conceal imbalances of power; it capitalizes on the opportunism of individualist career aspirations to the detriment of the collective.

Whereas critical/feminist theory counteracts the dominant discourse of education reform by consciously reclaiming the terms of discourse and examining the relationship between knowledge, authority, and power, critical/feminist praxis and feminist organizing suggest multiple ways of mobilizing collective socio-political action. In order to resist facile collusion with the ruling apparatus, teacher participation is crucial to formulate an alternative occupational strategy to the traditional androcentric constructions of professionalism and trade-unionism or business unionism. Teacher-participants in this study unanimously declare their allegiance to the OSSTF as best representing teachers' collective interests and defending public education, while unequivocally disavowing the OCT for its duplicity in the negative portrayal of teachers and in the punitive PLP program. This suggests that the government-controlled OCT must be abolished and that the greatest hope for teacher empowerment lies with the OSSTF and other teacher affiliates. I therefore propose a teacher-controlled occupational affiliation through a revitalized *federation* of teachers. This means retrieving the OTF from the brink of redundancy under education reform, and transforming it into a vital self-regulated association through grassroots mobilization premised on maximum participation and reciprocity. As originally conceived, the OTF was a self-regulated professional association embracing all four teacher affiliates, with jurisdiction over both union and professional matters. What has been missing during education reform is strong and united action by the affiliates acting together. A reclaimed OTF could coordinate socio-political activism in the community by fostering dialogue and facilitating action across multiple locations.

Within a hybrid federation, the artificial dichotomy between professionalism and unionism dissolves. The traditional professional preoccupation with the pursuit of status and prestige for the profession is seen as integrally connected with union protection through securing decent salaries and working conditions. The union function of collective bargaining co-exists with critical reflection on professional practice. Teachers collectively regain control over professional growth and monitor professional misconduct through peer review processes. If physicians and lawyers can be trusted to monitor professional conduct, then why not teachers? Many of the mechanisms remain in place for the OTF to resume functioning as the professional regulating body of teachers.[8] Acclamation of the OTF as teachers' professional association sidesteps the major obstacle of gaining teacher control over the OCT, and lays to rest its tainted complicity with education reform. My proposal for a revitalized OTF differs from the new unionism on the key aspect of maintaining independence and resisting alignment with management, or assimilation into the ruling apparatus. To counteract the trend towards 'academic capitalism' (Slaughter and Leslie, 1997), it incorporates a call for academic activism by resistance to the homogenization, corporatization, and privatization of public education through ongoing socio-economic criticism and active participation not only in formal politics but also in the local community.

In order to have an impact, a critical mass may be necessary; however, strength in numbers can also lead to bureaucratization in large organizations that tend to neutralize difference, stifle communication, and thwart formulating alternatives. To prevent the negative effects of amalgamation into a monolithic union that runs the risk of excluding marginalized groups and trading particular interests off against one another, a plurality of epicentres could form that foster responsiveness to the complexity and diversity of contemporary teaching practice. These epicentres may exist within or across the four affiliates. Principals and vice-principals could be incorporated back into the fold as an epicentre on an equitable footing with teachers. Unlike Wenger's 'communities of practice' (1998) that arose out of corporate funded research into organizational theory and knowledge management, the purpose is not restricted to garnering knowledge for the benefit the organization, but is geared to actively engaging people in an ongoing process of democratic participation and empowerment. Autonomous epicentres located outside the official channels of control are free to foster dialectical cultures of dissent and to participate in academic activism through politicization and connection to the broader socio-political community. As the need arises and depending on the issues at hand, a critical mass can be assembled by forming alliances and coalitions across epicentres and across difference with other groups, including parents groups, student groups, allied professions, other feminized professions, teachers in other locations nationally and internationally, as well as the labour movement at large. The Campaign for Public Education and the Need to Succeed Campaign offer local examples of community alliances among teacher, parent, and student groups dedicated to reinstating adequate funding to public education in Ontario. Based on issues arising out of local epicentres, such coordinated efforts towards building coalitions can counter the divisiveness orchestrated under education reform and amass resistance to the erosion of public education. Much can be gleaned from the inclusive practices of women's organizing and caucusing to enable working together across difference for genuine social change, without becoming enmeshed in large bureaucratic structures.

As educators, teachers embody the knowledge and know-how to engage in academic activism in a multiplicity of ways: first, reaching into the local community and engaging socio-political issues in the public realm as public intellectuals; second, bridging the gap between the academy and the real world of teaching practice and fostering cultures of dissent to formulate alternative discourses to the dominant discourse of education reform; third, exploring the forms academic activism can take through the curriculum and teaching students in the classroom. The intention of academic activism is to facilitate socio-economic criticism and public debate, and to politicize and democratize society and its institutions. The question then is how to democratize the institution of public education?

As an alternative to anti-democratic, hierarchically structured organizations, participatory democracy advocates horizontal relations in which power is shared in decision-making. As an early proponent of participatory democracy, Pateman (1970) centres citizens as active participants at all levels of decision-making in the workplace where socio-economic inequalities typically exclude democratic participation: 'One might characterise the participatory model as one where maximum input (participation) is required and where output includes not just policies (decisions) but also the development of the social and political capacities of each individual, so that there is 'feedback' from output to input' (p. 43).

This is a radical departure from the top-down management and control that construes 'capacity building' as increasing the efficiency of workers, with leadership power and benefit accruing in the opposite direction. Rather, participatory democracy in the workplace advocates reciprocity at all levels, such that decision-making is affected by the involvement of all participants (and vice versa). The educational element inherent in Pateman's proposition is that participation raises confidence and leads to greater involvement. Although participatory democracy undoubtedly demands time and energy, it increases political knowledge and efficacy, and also improves commitment toward collective decisions.

For inclusive decision-making to function democratically, it is important to distinguish between full participatory democracy and the illusion of democracy fabricated through pseudo or partial participation (Pateman, 1970), each of which can be utilized to manipulate people. *Pseudo-participation* is a manipulative management strategy used to enlist the compliance of workers by persuasion, and is akin to manufacturing consent after decisions have already been made. *Partial participation*, in which the parties enlisted in decision-making influence each other, nonetheless invests final decision-making power with one party. Both create the illusion of democratic participation but lack the crucial aspect of directly affecting decisions. To Pateman's typology I would add a third strategy of token participation that has been deployed in the divisive relations of education reform. *Token participation* occurs when a non-representative compliant sample of the population is selected or sequestered for input on behalf of the group (in this case, teachers). The participation of this chosen sub-group is cosmetic, lending the appearance of credibility and democratic process to final decisions. Used as evidence of consultation in the decision-making process, it creates the illusion of the group at large having been granted the opportunity to participate. Particularly susceptible to co-optation are career opportunists or neophytes who succumb to personal flattery and approval. In pursuit of their personal goals, both groups are inclined to be either disinterested or unaware of the larger socio-political context. These subgroups may be easily manipulated and participate minimally if at all in actual decisions, for that is not the intention of the enlisters nor the subgroup. Token participation individualizes input and conceals anti-democratic intentions. It is particularly destructive in working communities when the principle of divide and rule instills a climate of favouritism, distrust and betrayal.

Recognition of these strategies in operation is helpful in withdrawing complicity with the ruling apparatus, and striving for empowerment through full participatory democracy. It also applies to how we engender democratic values in students and raises the question: What is the relationship between democracy and education? Democracy operates in formal electoral politics, but in the larger sense it is also operates as a 'way of life' (Dewey, 1916). Like Carole Pateman, Portelli (2001) asserts the necessity for a reciprocal relationship between democracy and education that hinges on participation, where each affects the other. Both conservative (traditional, content-centred) and progressivist (child-centred) approaches to education claim to value democracy (Portelli). If we agree that it is important to educate students to foster democracy, then what does this mean for education in practice? How do we educate students to participate in a democratic society? While the notion of 'education for democracy' does not necessarily imply democratic schools, the notion of 'democracy in education' makes room for developing democratic practices and dispositions through education (Portelli, p. 280) – that is, in our schools and in our classrooms. In the interests of inclusiveness in a heterogeneous society, this means paying attention to the connection between equity and democracy. In the case of women teachers who have been denied authority in their own terms, the question is how to coordinate democratic classrooms without ceding authority altogether to students (Briskin, 1990) or to hierarchical bureaucratic structures of the institution of education.

Imbalances in relative power based on inequitable participation reproduce the dynamics of domination-subjugation or centre-periphery in society and its institutions. Invariably constructed around difference (gender, class, race/ethnicity, sexual orientation, age, ability and so on), socio-economic imbalances are complicated further by overlapping axes of difference. Hegemonic ideologies that privilege certain groups over others present systemic barriers to socio-economic equity and justice. Attention to difference is crucial to perceive the operation of inequitable social relations and to ensure equitable participation in the workplace, in our federation and in the classroom. The interlocking patriarchal, capitalist, and neo-colonialist ideologies that pervade the institution of education under reform in Ontario are undoubtedly compounded by other axes of difference, since the 'othering' isms tend to go hand-in-hand. To challenge education reform, not only can we teachers resist the constraints imposed variously on our lives and work through collective action and withdrawing complicity with the ruling apparatus, but through our work we can counteract the perpetuation of hegemonic ideologies in the next generation and work for social transformation. Integrating critical analysis, socio-political activism, and democratic practice proffers a proactive alternative to hegemonic dominance. This can occur in various ways depending on local context, personal location, and availability of time. As teacher-educators, we can begin in our own way from where we are – in our schools and in the everyday world of the classroom – as conscious agents practising critical pedagogy and fostering full participatory democracy in our everyday relations. It grows from there.

Afterword

Teaching does not end when the last bell rings; it is indeed an occupation that follows us like a silent shadow in the berry patch, on the bay, or into the middle of the night (Roland S. Barth, 1990, p. 4). At Big Bay one summer evening at sunset, I had occasion to meet a couple of teachers from London, Ontario, who had taken early retirement in the midst of education reform. Both felt that they had left teaching at the right time, as they could not participate in the reform agenda. Their personal reasons for making the decision were three-fold: having no control over their teaching assignments, being ruled by the clock, and being subjected to continual teacher bashing by government and the media. Rachel expressed similar sentiments when she announced her retirement in June 2003; yet an ongoing commitment to education is reflected in her work on mathematics games that she presented at a university conference and at a teacher workshop at the board. At present she is compiling her research with the intention of publishing a book. Whereas the accumulated expertise and acquired knowledge of these experienced teachers may be lost to the public education system, according to the 'earthworm theory of change' (Franklin, 1990), their success is immeasurably registered in the thousands of students whose lives they have touched over the years.

In June 2003 the double cohort of students graduated from high school amid fierce competition for university spots and higher than usual marks required for university entrance, while government statements claimed that spots were available for all 'willing and qualified' students. Among the qualified are public school graduates with the means to raise their averages by taking one or more private courses (usually in English or mathematics) at the 700 odd new private 'acade-mies' in Toronto. As distinct from established traditional private schools, these private 'credit mills' offer single credits, inflated marks, and charge high fees per course.[1] Who can afford to pay the high fees? High marks at graduation give students whose parents can afford the investment an advantage not only for spots, but also for scholarships. The equity issue eludes proponents of choice and/or entrepreneurs for whom the growth industry of private education represents a business opportunity and is fair game in the marketplace.

Since the focus group assembled for the book took place in 2002, restructuring proceeded with additional controls over teachers. The onslaught continued with a new Position of Responsibility Model (POR) model and two new teacher testing instruments: the Ontario Teacher Qualifying Test (OTQT) and the Teacher Performance Appraisal (TPA).

The new POR model of curriculum leaders restructures subject departments, reduces the overall number of headships, and amalgam-ates smaller departments together under the authority of 'superheads.' Geared towards managerial-administrative functions according to a competitive-business headhunter model of leadership, the new POR model supersedes the former collegial-academic model of school gov-ernance. Teachers' unions boycotted what amounts to demoting all existing heads of department, hand-picking new ones and download-ing responsibility onto teachers. The divisiveness of pitting former heads of smaller departments against one other in competition for fewer spots created tension among teachers. Under the POR model, curriculum leaders are appointed by school principals for a finite term of three years, which is likely to ensure compliance. Furthermore, an overall reduction in the number of positions limits prospects for career advancement; this was a factor cited as one of the disincentives for selecting teaching as career choice (McIntyre, 1998) and is likely to have a negative impact on teacher recruitment.

For teacher-graduates, the OTQT counted briefly for entry into the profession. Overseen by the ministry, it was conceived as a licensure test for all new teacher-graduates as a condition of registration with the OCT. This US-style test was designed by a private firm (Educa-tional Testing Service in New Jersey) in partnership with the OPC. Questions covered the gamut of subject specializations and program levels in the form of thirty-six multiple choice and fourteen short answer questions. Given such a broad scope, superficial questions related to classroom management or general knowledge prevail, such as who are adolescents most influenced by – teachers, parents or peers?[2] What purpose is served by generating a score from simplistic questions? Yet while it was in effect, the import of this test was such that it determined which teacher-graduates were permitted entry into the profession in of Ontario. Due to its limited validity to determine new teachers' 'readiness to teach,' the OTQT was declared temporarily in abeyance in 2005, pending the formulation of a 'new and improved' entry-to-practice assessment that satisfies government regulations and certification requirements of the OCT. New teachers are not off the hook. In a time of scarce resources, the ministry allocated $2.6 million over two years to testing teacher-graduates, but to what end? At an additional cost of tens of millions of dollars per year that escalates annually, EQAO student testing continues, despite lack of evidence that testing contributes to 'improving student learning' – that ill-defined catch-phrase of educational reform.

After graduation and registration with the OCT, perpetual teacher testing persists every three years with the cumbersome and time-consuming TPA process as specified in legislation. The evaluation is conducted by principals, vice-principals, or supervisory officers who rate teachers as exemplary, good, satisfactory, or unsatisfactory according to 16 competencies and up to 165 'look-fors,' as outlined in the *Teacher Performance Appraisal Manual and Approved Forms and Guidelines* (2002). The testing obsession is typified by the meticulous categorization and itemization of the TPA rubric, that instrumentalizes general descriptors of the 'skills, knowledge and attitudes' laid out in the OCT Standards of Practice. The onus of proof lies with the individual teacher to produce evidence for the competencies, as if on trial. Upon completion, the principal's final TPA report is relegated to file storage, unless the evaluation is unsatisfactory. In the latter case, an elaborate disciplinary process is mobilized, the punitive consequences of which include OCT decertification. It appears the main raison d'être of this laborious process for principals and teachers alike, is to weed out a few 'incompetent' teachers by regularly testing the thousands of public school teachers across the province. What does this say about public regard of teachers in Ontario? Are all guilty until proven innocent? The effort and expense invested in developing and implementing such an overwrought barrage of paperwork seems misspent and counterproductive given the scarcity of resources and time for the real work of teaching.

The flaw in the accounting logic becomes clear when contrasting the lavish expenditures of money, time and resources in teacher testing and student testing with the poverty of budgets to schools where student learning actually takes place. Government-appointed supervisor Paul Christie proved unable to balance the TDSB budget for 2002-3. Using 'cosmetic' accounting practices explicitly disallowed to school trustees, having cut school attendance counsellors and reduced the heating in schools by one degree, even Christie could find nothing left to trim. The illusion of democratic process was created by holding so-called public consultation sessions during the summer of 2003, with very limited attendance since teachers and students had dispersed for the summer.[3] What was the rationale for this timing? The few in attendance were placed in the position of begging for money to prevent any further cuts and closures. A picture was painted of schools in disrepair with leaking roofs, broken washroom facilities, limited supplies, insufficient or tattered textbooks, cuts to programs such as special education and African history (low priorities under education reform), and fears of further school swimming pool closures. One student recounted that next to the pencil sharpener at her school is a ruler; unless a pencil is shorter than five centimeters, students do not qualify for a replacement. The paradox of nickel-and-diming schools while paying undisclosed amounts to external accounting consultants (estimated to be in excess of $400,000 to Christie and his entourage alone, excluding what was paid to Al Rosen for his six-week audit of the TDSB) exposes the unconscionable logic of the accountability obsession. What has been accomplished? Who are the beneficiaries?

Among the usual suspects at the upper echelons of ruling structures identified in this study is Earl Manners. Having served as president of the provincial OSSTF throughout the period of hostile labour relations with the provincial government, he stepped down and landed the lucrative position of chief negotiator and grievance officer for the Trillium-Lakelands District School Board. Like Margaret Wilson before him, Manners turned power to personal advantage. A corollary to the familiar quote, 'Power tends to corrupt; absolute power corrupts absolutely' is that power is in inverse proportion to ethics (both attributed to Lord Acton). Members of the OTF are bound by its code of ethics, wherein the section on negotiations states, 'That it be unethical for a statutory member to act as a negotiator on behalf of a school board in negotiations conducted under the School Boards and Teachers Collective Negotiations Act.' The sense of betrayal in crossing the floor to management lies in giving employers the psychological advantage and marks the ascendancy of management rights over labour rights in collective bargaining.[4] Manner's windfall confirms that entrenched power at the upper echelons of ruling structures is ideologically aligned, even across the management-labour divide.

The so-called experts on education reform in Ontario, Andy Hargreaves and Michael Fullan, have benefited from glorified status in the United States and Britain. Hargreaves, director of the International Centre for Educational Change at OISE/UT, was appointed as Thomas More Brennan Chair at the Lynch School of Education, Boston College in the United States. In the news is Fullan, courted as an education consultant by British prime minister Tony Blair, and 'discovered' by the newly ensconced Liberal premier, Dalton McGuinty (Alanna Mitchell, *Globe and Mail* 4 October 2003, p. F2, and 1 May 2004 pp. F4-5). Imbued with star status as the change-management guru along the lines of Kotter and Senge, he has influenced the highest levels of education policy internationally Britain and the United States as well as Europe, Australia, and Hong Kong. This suggests that the ideology of education reform is carried far and wide through the authority of education research, and into the official annals of power where reform policies are formulated. Fullan's appointment as special education advisor to the premier strikes an ominous tone for things to come in Ontario, given his promotion of standardized testing of a common curriculum by the EQAO (as in Britain with the testing of the national curriculum under the Qualifications and Curriculum Authority). This is an early indicator that the Liberal government is falling in line with the tenets of neoliberal education reform predicated on standards-based accountability.

Appointed dean at OISE/UT under the NDP government, Michael Fullan held office throughout the PCs restructuring of education, thus remaining in favour across the mandates of all three official political parties. The final version of the report entitled *The Schools We Need: A New Blueprint for Ontario* (Leithwood, Fullan and Watson, 2003) was adroitly released in the last days of the PC regime. This report belatedly alludes to the failure of education policy reform in Ontario that precipitated unprecedented teacher protests across the province since the mid-1990s. Eight years after these policies began to be implemented, and six years after teachers took the drastic step of going out on strike to draw attention to the threat to public education, these academic leaders in education adapt by repackaging their ideas in manageable and marketable sound bites and re-present themselves as saviours of a failing system that they helped to create.

In *The Schools We Need*, education reform policy is criticized for ignoring research evidence and professional judgment in favour of the ideology of common sense that has had a neutral or negative effect on student learning. The authors propose five conditions (and seventeen related recommendations) for the schools we need: vision, governance, evidence, support for teachers, and adequate and flexible funding. Recommendations include: stop wasting resources on things that don't matter to students; refocus new policy initiatives on things that do matter for students; champion the development of healthy families in order to provide students with the 'social capital' and the 'capacity to succeed'; pay attention to 'uncommon sense' by questioning assumptions about what constitutes common sense; and revitalize the teaching profession through an induction program of 'mentor-teacher leaders.' In short, teachers are still regarded as passive and deficient, to be manipulated by selective 'pressure and support,' and hope remains vested in standardized testing and the leadership of principals.

On the contrary, as this study based on teachers' experience and institutional analysis shows, standardized testing is of negligible pedagogical value in practice, and top-down management not only undermines collegial relations and incites resistance, but most importantly denigrates the value of teachers' input in policy-making. The OPC inducts principals into the management mindset as a precondition of advancement up the hierarchy, and principals as a group have been co-opted as enablers and enforcers of education reforms at the level of the school. The role of principals as a group is not to deny the efforts of some individual principals who have taken a stand. However, the ideology of education reform and the Common Sense Revolution is actually so fully assimilated into the operations of the OPC such that conscientious objection is tantamount to heresy.

Still adhering to the ideology of neoliberalism and subscribing to the language of the boardroom, Leithwood, Fullan, and Watson (2003) propose social engineering of 'healthy families,' whatever that means! Research suggesting that parent involvement is the most reliable predictor of school success ignores the implicit assumption of the white middle-class family as the prototype; it discounts the parallels that exist between socio-economic disparity and class/ethnic differences – a parallel that may actually be exacerbated by education reform in favouring the interests and success of already advantaged groups in society. As any teacher knows, families – or parents/guardians – cannot be expected to compensate for inadequacies of the system. Some parents have joined the Ontario Parent Council and uncritically support education reforms that serve dominant groups in society; others through independent coalitions such as People for Public Education have actively opposed reforms; many have neither the time nor the resources to get involved, either collectively or with their own children. To shift blame onto parents for the failure of education reforms is another ruse to shore up a fundamentally flawed ideology of education.

The timing of the release of *The Schools We Need* is worth noting. It occurred amid mounting public criticism of mismanagement by the government in the run-up to the provincial election; it followed in the wake of criticism from the government's own Rozanski Report (by the Education Equality Task Force) on the funding formula, and Phase 2 of Alan King's *Double Cohort Study* (both in 2002). Referring to high failure rates in Grades 9 and 10 applied courses of the new curriculum, especially mathematics, and failure rates in excess of 20 per cent on the literacy test, King predicted that 'Graduation rates will almost surely decline in the new program in light of students' [diminished] credit accumulation already observed for the first two years of the program. This pattern could have the effect of reducing the pool of students eligible to apply to college but not likely to university' (p. 20). Phase 3 of King's (2003) research confirms what educators already know, as expressed by teacher-participants in the focus group, and what was anticipated back in 1996 when the OSSTF protested the haste with which ill-conceived policies were being rushed through. To summarize Kings conclusions, the common curriculum jeopardizes students' chances of graduating, especially students with learning disabilities, whose first language is not English, or who are not university-bound – now labelled as a catch-all category of 'students-at-risk'; these are the students about whom teacher-participants expressed their concern, as struggling with a curriculum that is not suited to them. It takes time for what is happening on the ground to register with the official channels of the ruling apparatus. While the leading academic researchers, like school board trustees before them, ought to be commended on belatedly exposing the flaws, one wonders how different things might have been had a critical perspective prevailed earlier, and had they listened to and valued teachers' first-hand knowledge in the classrooms across Ontario.

Some university deans have heeded the concerns of teachers. Initiated by the deans of education, an ad hoc Task Force on Professional Learning was formed in January 2003 to look into the 'stalemate' of the PLP program. Clearly, the teacher boycott was widespread and exerted an impact. The task force, chaired by Rosa Bruno-Jofré (dean of the faculty of education at Queen's University) included deans from faculties of education as well as representatives from the OTF and affiliates, the OCT, and the Ministry of Education.[5] Their report entitled *Proposal for an Alternative to the Professional Learning Program (PLP)*, released in November 2003, suggests a formalized version of annual learning plans to replace the provider-driven PLP model. The proposed plans are to be connected to the TPA process, with school boards reporting to the OCT if teachers do not comply. While this proposal reduces the OCT bureaucracy required for data management of the PLP program, the College retains authority over professional development according to its *Professional Learning Framework* and is empowered to execute punitive consequences for non-compliance. According to a union representative on the deans' task force, the OCT raised objections to the proposal during final negotiations, on the grounds of loss of their major mandate over professional development, and the significant investment in real estate, technology, and personnel to manage the PLP program (actually funded through teachers' fees); the College also came out in defence of the investment made by public/private course providers who set up some 2681 courses it had approved. Whose interests did the OCT represent on the task force?

Not only was teacher resistance successful in bringing an end to the reviled PLP program, but union action was successful in settling the pay dispute with the TDSB regarding the CUPE strike. After a protracted process that lasted almost two years, the collective grievance with the TDSB was resolved in December 2002 through expedited arbitration. The arbitrator's award ruled in favour of the OSSTF. The board was required to fully reimburse teachers who had submitted explanations, and to remove letters of discipline from teachers' records, replacing them with a sealed letter specifying the protocol to be followed in the event of a strike by another bargaining unit. A TDSB letter dated 29 January 2003 sent to teachers states: 'Teachers who did not reply to the letter(s) from Aubrey Amo, Superintendent - Human Resources in which she asked for written explanation for their absence, by the date of the arbitration order or who self-declared that they, as a matter of conscience did not cross the picket lines, will not be reimbursed for the pay deducted.' It is fair to say that although relieved the issue is closed, teachers felt little satisfaction with the outcome, and the experience left its mark. I wonder whether Helena, who did not comply with giving an explanation at the time, remains out of pocket a day's pay.

Teacher unions, among others, can also claim credit for successful canvassing against the PC regime in the 2003 election. On 2 October 2003 the Liberals came to power in Ontario on an election platform promising to restore the beleaguered healthcare and public education systems, and to replace cynicism with hope. The first move in education of the new Liberal government was to release Paul Christie and the other government appointment supervisors from their duties, thereby vindicating the 'no-cuts' school trustees and reinstating local democracy to school boards. For democracy to be restored, however, it requires more than lip-service; it also requires restoring funding to public education as outlined in the Rozanski Report. The other proposed moves that require legislative approval are to repeal the private school tax credit, and to repeal the PLP program following the recommendation of the deans' task force. These are welcome moves with no cost attached; the infusion of $112 million for so-called students at risk is a start, but insufficient to rectify years of fiscal neglect and mismanagement. Resorting to the all-too-familiar excuse of the unexpected discovery of a large deficit to renege on election promises has a disconcerting ring. There have been some gains, but the ruling structures and legislation orchestrated under education reform remain firmly ensconced.

As this book goes to print, in October 2005 the site of major contention shifted to British Columbia, where 38,000 elementary and secondary teachers went on strike for two weeks in protest against Bill 12 that enforced the conditions of their previous contract, without negotiation. Issues included the wage freeze, class sizes, and provisions for special needs students. Even though media reports indicated public support for teachers, they were found in contempt of court for defying a back-to-work order. The union's strike fund was frozen, and threats of hefty fines ensued. As punitive pressure escalated, teacher relations with Gordon Campbell's Liberal government resembled the dark days of the Harris/Eves PCs in Ontario. Clearly, the ideology of education reform runs across political parties, with teachers from coast to coast taking a stand against the deterioration of working conditions in schools and the erosion of public education; from the perspective of teachers, what is worth fighting for is an accessible, sustainable, and democratic system of education.

Amidst the turmoil of education reform in Ontario, the teacher-participants in this study sought hope. And so I leave them with the final word – and the last laugh – as they overcome acrimony by affirming the priorities from which they derive a sense of meaning and purpose in their everyday work:

ALICE: It's [government policy] all about money. And the rest is just 'noise' – I hope so.

RACHEL: So, you do your own thing.

JESSICA: But, you know, with all this government 'stuff,' you just have to keep in mind that you're there for the kids, and not for anybody else. 'Cause you're not making a fortune, that's for sure!

HELENA: Nobody is in this profession for money, let's face it.

JESSICA: It's a great profession and it's uplifting to be with kids. And you know, it's great, but you just can't afford to get bogged down in all that bitterness, because you turn into a bitter person (group laughter).

Appendix I-A OCT Letter

Ontario College of Teachers

Ordre des enseignantes et des enseignants de l'Ontario

October 15, 2001
Toronto, ON M4P 1T9

Registration #:

The Ontario legislature has recently passed Bill 80 requiring all teachers certified to teach in the province to successfully complete a program of professional learning that includes a selection of 14 courses – seven core and seven elective – every five years.

Under the implementation timelines outlined in both the legislation and the subsequent regulations, the College has been working diligently to make the Professional Learning Program (PLP) both useful to you in your teaching and a contributor to your professional growth.

In our August 13 letter to all members of the College, we indicated that, for about 30 per cent of the College membership, the five-year Professional Learning Program cycle would begin this year and end in 2006.

This is your official notice that you are in this first group. You must complete a Professional Learning Program of 14 approved courses by December 31, 2006 to maintain your Ontario teaching certificate.

When you begin to plan your individual Professional Learning Program for the next five years, you should keep in mind that a wide variety of traditional professional development courses like Additional Qualifications, MEd studies or other university courses may be eligible for PLP course credits if they meet certain conditions. Many of these courses will likely qualify for multiple PLP course credits.

You are in the first group who must complete PLP courses by December 31, 2006 because:

- you are one of 40,000 practising classroom teachers selected at random from the College register of teachers (Bill 80 requires the College to make this random selection)

   or

- you are employed as a classroom teacher and were first certified to teach in Ontario in 2001 (a further requirement in Bill 80).

Together We're Shaping The Future

Tous ensemble, nous bâtissons l'avenir

/...2

The rest of the College's members – including other classroom teachers, vice-principals, principals, consultants, superintendents, directors of education and Ministry of Education and College of Teachers employees who hold teaching certificates – must complete their 14 courses by December 31, 2007.

There are some key facts you should know about the Professional Learning Program.

You *may* have already accumulated credits towards your PLP course requirements. Additional Qualification (AQ) courses, university or community college courses, summer institutes or other professional learning completed after June 29, 2001 may count for one or more PLP requirements. Certain important conditions apply. Please see *Retroactive Credits – Professional Learning Program*, which is included in this mailing and is also posted on the College web site at *www.oct.on.ca* ➜ **Professional Learning Program.**

You can check the College web site to find out what providers have been approved to offer professional learning credits. If you engaged in professional learning after June 29, 2001 and think it should count for your professional learning, contact the provider to determine if they have applied for approved provider status with the College. By legislation, only courses delivered by providers approved by the College can be credited for the PLP.

Professional Learning courses must be a minimum of five hours long. They can be completed on a Professional Activity Day. Longer courses may be eligible for multiple PLP credits. For example, a 125-hour AQ course may provide learning opportunities in more than one of the seven core course areas – possibly curriculum, use of technology and teaching strategies. The College's new Professional Learning Committee will address guidelines for multiple course credits when it meets in mid-November and early December. Watch *www.oct.on.ca* ➜ **Professional Learning Program** and *Professionally Speaking* for more information.

You will be able to choose courses offered by many course providers. Dozens of respected educational institutions and organizations have already applied for approval as PLP providers. The list of approved providers is growing by the week. The College expects that hundreds of providers will be offering you approved courses within a year. For the list of approved providers visit *www.oct.on.ca/english/plp/providerslist.asp.*

There will be a wide selection of courses available throughout the province in both English and French. Many courses will be available online. You will be able to choose your courses by visiting *www.oct.on.ca/english/plp/catalog.asp.* All the courses will be listed there, with links to providers' web sites where you will find detailed information about locations, times, language(s) of instruction, method of delivery, length and fees if applicable. Providers may also advertise their courses through other means.

/ ...3

The College is committed to equity of access to courses in both official languages. In addition to accessibility, the College has consistently maintained the position that it wants your professional learning to contribute to your professional growth and reflect your professional needs.

You can complete your Professional Learning course credits at your own pace, as long as you accumulate 14 credits by December 31, 2006.

Your Professional Learning Program status is private. No information about the courses you take or how many credits you have accumulated will be made public by the College. The College will not inform anyone, including your employer, that you have begun your five-year PLP cycle. Whether you share this information with anyone is entirely up to you.

However, as required by law, any teacher whose teaching certificate is suspended for failure to complete the required 14 courses in five years will have the suspension and reasons recorded on the College's public register.

You will be able to keep track of your PLP credits through a secure individual password-protected account on the College web site. Watch *Professionally Speaking* for information on how to create your own private account, coming in 2002.

Starting in 2003, the College will mail you an annual statement of your PLP credits when you receive your Certificate of Qualification. Your PLP statement will not appear on your Certificate of Qualification – it will be a separate document.

Providers are responsible for notifying the College of your successful completion of courses. The process of recording the information about College members' participation in courses since June 29, 2001 will not be completed for several months. Providers will not inform the College about unsuccessful participants in courses. The College will only record successful completions.

All courses must:

- support the *Standards of Practice for the Teaching Profession* and the *Ethical Standards for the Teaching Profession* (available on the College web site)

- have outcomes that include improving student achievement

- contain a formal assessment mechanism.

You must successfully complete at least one course in each of seven core course areas: curriculum, student assessment, special education, teaching strategies, classroom management and leadership, use of technology, and communication with parents and students.

/ ...4

Providers will design and offer a wide variety of courses that fall under each of the seven categories, so you will be able to choose the particular course that meets your own learning needs.

In addition, you must complete seven elective courses for a total of 14 courses. These may be additional courses in the core areas, or in other approved areas. The Professional Learning Committee will develop the criteria for elective courses in the next few months. Watch the web site and *Professionally Speaking* for more information.

The legislation that requires teachers to complete this program also provides for exemptions, which are to be set out in a regulation by the government. We expect these exemptions – actually extensions to the timelines for PLP requirements – to be quite limited, so they would apply only in specific cases such as long-term medical leaves.

We now expect to receive this regulation in the next few months. When the regulation is passed, it will be available on the provincial government web site at *www.e-laws.gov.on.ca*. The College will also make a plain-language explanation available on our web site at *www.oct.on.ca* ➜ **Professional Learning Program** and in *Professionally Speaking*.

We welcome your input about this new program. If you have not already done so, please fill out the survey that you will find in the professional learning section of the College web site. You can also find many useful questions and answers at *www.oct.on.ca/english/plp/memberqa.asp*.

We recognize that we are not able to answer all your questions yet because the Professional Learning Program is still in its very early stages of development. However, the College is required under Bill 80, which established this program, to send you this notice at this time.

Sincerely,

Larry M. Capstick
Chair

J.W. (Joe) Atkinson
Registrar

P.S. The latest information about the implementation of the Professional Learning Program will always be available on the College web site at *www.oct.on.ca*. Use the web site to check on lists of approved providers and their courses. These lists will be updated regularly.

Appendix I-B TDSB Letter

Toronto
District
School
Board

Human Resources Services – Secondary Teaching Office
155 College Street, Toronto, Ontario M5T 1P6 Tel: (416) 397-3580 Fax: (416) 397-3484

June 22, 2001

Lindsay Kerr

Dear Lindsay Kerr:

It has come to our attention that you were not present at your work site as required on **Apr. 5/01** and have not delivered a medical certificate explaining your absence.

As you are aware, the bargaining unit to which you belong was not in a legal strike position at that time. Therefore, your refusal to be at your work site as required was in violation of the collective agreement between your union and the Board. In addition, the failure to attend at your work site as required is a breach of your legal duties, including those under the *Education Act* and its Regulations.

Accordingly, please be advised as follows:

- you will not be paid for your unauthorized absence;
- the appropriate deduction from your salary will be taken from your pay before the end of the current school year;
- this letter will be placed in your Personnel File.

If you feel that your absence was justified, I would be pleased to receive a written explanation and have that reviewed. Please send the explanation by hard copy or e-mail. Your written explanation must reach my office not later than noon on August 1, 2001. The explanation may be submitted as follows:

Address: Audrey Amo
                Secondary Teaching Office, 4th floor
                155 College Street
                Toronto, Ontario
                M5T 1P6

        E-mail: audrey.amo@tdsb.on.ca

However, if no satisfactory written explanation is received as above-mentioned, please be advised that the decision as outlined above will stand. If the written explanation is accepted, we will reimburse the appropriate amount in September.

Yours truly,

Audrey Amo
Superintendent, Human Resources

c. School Principal
   School Superintendent
   Personnel File

Appendix I-C Remedial Support Program – Teacher Log

Forest Hill Collegiate

Remedial Support Program – Teacher LOG

Teacher: _____

Date	Time	Student Name	Home Form	Topic/Activity

TOTAL TIME LOGGED: _____

Please return this form to _____ *Main Office, on the last Friday of each month.*

Appendix I-D Letter from OISE/UT

ONTARIO INSTITUTE FOR
STUDIES IN EDUCATION
OF THE UNIVERSITY
OF TORONTO
252 Bloor Street West
Toronto, Ontario
Canada M5S 1v6
Telephone: (416) 923-6641

February 12, 2002

The Honourable Janet Ecker
Minister of Education, Ontario
Mowat Block, 900 Bay Street
Toronto, ON M7A 1L2

Dear Minister Ecker,

Because of its opposition to the Professional Learning Program, the Ontario English Catholic Teachers Association has passed a motion to advise all its members not to accept teacher candidates in practicum settings after February 25, 2002 from those faculties who have registered for the Professional Learning Program. A copy of their letter is appended.

The Representative Council of the Elementary Teachers' Federation of Ontario has passed a similar motion and will be bringing it to their Executive on March 1-2, 2002.

Essentially we see this as a matter to be resolved by the Ministry and the teacher associations. We are also very much committed to contributing to the continuous development of teachers through the Professional Learning Program. However, the actions of OECTA and possibly ETFO have extremely serious consequences to the teacher candidates at OISE/UT, one of the faculties which has registered to be part of the Professional Learning Program.

Unlike some programs in other faculties of education, our Bachelor of Education program is scheduled in such a way that our teacher candidates have yet to complete their second practicum (February 18 - March 28) and their required internship (April 29 - May 30).

The possibility of the action contemplated by the two teacher associations is having an enormous negative effect on our teacher candidates, especially in this year where they must prepare for the new Initial Teacher Qualifying Test at the same time as they are engaged in seeking employment for next year.

In light of their vulnerability, we would have to seriously consider deregistering as a provider of the Professional Learning Program, an action we would find difficult in light of the support OISE/UT has always had for ongoing teacher development.

I would very much appreciate your advice as to how we should proceed in this difficult situation. It would be most helpful to hear from the Ministry before February 20, 2002, when we have scheduled a major meeting with all 1300 of our teacher candidates.

Yours sincerely,

Michael Fullan
Dean

Enclosure

cc. Ms Suzanne Herbert, Deputy Minister
Ms Susan Langley, Secretary-Treasurer, Ontario Teachers' Federation
Mr. Joe Atkinson, Registrar, Ontario College of Teachers

Notes

1. Introduction

1 The sense in which globalization is used here is as a set of corporate-capitalist relations that dominates the political economy internationally. These relations serve the interests of big business in competition for markets and resources across borders, at the expense of local economies and peoples. The accumulation of wealth by a few powerful transnational companies with their headquarters in the first world is mirrored by increasing poverty and hunger in the third world. As an exponential extension of colonialism, globalization rose to dominance during the 1980s and 1990s, under Reagan (in the United States) and Thatcher (in the United Kingdom). A corollary to economic globalization is the globalization of culture. The cultural imperialist aspect of globalization induces a 'monoculture' of mind that brings people in line with the dominant ethos. Since this creates conditions conducive to foreign investment, cultural and economic globalization operate hand-in-hand.

2 The theoretical basis for neoliberalism can be found in the work of two Nobel prize winners at the University of Chicago School of Economics, Frederick Hayek and Milton Friedman. Inherent in this doctrine is prominence for the basic value of individual freedom to determine one's own destiny. Inequality is accepted as inevitable in a competitive free market that rewards initiative. Neoliberal ideology subscribes to supply-side economic theory that originated with Arthur Laffer, famous for the Laffer Curve. According to this theory, economic growth is deemed to be stimulated by decreasing taxes so as to increase investment, with no resultant decrease in net tax payments or fall in overall revenues. Economic policies geared to speculative investment create the illusion of economic growth at the

expense of the poor and other disadvantaged socio-economic groups in society.

3 The Collective Agreement (2000–2) was ratified by only 53 per cent of the membership of the OSSTF (District 12).

4 Downshifting refers to stepping down the career ladder, for example by relinquishing positions of responsibility (headships), changing to part-time or casualized supply teaching, or requesting less demanding teaching assignments.

5 The findings of the Institute for Public Policy Research was reported on BBC News, Tuesday 4 September 2001, http://newssearch.bbc.co.uk/hi/ english/education/newsid_1523000/1 523478.stm

6 The Toronto Board of Education was renamed the Toronto District School Board under amalgamation. To mention a few initiatives: as co-author of the draft document entitled *The Facilitator's Manual of All School Enrichment* (with Glen Way and Bernice Slotnik); a $10,000 grant for a project entitled *Teleconferencing using Laptops* predicated on integrating computers into the classroom curriculum; and as a team member for a pilot project developing a new course on communications technology for which my contribution was a unit on *Videography* (including pre-production, production and post-production). Funding for such projects has largely dried up under education reform, relying instead on the formation of individual 'partnerships' with businesses for sponsorships.

7 Leaders (for example, principals) here refers to asymmetrical constructions of power favoured under education reform, where leaders are legitimized by legislation and appointed by higher levels to control lower levels within a hierarchical, bureaucratic system, using coersion or manipulation. More egalitarian, inclusive, and democratic constructions of leadership favour participation, election of leaders, and/or rotation of the role; this kind of leadership fosters collegial, horizontal relations and power-sharing.

8 Work intensification refers to neoliberal economics policies that impose more work in less time on fewer employees.

9 The term 'third world' does not imply a hierarchy. Rather it implies a different worldview from first world capitalist nations and second world socialist nations. The self-designated term of the 'third world' originates from the 1955 Bandung Conference of non-aligned African and Asian nations that share an anti-colonial perspective. Although these distinctions are no longer clear, alternative terms such as East and West, or more recently North and South, have associations with geographic location rather than accentuating socio-political differences.

2. The Socio-Political Context of Ontario

1 See United Nations, Universal Declaration of Human Rights, (http://www.un.org/Overview/rights.html).

2 The BNA Act harks back to the founding nations of English/Protestants and French/Catholics. At that time when schools were religious-based, it protected minority rights to education. Not only does it subsume the First Nations, but with the advent of secular public education in a heterogeneous society, it disregards the diversity of religious affiliations. The court challenge based on the violation of the Canadian Charter of Rights and Freedoms was overturned by both the Ontario Court of Appeal and the Supreme Court of Canada. However, a United Nations ruling found Ontario in contravention of the UN Covenant on Civil and Political Rights, for discriminating in favour of one faith over others. Quebec and Newfoundland-Labrador eradicated separate systems during the restructuring of education in the late 1990s, whereas Alberta funds Roman Catholic schools. In Ontario, the precedent of financing Roman Catholic schools garnered some public support for Bill 45, in the form of tax breaks to parents of children who attend private/parochial schools, thus contributing to a double drain on public education funds.

3 The legacy of colonialism in the Canadian education system is also reflected in special provisions for the education of First Nations children. Although there is no federal Ministry of Education, an exception pertains under the Indian Act that regulates the system of native reservations. The federal minister of the Department of Indian Affairs and Northern Development (DIAND) is responsible for the provision of education to Indian or Inuit children. DIAD funds on-reserve schools, and also reimburses costs for students who reside on-reserve but attend provincial schools. The Indian Act is contested by the First Nations as paternalistic, out-dated, and obstructive to self-government. The responsibility of reparations for past child abuses in residential missions schools continues to be shuttled between church and federal authorities.

4 Along with teaching and nursing, social work is also largely a feminized profession. Social workers are subject to similar dynamics and have suffered the negative effects of restructuring and cutbacks. Their non-union status as a group has meant that relations with government have been less confrontational and could explain why social workers have been less visible in the media than teachers or nurses. Social workers were in the process of unionizing as a group during the period of restructuring public services.

5 In February 1993, under Bob Rae's NDP government, a new 'superminis-

try' was formed and named the Ministry of Education and Training, with Dave Cooke as minister. This ministry lumped together schools, skills-training programs, and colleges and universities under one umbrella. It was subsequently renamed and reconfigured as the Ministry of Education/ Ministry of Training, Colleges and Universities.

6 The five commissioners of the Royal Commission on Learning were Monique Bégin and Gerald Caplan (co-chairs), with Manisha Bharti, Avis Glaze, and Dennis Murphy (commissioners). Raffaella Di Cecco was the executive director.

3. Research Methodology

1 One of the potential participants suffered a serious medical condition requiring hospitalization and lengthy rehabilitation that prevented her participation in the focus group. This raises the possible question of stress associated with the pressure of increased workload affecting teachers' physical health. Her input based on field notes from initial telephone contact has been included in this study.

2 The term 'aspiring administrator' is derived from vernacular teacher-talk. It describes teachers perceived as upwardly mobile career opportunists, with the personal ambition of rising up the hierarchy to become administrators but without allegiance to place or people. In the presence of presumed aspiring administrators, conversation among regular classroom teachers is measured or the subject changed, a dynamic sometimes observed in the staff room or departmental offices. This was obviated in the focus group, where the openness of exchange indicates no fear or suspicion of 'informants.' In my personal experience, this divisive dynamic has become particularly pronounced under restructuring, to the point where I needed to reassure a colleague that my post-graduate work at OISE/UT, though under the Department of Theory and Policy Studies, was *not* under the auspices of the administrators' program, but in Higher Education.

4. Ruling Structures and Relations

1 Liz Sandals' speaking notes, Queen's Park Media Studio, 30 January 2002, http://www.tdsb.on.ca/boardroom/boardroom.

2 A deal struck in 1998 between the OTF and the provincial government permitted a 50:50 sharing of the Ontario Teachers' Pension Plan surplus of $17.8 billion. Whereas there were rumours of the government attempting to appropriate their share to balance the budget prior to the 1999 provincial

election, it was used to eliminate unfunded liability for teachers. Teachers retain control over how their portion is distributed to improve pension benefits (see 'Changes to teachers' pension plan: The 1998 deal,' *Update* 28[11], 27 March 2001).

3 For two years a fee dispute waged in the courts between the OTF and the OSSTF (provincial) over OSSTF withholding membership fees from the OTF. In the first ruling the OSSTF won. The appeal court decision of June 2002 ruled in favour of the OTF. The dispute revolved around whether the OTF can claim union dues if it is not a union. In addition, relations between the provincial OSSTF and OSSTF (District 12) have been strained, exacerbated by different approaches to contesting inadequate provincial government funding to education.

4 The OTF affiliates such as the OSSTF can be compared with the Ontario Medical Association (OMA) or more appropriately, with the Ontario Nurses Association (ONA), which is also a feminized group. The OMA and ONA are the bargaining units for doctors and nurses respectively. Just as nurse-managers are split off from the ONA, principals and vice-principals have been split off from the OSSTF since the formation of the OPC under education reform.

5 In the case of the Collective Agreement (2000–2) between OSSTF (District 12) and the TDSB, negotiations broke down and the provincial OSSTF was called in to settle.

6 See the OTF report entitled 'Major concerns of the Ontario Teachers Federation pertaining to the Education Quality and Accountability Office,' January 2002 at http://www.otffeo.on.ca/news/inter/eqao.pdf; and the Elementary Teachers' Federation of Ontario (ETFO) report entitled 'Adjusting the Optics: Assessment, Evaluation and Reporting' at http://www.etfo.ca/documents/adjustingtheoptics.pdf .

7 See the EQAO website at http://www.eqao.com/eqao/home_page/01e/1_4e.html. An update reveals a ratio shift of women to men to 4:4 in January 2002. However, the clearly identifiable corporatist ideological congruence remains.

8 Freire's critique of the traditional 'banking model' of education, in which information and/or official knowledge is deposited into the empty accounts of passive students, is that it leads to the domestication of students to accept external authority passively, and so serves to perpetuate the status quo. His alternative critical pedagogy of 'conscientization' awakens critical awareness through active participation, dialogue, and praxis, and leads to liberation from the socio-political forces of domination.

9 Information about the operations and structure of the Toronto Learning

Partnership was derived in large part from its report, *Return on Investment* (2003) at http://www.thelearningpartnership.ca/ROI_2003.pdf.

10 The long list of corporate sponsors of the TLP include: Adobe Systems Canada, Apple Canada Inc., BMO Financial Group, Bell Canada, Borden Ladner Gervais LLP, Campbell Soup Co. Ltd., Canada Post Corporation, Canadian Tire Corporation, Cara Operations Limited, Celestica Inc., Enbridge Consumers Gas, Ernst & Young, Hewlett-Packard (Canada) Ltd., Hudson's Bay Company, Hydro One Networks Inc., IBM Canada Ltd., Imperial Oil Ltd., Kodak Canada Inc., Manulife Financial Corporation, Microsoft, Miller Dallas Inc., Ontario Power Generation, Pearson Education Canada, RBC Dominion Securities Inc., RBC Financial Group, Royal & Sunalliance, Scotiabank Group, Shibley Righton LLP, Sprint Canada, Sun Life Financial, Toronto Hydro, Xerox Canada Limited (from http://www.thelearningpartnership.ca/, Members).

11 The senior manager at the time of this study was Baiba St John. For an organizational chart of the OKNL, see http://oknl.edu.gov.on.ca/eng/pdf/1_4_1.pdf.

12 See 'College registrar's conduct at dinner raises questions,' *D12 Voice* 1(5), p. 5. April 2000 issue at http://www.osstfdist12.com/archive/d12voice/Voiceapril.pdf. This journal is published by the OSSTF (District 12).

13 Faculty at OISE/UT sanctioned as harbingers of the kind of educational change envisioned by the royal commission also include Michael Fullan and Suzanne Stiegelbauer (vol. 4, p. 124).

5. Teachers in Texts and Text-Mediated Relations

1 The *Standards of Practice for the Teaching Profession* (1999) and *Ethical Standards for the Teaching Profession* (2000) that were in effect during this study have undergone review. Revisions are contained within *Foundations of Professional Practice* (2005) that incorporates three previously separate documents: the above two, as well as the Professional Learning Framework. The contentious issue of professional learning is thus enshrined in the primary regulations of the OCT.

2 An inside source at the OCT reports that the college applied to the provincial government to cover set-up costs for the PLP program, further confirming close ties with government that belies OCT claims to be a self-regulating body. Set-up however does not cover long-term costs of maintenance for the program. College fees were increased by 33.65 per cent and later by more than 54 per cent to defray expenses associated with this program.

3 For Foucault, relations of domination are fixed in a system of rules and

beliefs that assume a 'naturalness,' reinforced 'in rituals, in meticulous procedures that impose rights and obligations. It establishes marks of its
power and engraves memories on things and even within bodies' (in
Rabinow, 1984, p. 85)

4 Ontario College of Teachers public register can be found at http://
www.oct.on.ca/pr/english/info.htm .

5 Some other professions are subjected to annual recertification. In the case of
the feminized profession of pharmacists, an annual sticker is applied to the
licence displayed on the pharmacy wall. Given pharmacy's close ties with
the pharmaceutical industry, gender and corporate relations intersect here.

6 I noticed that a self-declared private provider attended a course given at
OISE/UT on school renewal, raising the possibility of private companies
gathering material to offer the same or similar courses, as well as drawing
students away from university courses. The private provider's interest in
school renewal suggests it fits ideologically with private corporate constructions of organizations. This is discussed further in chapter 6.

7 Michael Fullan's letter was located at www.otffeo.on.ca/news/inter/
oiseutp_ltr.pdf .

8 OECTA proceeded with this boycott action whereas the ETFO did not.

9 Soon after the election of the new premier, Ernie Eves, it was announced in
the media that teacher-graduates would still have to write the Ontario
Teacher Qualifying Test, but that it would not count in the first year. This
temporary reprieve is typical of ruling relations in Ontario that instill compliance by sudden edict, catching people off-guard; when objections arise,
postponement without backing down is the strategy for deflecting revolt,
like the proverbial frog that stays in water as it rises to boiling point. Similar to the strategy of divide and rule, it diffuses opposition and prevents
united collective action.

10 Not only are divisions between the OTF versus affiliates marked by professionalism versus unionism, but within the two levels of affiliates – provincial OSSTF and OSSTF District 12 – different constructions of unionism
prevail: bureaucratic, business unionism (at the provincial level) as against
radical, grassroots unionism (in Toronto). The distinction between them can
be characterized as follows: business unionism is concerned with growth in
membership and formal standing with the rest of the labour movement, but
is not opposed to privatization and corporate partnerships; grassroots
unionism favours not only affiliation with the labour movement but also
broad-based public education alliances with parents and other teachers
unions, and it is opposed to privatization and corporate sponsorships (see
Doug Little, 'District 12 changes direction,' *D12 Voice* 1[1], November 1999).

The conflict between the provincial OSSTF (under Earl Manners) and OSSTF District 12 (under Jim McQueen) became so polarized that there was talk of District 12 splitting off from the provincial OSSTF.

11 A copy of the Collective Agreement (2000–2) may be located at the OSSTF District 12 website at http://www.osstfdist12.com/ca_2000_02.htm .

12 The '4 over 5 Plan' is a leave-savings plan whereby teachers work for four years at 80 per cent pay in order to take leave in the fifth year, while continuing to receive pay and benefits. The separate letter sent to teachers involved in the plan was copied to the principal, pension administration, and benefits.

13 A follow-up letter from the TDSB, dated 16 November 2001, announced that having reviewed the circumstances as explained by individual teacher's responses, certain teachers would be 'reimbursed for 0.5 of the pay that was deducted from your salary.' Regardless of sign-in time and beholden to the good graces of senior officials, this arbitrary, piecemeal reimbursement epitomizes a military style of command designed to instill unquestioning compliance. (For an update see Afterword.)

14 By comparison, in reputable private schools, teachers are typically timetabled to teach five out of eight periods, with significantly smaller class sizes and more homogenous groupings than in the public system.

6. Counteracting Despair with Hope

1 See John Fisher, 'Africa,' in Charlton and Charlton (2001, pp. 199–211). Other chapters cover various places in the world and make it clear that similar patterns are occurring globally. Also see George J. Sefa Dei, *Schooling and Education in Africa: The Case of Ghana* (Trenton, NJ: Africa World Press, 2004). A local case in point is North Toronto Collegiate Institute; this historic school building has been so poorly maintained that the architect-developer consultants report that it is cheaper to demolish and rebuild than to repair the existing building. The proposed deal with developers is complex and warrants further investigation.

2 During the writing of this study, I wondered whether I would be shooting myself in the foot by including a critique of these influential scholars in education at OISE/UT. The conventional wisdom within the hierarchical structure of academia is that 'Little fish should not take on the big fish.' However, according to Smith (1987) the obligation of the researcher in institutional ethnography is to be 'truthful.' This work is also an autoethnography and so I decided to take the risk of including this piece, since it is an important part of the process that unfolded for me in mapping ruling rela-

tions in education in Ontario. Why should the big fish go unchallenged and continue to benefit? As a teacher (a little fish as far as reform pundits are concerned), my bristling reaction to this work is a marker of the operation of ruling relations and may clarify for others how we teachers can be drawn into complicity with the ruling apparatus in ways that induce us to act against our own interests and /or those of teachers as a group.

3 Hargreaves acknowledges the criticism and the problem of contrived collegiality in *Changing Teachers, Changing Times* (1994), but fails to integrate the distinction so as to move beyond an apolitical collegiality of 'happy campers' whose complicity is elicited in the educational reform agenda.

4 The policy of moving principals around the system in the so-called 'Christmas Package' was terminated, conceivably to instate principals as permanent authoritative 'leaders' within individual schools.

5 For a critique of Noddings, see feminist ethicists Claudia Card and Laura Purdy: in particular, Claudia Card, 'Caring and evil,' *Hypatia* 5 (Spring 1990), pp. 101–8; and Nel Noddings, 'A Response,' ibid., pp.120–6.

6 Autonomy as usually understood values individual independence and is contested as a masculinist construct by relational feminists who value relational interdependence. It is beyond the scope of this chapter to engage in the complexities of the debate surrounding the ethics of care among feminists. Clement's definition of autonomy however makes the point here.

7 Three of the four teacher-participants in this study are casualized by having downshifted to part-time (Rachel and Jessica) or to supply teaching (Alice). Although this group is far too small to make generalizations, further investigation would determine whether there is a similar trend in Ontario as in Alberta, where teaching is becoming part-time casualized work for women.

8 The OTF has a code of ethics and is physically and procedurally distinct from the affiliates. As stated in chapter 4, teachers currently hold dual membership in the OTF and the designated affiliate. Founded as the location of teachers' professional identity with responsibility over disciplining professional misconduct, it formerly performed functions usurped by the OCT. The mechanisms remain in place and the OTF continues to hear cases initiated prior to 1997 in a peer review process. Teacher certification was however under the purview of the ministry.

Afterword

1 In my experience as a guidance counsellor, comparing the track record of students in public school who take individual credits outside the school, marks at these private academies are 20 to 40 per cent higher. Whereas stu-

dents recognize the 'joke' of some of these academies with limited teaching, multiple attempts at the same test, easy marking, and rampant plagiarism, they argue that it could make the difference between getting into university or not. What message are we giving students if the institution continues to turn a blind eye? Whereas guidance counsellors have alerted the ministry and the universities about the issue, no action has been taken to regulate this practice that emerged with the fierce competition for marks. It is not sufficient for the ministry to conduct occasional hit-and-miss inspections. See the newspaper article by Alanna Mitchell, 'Are some students "buying" a spot at university?' *Globe and Mail*, 3 January 2004, pp. M2–M4.

2 For sample questions, see the Educational Testing Service website at http:/ /www.ets.org/otqt/pdfs/einfobooklet.pdf

3 I personally attended the session at Jarvis Collegiate in July 2003 in order to see public consultation in action. At that session there were an estimated thirty to forty people in attendance, occupying scattered seats in the first few rows of the otherwise empty school auditorium. Nevertheless, Christie (and his assistant) presided over the session from the elevated podium. It did not escape notice that Christie responded positively only to the proposal of a private-sector organization offering its assistance to the TDSB to operate within the confines of the funding formula by capitalizing on the free labour of volunteers. The exploitation inherent in using volunteers as substitutes for paid workers whose survival is at stake, and the transience of volunteers coming and going, suggests that volunteerism is neither an ethical nor reliable solution to the financial problems of the public education system.

4 For the OSSTF perspective, see Ahmed Abdolell, 'Manners betrayal wake up call,' *D12 Voice*, 5(3) (December 2003), p. 2.

5 According to the OSSTF representative, Michael Fullan was not a participant at meetings of the deans' task force.

Bibliography

Acker, Sandra (1994a). *Gendered education*. Toronto: OISE Press.

Acker, Sandra (1994b). *Gendered learning: Sociological reflections on women, teaching and feminism*. Buckingham: Open University Press.

Acker, Sandra (1999). Caring as work for women educators. In Elizabeth Smyth, Sandra Acker, Paula Bourne, and Alison Prentice (Eds.), *Challenging professions: Historical and contemporary perspectives on women's professional work* (pp. 277–95). Toronto: University of Toronto Press.

Alexander, M. Jacqui, and Chandra Talpade Mohanty (Eds.) (1997). *Feminist genealogies, colonial legacies, democratic futures*. New York: Routledge.

Altbach, Philip, Gail Kelly, and Lois Weis (1985). *Excellence in education*. Buffalo, NY: Prometheus Books.

Anthias, Floya, and Nira Yuval-Davis (1993). *Racialized Boundaries: Race, nation, gender, color and class and the anti-racist struggle*. New York: Routledge.

Apple, M.W. (1986). *Teachers and texts: A political economy of class and gender relations in education*. New York: Routledge and Kegan Paul.

Apple, M.W. (1993). Constructing the 'other:' Rightist reconstructions of common sense. In C. McCarthy and W. Crichlow (Eds.), *Race, identity and representation in education* (pp. 24–39). New York: Routledge.

Barlow, Maude, and Heather-Jane Robertson (1994). *Class warfare: The assault on Canada's schools*. Toronto: Key Porter.

Barthes, Roland (1977). *Image–music–text*. Trans. by Stephen Heath. New York: Farrar, Straus & Giroux.

Barth, Roland S. (1990). *Improving schools from within: Teachers, parents and principals can make a difference*. San Francisco: Jossey-Bass.

Bascia, Nina (1994). *Unions in teachers' professional lives: Social, intellectual, and practical concerns*. New York: Teachers College Press.

Bascia, Nina (1998). Women teachers, union affiliation and the future of North

American teacher unionism. *Teaching and Teacher Education*, 14 (5): 551–63.

Bascia, Nina (2001). Learning through struggle: How the Alberta Teachers' Association maintains an even keel. *New Approaches to Lifelong Learning*, Working Paper No. 44.

Bascia, Nina, and Andy Hargreaves (Eds.) (2000). *The sharp edge of educational change: Teaching, leading and the realities of reform*. New York: Routledge-Falmer.

Blackmore, Jill (1999). *Troubling women: Feminism leadership and educational change*. Philadelphia: Open University Press.

Briskin, Linda (1990). *Feminist Pedagogy: Teaching and learning liberation*. Ottawa: Canadian Research Institute on the Advancement of Women.

Broadbent, Jane, Michael Dietrich, and Jennifer Roberts (1997). *The end of the professions?* London: Routledge.

Burke, Ronald, Esther Greenglass, and Ralf Schwarzer (1996). Predicting teacher burnout over time: Effects of work stress, social support and self-doubts on burnout and its consequences. *Anxiety, Stress, and Coping: An International Journal*, 9 (3): 261–75.

Butler, Judith (1990). *Gender trouble: Feminism and the subversion of identity*. London: Routledge.

Buttigieg, Joseph, and Antonio Callari (Trans.) (1975). *Antonio Gramsci: Prison notebooks*. New York: Columbia University Press.

Canada. Human Resources Development (2002). *Knowledge matters: Skills and learning for Canadians*. Hull, QC: Author. www11.sdc.gc.ca/sl-ca/doc/knowledge.pdf

Casey, Kathleen (1993). *I answer with my life: Life histories of women teachers working for social change*. New York: Routledge.

Charlton, Emma, and John Charlton (Eds.) (2001). *Anti-capitalism: A guide to the movement*. London: Bookmarks Publications.

Chossudovsky, Michael (1997). *The globalization of poverty: Impacts of IMF and World Bank reforms*. London: Zed Books.

Clarke, Tony (1997). The transnational corporate agenda behind the Harris regime. In Diana Ralph, André Régimbald, and Néréé St-Amand (Eds.) *Open for business / Closed to people: Mike Harris's Ontario* (pp. 28–36). Halifax: Fernwood Publishing.

Clement, Grace (1996). *Care, autonomy and justice: Feminism and the ethic of care*. Boulder, CO: Westview Press.

Clune, W. (1990). Three views of curriculum policy in the school context: The school as policy mediator, policy critic, and policy constructor. In M. McLaughlin, J. Talbert, and N. Bascia (Eds.) *The contexts of teaching in secondary schools: Teachers' realities* (pp. 256–70). New York: Teachers College Press.

Corporate Council on Education et al. (1992). *Employability skills profile: The critical skills required of the Canadian workforce.* Ottawa: Conference Board of Canada.

Cowley, Peter, and Shahrokh Shahabi-Azad (2001). *Report card on Ontario's secondary schools.* Vancouver: Fraser Institute. http://oldfraser.lexi.net/publications/studies/education/report_card/2001/ont/section_06.html.

Datnow, Amanda (2000). Gender politics in school reform. In Nina Bascia and Andy Hargreaves (Eds.) *The sharp edge of educational change: Teaching, leading and the realities of reform* (pp. 131–55). New York: RoutledgeFalmer.

Denzin, Norman K., and Yvonna S. Lincoln (Eds.) (2000). *Handbook of qualitative research* (2nd ed.). Thousand Oaks, CA: Sage Publications.

Dewey, John (1997). *Democracy and education: An introduction to the philosophy of education.* Simon & Schuster (original copyright, 1916).

Ellis, Carolyn (1997). Evocative autoethnography: Writing emotionally about our lives. In W.G. Tierney and Y.S. Lincoln (Eds.) *Representation and the text: Re-framing the narrative voice* (pp. 115–39). Albany: State University of New York Press.

Elmore, R. (1977). Backward mapping: Implementation research and policy decisions. *Political Science Quarterly,* 94 (4): 601–16.

Engler, Allan (1995). *Apostles of greed: Capitalism and the myth of the individual in the market.* Halifax: Fernwood Publishing.

Foucault, Michel (1972). *The archaeology of knowledge.* London: Tavistock Publications.

Foucault, Michel (1979). *Discipline and punish.* Trans. by A. Sheridan. London: Peregrine Books.

Franklin, Ursula (1990). *The real world of technology.* Toronto: CBC Enterprises.

Freidson, Eliot (1985). The reorganization of the medical profession. *Medical Care Review,* 42 (1) Spring: 11–35.

Freire, Paolo (1972). *Pedagogy of the oppressed.* Harmondsworth: Penguin.

Fullan, Michael, and Andy Hargreaves (1991). *What's worth fighting for? Working together for your school.* Toronto: Ontario Public School Teachers' Federation.

Fullan, Michael and Andy Hargreaves (1998). *What's worth fighting for in education? LPD Video Journal of Education,* vol. 8 (1). Salt Lake City: Linton Professional Development Corporation.

Gallen, V., B. Karlenzig, and I. Tamney (1995). *The workload and worklife of Saskatchewan teachers: Full-time teachers, 1994–95.* Saskatchewan Teachers' Federation.

Garfinkel, Harold (1967). *Studies in ethnomethodology.* Englewood Cliffs, NJ: Prentice Hall.

Gidney, R.D. (1999). *From hope to Harris: The reshaping of Ontario's schools.* Toronto: University of Toronto Press.

Gidney, R.D., and W.P.J. Millar (1990). *Inventing secondary education: The rise of the high school in nineteenth-century Ontario.* Montreal: McGill-Queen's University Press.

Gidney, R.D., and W.P.J. Millar (1994). *Professional gentlemen: The professions in nineteenth-century Ontario.* Toronto: University of Toronto Press.

Giguère, Denys (1999). Gender gap widening among teachers. *Professionally Speaking,* June. http://www.oct.on.ca/english/ps/june_1999/gap.htm

Gilligan, Carol (1982). *In a different voice: Psychological theory and women's development.* Cambridge: Harvard University Press.

Giroux, H.A. (1988). *Schooling and the struggle for public life: Critical pedagogy in the modern age.* Minneapolis: University of Minnesota Press.

Giroux, H.A. (1994). *Disturbing pleasures: Learning popular culture.* New York: Routledge.

Giroux, H.A. and P. McLaren (Eds.) (1994). *Between borders: Pedagogy and the politics of cultural studies.* New York: Routledge.

Gordon, Colin (1972). *Power/knowledge: Selected interviews and other writings, 1972–1977, by Michel Foucault.* New York: Pantheon Books.

Greven, Michael, and Louis W. Purdy (2000). *Democracy beyond the state: The European dilemma and the emerging world order.* Toronto: University of Toronto Press.

Hall, E.M., L.A. Dennis et al. (1968). *Living and learning - the report of the provincial committee on aims and objectives of education in the schools of Ontario.* Toronto: Newton Publishing Company.

Haney, Walt (2000). The myth of the Texas miracle in education. *Education Policy Analysis Archive* 8(1). http://epaa.asu.edu/epaa/v8n41/

Hargreaves, Andy (1994). *Changing teachers, changing times: Teachers' work and culture in the postmodern age.* Toronto: OISE Press.

Hargreaves, D.H. (1994). The new professionalism: The synthesis of professional and institutional development. *Teaching and Teacher Education,* 10(4): 423–38.

Harrison, Trevor W., and Jerrold L. Kachur (Eds.) (1999). *Contested classrooms: Education, globalization, and democracy in Alberta.* Edmonton: University of Alberta Press.

Heritage, John (1984). *Garfinkel and ethnomethodology.* New York: Polity Press.

Holquist, Michael (Ed.) (1981). *The dialogic imagination: Four essays by M.M. Bakhtin.* Trans. by C. Emerson and M. Holquist. Austin: University of Texas Press.

hooks, bell (1994). *Teaching to transgress: Education as the practice of freedom.* New York: Routledge.

Human Resource Development Canada (2002). *Knowledge matters: Skills and learning for Canadians.* http://www.hrdc-drhc.gc.ca/sp-ps/sl-ca/doc/report.shtml

King, A.J.C., and M.J. Peart (1992). *Teachers in Canada: Their work and quality of life.* Ottawa: Canadian Teachers' Federation.

King, Alan (2002). *Double cohort study: Phase 2.* www.edu.gov.on.ca/eng/document/reports/dcohortp2.html

King, Alan (2003). *Double cohort study: Phase 3 report.* http://www.edu.gov.on.ca/eng/document/reports/phase3/

Klein, Naomi (2000). *No logo: Taking aim at the brand bullies.* Toronto: Vintage Canada.

Laxer, Gordon, and Trevor Harrison (1995). *The trojan horse: Alberta and the future of Canada.* Montreal: Black Rose Books.

Laxer, James (1993). *False god: How the globalization myth has impoverished Canada.* Toronto: Lester Publishing.

Leithwood, Kenneth, Michael Fullan, and Nancy Watson (2003). *The schools we need: A new blueprint for Ontario Final Report.* http://schoolsweneed.oise.utoronto.ca/textonly.pdf

Levin, Benjamin, (1997). The lessons of international educational reform. http://home.cc.umanitoba.ca/~levin/res_pub_files/lessons_of_international.pdf

Levin, Benjamin, and J. Anthony Riffel (1997). *Schools and the changing world: Struggling toward the future.* London: Falmer Press.

Livingstone, David W. (1999). *The education-jobs gap: Underemployment or economic democracy.* Toronto: Garamond Press.

Livingstone, David W. (2000). Exploring the icebergs of adult learning: Findings of the first Canadian survey on informal learning practices. *New Approaches to Lifelong Learning,* Working Paper No. 10. www.oise.utoronto.ca/depts/sese/csew/nall/res/10exploring.htm

Livingstone, D.W., D. Hart, and L.E. Davie (1999). *Public attitudes towards education in Ontario 1998: The twelfth OISE/UT survey.* Toronto: University of Toronto Press.

Lorde, Audre (1984). *Sister outsider.* Freedom, CA: Crossing Press.

Mackenzie, Hugh (2002) *Cutting classes: Elementary and secondary education funding in Ontario 2002–2003.* Ottawa: Canadian Centre for Policy Alternatives.

Margolis, Eric (Ed.) (2001). *The hidden curriculum in higher education.* New York: Routledge.

Martell, George. 1995. *A new education politics: Bob Rae's legacy and the response of the Ontario Secondary School Teachers' Federation*. Toronto: James Lorimer.

McIntyre, Frank (1998). Teacher shortage looms. *Professionally Speaking*. http://www.oct.on.ca/english/ps/december_1998/cover.htm

McLaren, P. (1993). *Critical pedagogy and predatory culture: Oppositional politics in a postmodern era*. London: Routledge.

McQuaig, Linda (1995). *Shooting the hippo: Death by deficit and other Canadian myths*. Toronto: Viking.

Mitter, Swasti (1986). *Common fate, common bond: Women in the global economy*. London: Pluto Press.

Mohanty, Chandra Talpade (1997a). Dangerous territories, territorial power, and education. In Leslie Roman and Linda Eyre (Eds.) *Dangerous territories: Struggles for difference and equality in education* (pp. ix–xvii). New York: Routledge.

Mohanty, Chandra Talpade (1997b). Woman workers and capitalist scripts: Ideologies of domination, common interests and the politics of solidarity. In M. Jacqui Alexander and Chandra Talpade Mohanty (Eds.) *Feminist genealogies, colonial legacies, democratic futures* (pp. 3–29). New York: Routledge.

Morgan, David L. (1988). *Focus groups as qualitative research*. London: Sage.

Muzzin, Linda (2001). 'Powder puff brigades': Professional caring vs. Industry research in the pharmaceutical sciences curriculum. In Eric Margolis (Ed.) *The hidden curriculum in higher education* (pp. 135–54). New York: Routledge.

Muzzin, Linda, Claudia Lai, and Pat Sinnott (1999). Pawns among patriarchies: Women in pharmacy. In Elizabeth Smythe, Paula Bourne, Alison Prentice, and Sandra Acker (Eds.) *Challenging professions: Historical and contemporary perspectives on women's professional work* (chap. 13). Toronto: University of Toronto Press.

Nash, Terre. (1995). *Who's counting? Marilyn Waring on sex, lies and global economics*. Montreal: NFB Canada (video recording).

Naylor, Charlie (2001). *Teacher workload and stress: An international perspective on human costs and systemic failure*. BCTF Research Report, September 2001. Vancouver: B.C. Teachers' Federation. http://www.bctf.ca/researchreports/2001wlc01/report.html

Newson, Janice, and Howard Buchbinder (1988). *The university means business*. Toronto: Garamond Press.

Neysmith, Sheila (Ed.) (2000). *Restructuring caring labour: Discourse, state practice and everyday life*. Toronto: Oxford University Press.

Nias, Jennifer (1999). Primary teaching as a culture of care. In J. Prosser (Ed.), *School culture* (pp. 66–81). London: Paul Chapman Publishing.

Nias, Jennifer, and C. Biott (Eds.) (1992). *Working and learning together for change*. Buckingham: Open University Press.

Noddings, Nel (1992). *The challenge to care in schools*. New York: Teachers College Press.

Noddings, Nel (1990). Feminist critiques in the professions. In Courtney B. Cazden (Ed.) *Review of Research in Education 16*. Washington DC: American Educational Research Association.

Ontario. Education Equality Task Force (2002). *Investing in public education: Advancing the goal of continuous improvement in student learning* (Rozanski Report). http://www.edu.gov.on.ca/eng/document/reports/task02/report.html

Ontario College of Teachers (2000). *Ethical Standards for the Teaching Profession* (OCT website) http://www.oct.on.ca/english/publications/ethics.pdf

Ontario College of Teachers. (1999) *Standards of Practice for the Teaching Profession* (OCT website) http://www.oct.on.ca/english/professional_affairs/standard.pdf

Ontario. Premier's Council (1988). *Competing in the new global economy*. Toronto: Author.

Ontario. Premier's Council (1990). *People and skills in the new global economy*. Toronto: Author.

Ontario. Royal Commission on Learning (1994). *For the love of learning*. Vols. 1, 2, 3, 4 and short version. Toronto: Queen's Printer for Ontario.

Ontario. Royal Commission on Learning (1994). *For the love of learning*. Recommendations. www.edu.gov.on.ca/eng/general/abcs/rcom/main.html

Pateman, Carole (1970). *Participation and democratic theory*. Cambridge: Cambridge University Press.

Pettman, Jan Jindy (1996). *Worlding women: A feminist international politics*. London: Routledge.

Portelli, John P., and R. Patrick Solomon (Eds.) (2001). *The erosion of democracy in education in Canada*. Calgary: Detselig Enterprises.

Rabinow, Paul (Ed.) (1984). *The Foucault reader*. New York: Pantheon.

Ralph, Diana, André Régimbald, and Néréé St-Amand (Eds.) (1997). *Open for business/Closed to people: Mike Harris's Ontario*. Halifax: Fernwood Publishing.

Rebick, Judy (2000). *Imagine democracy*. Toronto: Stoddart Publishing.

Richardson, Laurel (1997). *Fields of play: Constructing an academic life*. New Brunswick, NJ: Rutgers University Press.

Robertson, Heather-Jane (1998). *No more teachers, no more books: The commercialization of Canada's schools*. Toronto: McClelland & Stewart.

Rowbotham, Sheila (1993). *Women in movement: Feminism and social action*. New York: Routledge.

Schön, Donald (1987). *Educating the reflective practitioner.* London: Jossey Bass.

Slaughter, Sheila, and Larry L. Leslie (1997). *Academic capitalism.* Baltimore: Johns Hopkins University Press.

Smith, Dorothy (1987). *The everyday world as problematic: A feminist sociology.* Toronto: University of Toronto Press.

Smith, Dorothy E. (1999). *Writing the social: Critique, theory and investigations.* Toronto: University of Toronto Press.

Smith, Dorothy E. (2005). *Institutional ethnography: A sociology for people.* Lanham, MD: AltaMira Press.

Tannen, Deborah (1990). *You just don't understand: Women and men in conversation.* New York: William Morrow.

Taylor, Alison (2001). *The politics of educational reform in Alberta.* Toronto: University of Toronto Press.

Tudiver, Neil (1999). *Universities for sale: Resisting corporate control over Canadian higher education.* Toronto: James Lorimer.

Turk, James L. (1997). Days of action: Challenging the Harris corporate agenda. In Diana Ralph, André Régimbald, and Néréé St-Amand (Eds.), *Open for business / Closed to people: Mike Harris's Ontario* (pp. 165–76). Halifax: Fernwood Publishing.

Turk, James (Ed.) (2000). *The corporate campus.* Toronto: James Lorimer.

University of Toronto Forum Series (1995). *Royal Commission on Learning.* Vols. 1–4 (audiotapes).

Veblen, Thorstein. (1979). *The theory of the leisure class.* New York: Penguin Books (first published 1918).

Weinroth, Michelle (1997). Deficitism and neo-conservatism in Ontario. In Diana Ralph, André Régimbald, and Néréé St-Amand (Eds.), *Open for business / Closed to people: Mike Harris's Ontario* (pp. 54–67). Halifax: Fernwood Publishing.

Wenger, Etienne (1998). *Communities of practice: Learning, meaning, and identity.* Cambridge: Cambridge University Press.

Witz, Anne (1992). *Professions and patriarchy.* London: Macmillan.

Woods, Peter, Bob Jeffrey, Geoff Troman, and Mari Boyle (1997). *Restructuring schools, reconstructing teachers: Responding to change in the primary school.* Buckingham: Open University Press.

United States. National Commission on Excellence in Education (1983). *A nation at risk: The imperative for education reform.* Washington: U.S. Government Printing Office.

Yee, Sylvia Mei-Ling (1990). *Careers in the classroom: When teaching is more than a job.* New York: Teachers College Press.

Index